*From Grandmother to
Granddaughter*

From Grandmother to Granddaughter

SALVADORAN WOMEN'S STORIES

MICHAEL GORKIN

MARTA PINEDA

GLORIA LEAL

UNIVERSITY OF CALIFORNIA PRESS
Berkeley   Los Angeles   London

University of California Press
Berkeley and Los Angeles, California

University of California Press, Ltd.
London, England

Library of Congress Cataloging-in-Publication Data

Gorkin, Michael.
    From grandmother to granddaughter : Salvadoran women's stories /
Michael Gorkin, Marta Pineda, and Gloria Leal.
        p. cm.
    ISBN 0-520-21165-0 (cloth : alk. paper)—ISBN 0-520-22240-7 (pbk. :
alk. paper)
        1. El Salvador—History—20th century.   2. Women—El Salvador—
Social conditions—20th century.   3. Oral history.   I. Pineda,
Marta.   II. Leal, Gloria.   III. Title.

    F1488 .G67 2000
    972.8405'2—dc21   99-049789

Manufactured in the United States of America

09 08 07 06 05 04 03 02 01 00
10 9 8 7 6 5 4 3 2 1

For our children,
Talya, Maya, Josemaría, Wendy, Natalie

Contents

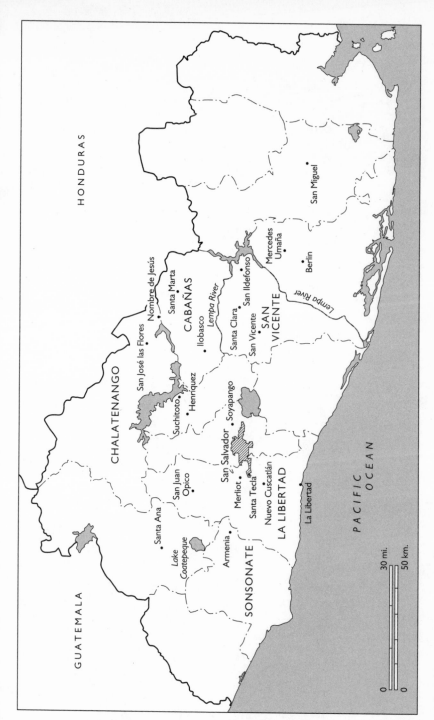

El Salvador

Acknowledgments

We are deeply thankful, above all, to the nine women who agreed to share with us their time and their stories, and who have made it possible to write this book. Though none of them appear here in their own names, we hope we have made clear to them privately the fullness of our gratitude.

In addition, there were many Salvadorans who gave us help and encouragement in producing this book, and we wish to thank them warmly: Marta Alicia Castro, Carlos Romeo Domínguez, David Escobar Galindo, Luis Gonzalez, Daniel Guttfreund, Julia de Leal, Ricardo Leal, Rómulo Leal, Marta Eugenia de Luna, Amparo Marroquín, Julia de Mendoza, Pedro Mendoza, Roxana Vides.

To the Fulbright Scholar Program that made it possible for Michael Gorkin to come to El Salvador, and to TACA Airlines that provided much of the transportation, we also extend our appreciation.

And finally, to the fine and friendly staff at the University of California Press—Lynne Withey, Edith Gladstone, Sue Heinemann, and Ina Clausen—we are thankful for helping us do this book as we wanted and hoped.

Introduction

BY MICHAEL GORKIN

For the second time in three years I find myself writing a book about women. I have asked myself repeatedly (as psychologists are wont to do) why my work has taken this particular direction. And I am now convinced that the two main reasons are the two individuals I name in the dedication to this book—my daughters, Talya and Maya. In short, the process of becoming and being a father to two girls seems to have moved me to the point where women's lives and writing about women have become an absorbing interest. Call it "feminism," I guess; and while I absolve them of any blame for the opinions expressed here, I consider Talya and Maya basically and blessedly responsible for the fact that I am involved in writing this book at all.

Why, then, write about Salvadoran women? The answer goes back to a serendipitous trip I made shortly after finishing the book on Palestinian women.[1] In the spring of 1996 I was invited to give some lectures to the staff of the Student Counseling Services of Universidad Doctor José Matías Delgado in El Salvador. Never having been to El Salvador, I was

I

curious and decided to go. In the obscure and magical way these things sometimes happen, I felt drawn to the country. By the time I left three weeks later, I already had in mind the possibility of doing a book about Salvadoran women and of collaborating with several women, colleagues I'd met on the counseling staff.

For me, part of the appeal of doing such a book was that El Salvador in some ways resembled the society and country about which I had just written—Palestine. Here too, I discovered, male dominance (*machismo*) was not only a pervasive pattern but was undergoing a serious challenge from increasing numbers of women. Moreover, as in Palestine, there had been a recent upheaval—the civil war that lasted from 1980 to 1992. To what extent, I wondered, had this war affected the role and perception of women in Salvadoran society?

Alongside the similarities, one marked difference between the two countries immediately struck me: the significance of social class. In Palestine the common struggle against Israel mutes class differences, but in El Salvador these differences are sharp and obvious. I began wondering how much solidarity—or if not solidarity, then a feeling of similarity—these class barriers allow Salvadoran women to experience.

Apart from these intriguing comparisons and contrasts between Palestinian and Salvadoran society, there was the challenge of once again trying to write a book *on* women, and *with* women (on some of the difficulties that face a man who wishes to do this kind of work, see my comments below). And the opportunity to gather and convey women's life stories in a meaningful way—despite the obstacles, both personal and technical—was one I found irresistible.

My next step was to contact possible coauthor(s). I had no interest in trying to do the book alone. I spoke enough Spanish *para defenderme* (to defend myself—to get along, in other words) and to conduct interviews but lacked a deeper understanding of the language and its subtleties. Even more crucial, as a man I could not alone meet or interview the majority of the women in the study. Hence, I turned to Marta Pineda and Gloria Leal, both psychologists, and asked if they would be willing to coauthor the book with me. Neither had been involved in gathering oral narratives, but with a mixture of enthusiasm and hesitation, they agreed. Their experience as psychologists made it likely that both might be skillful interviewers—and so they were, even beyond all our expectations.

As the title of this book suggests, we decided to write about families. Specifically, we settled on three families, and our subjects are a trio of grandmother-mother-granddaughter from each family. In writing about Palestinian mother-daughter pairs I took a similar approach. This time, I thought the addition of another generation might enhance the collective portrait of the families and the society. No doubt, part of my—and my colleagues'—inclination to choose families as our focus reflects the fact that we are psychologists. Thus, the interplay of family members has a special attraction for us. But beyond that, the focus on multigenerational families allows us to see how changes occur over time in each family and perhaps, by implication, in the society at large. Moreover, as oral historians are well aware, there is a subjective element to all storytelling. The focus on families, with each member bringing her own slant on one event or another, has the advantage of underscoring this subjectivity. Because I have worked in Arab and Latin cultures, I am now inclined to find a more poignant "reality" precisely in this so-called subjectivity.

For various reasons, then, the three of us were drawn to focus on families as our subjects. The question was, *which* families? We picked social class as the most significant criterion. More than any other factor except gender, social class differentiates among individuals. To be sure, these social classes are not equally represented in Salvadoran society. About 65 to 70 percent of Salvadorans belong to the lower class, with the middle class making up 20 to 25 percent, and the upper class 5 to 10 percent.[2] Yet despite the disproportionate percentages, this criterion provides a wide and varied picture of Salvadoran women's experiences and, by extension, a sense of Salvadoran society as a whole.

In choosing the three families, we felt that the women would be most open if they were talking to interviewers who were strangers to them.

Thus, in all three cases we made contact through intermediaries. With the upper-class family, one of our colleagues at the Student Counseling Services knew the mother; with the middle-class family a friend of Marta's introduced us to the granddaughter; and with the lower-class family a colleague of Gloria's cousin led us to all three women in the family.

To our surprise, the easiest family to locate and to begin interviewing was the upper-class family: la familia Nuñez.[3] The conventional wisdom in oral history predicts that interviewers (who, as a rule, are middle class) will find it easier to gain access and to interview "across" or "down"— middle-class and lower-class individuals[4]—rather than "up." But it didn't fit our experience. La familia Nuñez was the first and only upper-class family we met, and all parties immediately agreed to work together. Perhaps the fact that we three are psychologists and I am a U.S. citizen gave our project a measure of social status in their eyes. In any case, the family members invited us to visit them and to attend several fiestas at their sugarcane plantation. Niña Cecilia de Nuñez, the grandmother, still has a hand in managing this plantation, since her husband no longer chooses to do so. The 75-*manzana* plantation (some 128 acres) is only one of Niña Cecilia's assets. She and her husband have considerable sums in bank accounts—enough to enable them to enjoy the plush style of El Salvador's upper class. Her daughter, Monica, also partakes of the upper-class privileges and prerogatives. Married to a man who owns 50 manzanas of coffee land and is a partner in a lucrative business, Monica lives in one of the capital's exclusive neighborhoods. She considers herself simply "a housewife" and comes across as an unpretentious, down-to-earth individual. Her only child, Paulina, is currently finishing high school in one of El Salvador's most prestigious private schools. At the moment, Paulina thinks she'd like eventually to take over the reins from her father; or if not that, she says, "at least to do something important with my life—*not* be a housewife like my mother!"

The second family appearing in the book, la familia García, resides at the opposite end of the social spectrum. They are *campesinas* (peasant women) who, as it happens, all fought or collaborated with the guerrillas in El Salvador's civil war. Currently they all live in a new community

35 kilometers (21 miles) from the capital and with varying degrees of success are rebuilding their lives after the war. A community organizer who works with their settlement gave us access to them. Before meeting them, we had talked with two or three other lower-class families, both rural and urban. But none of the others, we sensed, were willing to open up to strangers, especially not about their political views. La familia García, on the contrary, showed little hesitation in discussing politics or any other subject. And thus we decided that Niña Dolores García, her daughter Lupe, and granddaughter María were a family who could provide a rich portrait—though not the only possible portrait—of lower-class family life in El Salvador.

The book's third trio comes from a middle-class family, la familia Rivas. Theirs was the most difficult family for us to locate and choose. And here we surprised ourselves. Since both Gloria and Marta come from the Salvadoran middle class, we all expected it to be easiest to find a middle-class family to interview. To some degree our difficulties must reflect chance. Several times we found two members of a family we would have liked to work with, but the third—usually, the grandmother—was unavailable. Apart from this, I think it was perhaps because Marta, Gloria, and I are from this class that we were somewhat quick to dismiss possible subjects on the basis that their stories seemed too familiar. And thus the family we chose is unusual in some respects: above all, in the fact that both the mother, Dulce, and the granddaughter, Sara, are socially committed individuals. One is a teacher who works in a poor neighborhood, and the other a university student with plans to "make a contribution" to her community. In contrast, the grandmother, Niña Julia Rivas, is a quietly apolitical individual. Her father, a middle-class farmer, did not support Niña Julia's mother and the five children. Niña Julia wound up working as a maid for much of her life, until her daughters managed to extricate her from this position and make it possible for her now to have some of the comforts of middle-class life. This struggle, which *is* typical of middle-class families in El Salvador, is what caught our attention and convinced us that la familia Rivas would be the trio to interview.

Whether it was in the grand salon of la familia Nuñez or the cramped dining room of la familia Rivas or the porch of one of la familia García, we used the same procedure in interviewing the women from all three families. We always brought along two tape recorders (in case one failed) and conducted each session in Spanish. To enable the women to speak most freely, we interviewed them separately and discouraged intrusions, though—especially with the *campesina* family—at times some of the children lingered nearby to observe the strange goings-on.

An interview usually lasted about one hour, with an additional half-hour or so of (untaped) socializing before and after. We had between six and nine interviews with each woman. With la familia Nuñez, the sessions were recorded from September 1996 to December 1997; with la familia García, from April 1997 to April 1998; and with la familia Rivas, from October 1997 to June 1998.

While at times all three of us would interview together, we generally went in pairs, an arrangement that we felt worked best. And in two cases Marta did much of the interviewing alone, since it became apparent that she had developed a special rapport with these women. In brief, we decided to be flexible about who interviewed whom; our procedure may be open to criticism on certain technical grounds, but we intuitively felt it would lead to greater openness from our subjects.

In this regard, I would like to make a few observations about how my participation added to, or detracted from, our subjects' willingness to speak openly about themselves. To the simple and blunt question, Can a man interview women as successfully as a woman can? I now reluctantly say, No, he cannot. Before I began to gather oral narratives from women, my clinical experience in working with women and my personal friendships with women persuaded me that women felt comfortable enough to talk freely with me. But the experience of these two books has made me see that a man is at a distinct disadvantage in interviewing women. Even when social conventions allow him access to them, women almost invariably talk less freely, *and* differently, to him than they do with female interviewers. And, I think, two related factors help explain the difference. First, as Gluck and Patai suggest, female interviewers generally take care to set up an atmosphere of rapport with their subjects whereas male interviewers, in their goal-orientedness, are more likely to hunt for information and neglect this vital element of rapport (sadly, their comment fits my interviewing style versus my collaborators' in all three cases).[5] Second, women have a prejudice—or maybe the word is "awareness"—that another woman will understand and appreciate what they relate of their lives far better than a man will, because he is less likely to be interested in their experience. And as a consequence, when a man attempts to interview women, the stories he hears are generally less full, less free, and ultimately less fascinating.

I first stumbled across this realization while doing the book on Palestinian women with Rafiqa Othman. With one of the three mother-daughter pairs, the mother (out of respect for her deceased husband) was unwilling to sit with me, a man. Rafiqa had to do the interviewing alone. She was a much less experienced interviewer than I was, but the material she received from this woman and her daughter was more frank and elaborate than most of what we had gathered together.

Having noticed this fact, I decided for the present book on Salvadoran women that it might be wise for Marta and Gloria to do some of the interviewing without me. They protested at first but then—with some eagerness—agreed to try it out. And once again, most often the interviews they gathered together were fuller and richer in detail than the material we gathered when I was present. The most notable exceptions (and thank goodness, there *were* some) came in a few of our sessions with the *campesinas* and the middle-class social activist. Here, the fact that my political sympathies are more leftist and those of both Marta and Gloria are more rightist led to a certain irony: a gringo got information about the political involvements and beliefs of these leftist women that Marta and Gloria might have missed. And in a few other areas, too, my personal interests led to some elaboration of material that, perhaps, would have gone unspoken. Yet overall I must admit that the intimate details and elaborate descriptions in this book primarily reflect the fact that Marta and Gloria were there and, often enough, without me. And because of their joint interviewing, the stories of these women's lives emerge clearly and, I think, compellingly.

To help the reader understand and follow the women's narratives, we append a short historical chronology of El Salvador's history to the book. Beyond that, I think it is worth sketching in here, however briefly, some of the features of the main upheaval in the country's recent history—namely, the civil war that took place between 1980 and 1992. Like almost everyone else in El Salvador, all nine women in the book were profoundly affected by this war. It enters all their life stories. Each woman has her own perspective on the war's causes and outcome, and I prefer to let the readers form their judgments from the stories themselves. Here, I wish only to indicate some of the principal aspects of this national upheaval.

The combatants in the twelve-year war were almost entirely Salvadorans: the government's armed forces, the Fuerza Armada, on one side; and the guerrillas, the Frente Farabundo Martí para la Liberación Nacional (FMLN), on the other side.[6] Yet the war also had a significant international dimension, and forces from the outside promoted and abetted one side or the other. Fearing the prospect of another leftist Sandinista-type victory such as had just occurred in Nicaragua (1979), the United States contributed vast sums of money and matériel, as well as technical advisors, to the government's forces.[7] And attempting to promote just such a revolution, Nicaragua and Cuba sent large quantities of arms and some volunteers to the Salvadoran guerrillas.

The war ebbed and flowed until 1992, at which time the United Nations, firmly supported by the United States, was able to negotiate a peace agreement between the two sides. The settlement remains intact, seven years later. Both sides achieved some gains. The government, which represented the political right and center, remained in power. And on the whole, the upper and middle classes kept their assets. But the guerrillas also made substantial gains. The FMLN got recognition as a legal political party and the passage of a good deal of social legislation it supported, including more land reform.[8]

No matter how we evaluate the gains of the war, nobody in El Salvador overlooks the losses. By any standard, the war's cost was devastating. Some 75,000 Salvadorans (1.5 percent of the population) died; at least 400,000 people, principally poor *campesinos*, lost their homes; and at least 500,000 Salvadorans fled the country. In sum, the upheaval devastated the country. And while a renewal of the war now seems unlikely, the country is still suffering from its aftereffects—as the various stories of the women in this book so vividly underscore, no matter where they appear along the political spectrum.

Other vast changes have occurred in the lives of Salvadoran women during this century. Our focus on multigenerational families highlights some of these shifts. One is the dramatic expansion of educational opportunities for women (for men as well, but the change is less remarkable). Two generations ago education was the prerogative of the upper class, and middle-class and lower-class women now value and seek it too. We see this trend clearly in the lives of the women in our study. In the generation of the grandmothers, only one-third of Salvadoran women were literate; today, at least three-quarters are literate. Moreover, while it was almost unprecedented for women to receive a university education in the era of the grandmothers, now two of every hundred women (and three of every hundred men) attend universities.[9] As a result of this increased level of education for women, their opportunities for productive work outside their homes are better too.

In the era of the grandmothers, an upper-class woman did not work outside her home. If she received some schooling, she was not expected to pursue a career; to be a housewife and attend to her husband's and children's needs was her prescribed role. The past two generations have seriously challenged this limiting perspective, and there has been a growing influx of women at all levels of the workforce. And perhaps most promisingly, more and more women appear even at the top of the occupational structure. We note, for example, that today fourteen of the eighty-four deputies in the Salvadoran Parliament are women; in 1961 they numbered two out of fifty-six. And within the professions, this trend is also impressive. Women still do the lion's (and lioness's) share of the housework and child-rearing. But even in this area, as the stories in this book suggest, male privileges are eroding. In short, we are witnessing a shift in women's occupational and work roles in El Salvador, and it seems to be irreversible.

In one significant realm, however, change seems to be occurring more slowly and painfully: sexual freedom. Here the ideology of *machismo* sways the minds of all Salvadorans, women included. In the era of the grandmothers, parental advice and consent were expected and accepted. Women today are substantially freer to meet and choose a marriage partner. And yet a sexual double standard prevails. At *all* social levels, women are still expected to be virgins when they marry or first enter a common-law relationship (become *ajuntada*) with the man of their choice. As some of the narratives in this book make vividly clear, the loss of virginity before marriage has a high price. And only a small number of women, usually those with higher education, are willing to defy this entrenched social norm.

In evaluating these trends in the social and personal lives of Salvadoran women, I found myself comparing them to what I had noted in Palestinian society. On the whole, the similarities are more prominent than the differences. Educational and occupational opportunities for women exist in both countries. And the area of least change in either country is that of sexual freedom for women; premarital sexual relations still carry the same stigma, if not quite the same danger, as in previous generations.

In addition, in both countries there is a burgeoning women's movement, with increasing numbers of women's organizations challenging male dominance and standards. Likewise, in both societies social upheaval (in Palestine the *intifada*, in El Salvador the civil war) provided an impetus for women's groups to gather strength.[10] Now that the heat of the war has passed in El Salvador and subsided in Palestine, the women's organizations continue to gather strength. In El Salvador, they remain small in actual membership numbers—smaller than in Palestine—but their potential impact should not be underestimated; they are, I think, the vanguard of changes that are likely to go on into the future.

Yet there are also some significant differences. In Palestine the patrilineal extended family still has a far greater influence in the society as a whole and, by extension, also a greater influence on the lives of women than in El Salvador. The common practice in El Salvador of women living and raising children alone, having been abandoned by their husbands or partners, and also by the men's families, is scarcely to be found in Palestine, where such behavior would be considered an *aeb* (shame).[11] Among the women in our small sample, three of the seven who bore children were abandoned by their spouses or partners, either permanently or temporarily. And while this phenomenon is more common in poorer families—as in our sample—it is present at all levels of the society. Its social and psychological price is amply illustrated in some of the women's life stories (see also our Afterwords).

And yet in El Salvador the lack of "protection" from the patrilineal extended family seems to have led to a relatively greater aversion to male hegemony on the part of Salvadoran women than I observed in Palestine. As a consequence, Salvadoran women have sought and achieved a greater measure of individual freedom. From a psychological perspective, it seems to me that Salvadoran women define themselves more in terms of "I" than do Palestinian women. For the latter, more often the sense of self is entwined in the group self of the extended family, that is, a "we-self."[12] Palestinian women almost always have to negotiate their freedom with an eye toward male censure. (Indeed, it was far harder to find women subjects to interview in Palestine than in El Salvador, and Salvadoran women seem to feel freer to express their feelings and views, to disclose their loves and even lusts.) With the relative absence of control from the patrilineal extended family, women in El Salvador are more able to navigate their own destinies than are women in Palestine. And I would speculate that the prospects are better in El Salvador than in Palestine for a continued expansion of such individual freedom for women.

Before turning to the stories of the nine women in this book, I would like to comment on a couple of other matters that are of concern to those who gather and present oral narratives. We ask ourselves, as indeed we must, how accurately the material we present in written form does in fact reflect the lives of the people we met. Furthermore, as we ask ourselves this question we cannot and must not avoid asking whether the work we are doing, the transmitting of these accounts, is a worthwhile *and* ethical process. Much has been written about both these issues.

Let me start with the issue of whether the narratives here, as I have edited them, can be said to reflect the lives of our subjects. Certainly these written products are the result and reflection of both the interviewee and interviewer; and—as practitioners of oral history remind us—their very wording also anticipates the potential audience, the reader(s), for whom the narratives are intended.[13] To me, this view is correct. Hence, what the reader will find here is *a* version—not *the* version—of each of the nine women's lives. With another public in mind than the North American, another interviewer would undoubtedly write a different work.

Inasmuch as the narratives are the product of a dialogue, some researchers argue that one should present the narratives in dialogic form.[14] I, however, rejected this suggestion because my impression is that the dialogic presentation is less readable, that is, narratively less interesting, than a monologic presentation of material. But I try to indicate within the flow of the text some of the moments when we were asking direct questions and keep many comments that the interviewees addressed to us about the interviewing process. Thus, I hope readers will experience an intimate conversation they are invited to overhear. That, and not a monologue uttered in a megaphonelike manner to an anonymous audience, has been my aim in technically editing the material.

Whether in dialogic or monologic form, the material brings up technical problems that are in some ways insurmountable. We cannot avoid editing the oral material, and thereby changing to some degree precisely what was said. The repetitions, ramblings, and detours that are present in all storytelling, with educated and illiterate subjects alike, will not form a readable text. All that the editor can hope to do is shape the text with a delicate and true hand—"true" in the sense of keeping the essential style and voice of the subject.

The task of keeping the voice of the subject is even more difficult in translation from one language to another. With the more educated subjects, translation from Spanish into English has been relatively manageable. But with the less educated women, the *campesina* family in particular, I found it impossible to retain the richness of their language, even with Marta and Gloria, who are quite fluent in English, peering over my shoulder. All three women in the *campesina* family speak a dialect distinct from that of almost all the other women—as different as an Appalachian farmer's speech from that of a New York schoolteacher. To capture this difference proved at times impossible. I believe, however, that the voices of the individual *campesina* women do come through; at least the personal manner and style of telling their stories remain. And thus, I feel that the personalities of these women are adequately reflected, even though the beauty of the dialect is often lost in translation.

Finally, I would like to comment briefly on some of the troubling ethical issues that arise when gathering and writing up oral narratives. To my mind, nobody has put this matter more forcefully than Daphne Patai in her essay "U.S. Academics and Third World Women: Is Ethical Research Possible?"[15] Basically, her argument is that the U.S. academic is in a more "powerful" and "privileged" position than a third-world subject, and she or he has more to gain in "prestige" and "economic" terms than does the subject; and consequently, an element of exploitation is unavoidable. As Patai concludes, "in an unethical world we cannot do truly ethical research."

In addition, I think it is true that no matter how clearly we explain to our subjects what we are doing and how we are doing it, many of them—especially the less educated—have only a partial and vague idea of how their stories, with all the self-revealing details, eventually come into the hands of strangers. We, as transmitters of these stories, have a need and even an obligation to the reader to provide narratives that are self-revealing. At times, with *all* subjects we try to garner information that the subject herself would prefer to hide. This tension is inevitable, and I imagine for most of us it arouses a certain ethical uneasiness.

Then how can we justify doing this work? The answer for me lies in the belief that though an element of exploitation, or using the other, is inevitable, we also provide our subjects with some benefits. I am not referring to monetary gains. Although one could legitimately pay interviewees, we did not do so. It was our judgment that interviewees who chose to participate in the project would ultimately be more open, and more truly involved, if their reason for doing so was not one of material gain.

The historian Paul Thompson points to the salutary effects for the subject in participating in an oral history project.[16] He emphasizes two psychological benefits that subjects often receive from the process of recollecting their lives. First, the act of remembering, even while painful in some instances, has a cathartic effect for many interviewees. Second, the process of recounting the past to an attentive listener is a meaningful and self-enhancing experience for subjects who perhaps have never had such an experience. As a psychologist, I agree with Thompson. Patai is similarly aware of these factors, but it seems to me that she underestimates their value for the subject.

My experiences with the women I interviewed persuade me that it is primarily these psychological benefits that motivate the interviewees to talk and reveal so much about their lives. As a psychologist, I by no means attempt to do "psychotherapy" with the subjects. Yet the listening process and what happens *to me* as a listener of the stories is substantially the same as when I am doing psychotherapy with patients. By interviewing each woman several times over a long period, and meeting other members of her family as part of the project, I find that sooner or later I develop an empathic understanding of who she is. Whether her political, social, and personal predilections mesh or clash with mine, I strive—just as with patients—to see the world through her eyes. And simply expressed, I almost always come to like the person. Naturally, with some subjects this empathic understanding comes quicker than with others. But I take it as my task to strive for this understanding.

Once I feel I have substantially achieved this position with the subject, I feel I can put together a fair, *and* ethical, narrative of her life.

And then I begin writing. And then I begin hoping that out there, somewhere, are those individuals (women and men too) who will have the interest and time to listen in. And finally, I admit, I find myself wondering as I write what Maya and Talya, now eleven and five years old, will someday think when they read these stories—stories that their father has written up, in the deepest sense, for them.

NOTES

1.   Michael Gorkin and Rafiqa Othman, *Three Mothers, Three Daughters—Palestinian Women's Stories* (Berkeley: University of California Press, 1996).
2.   The principal criterion used here for designating social class is an economic one. In the absence of reliable data on personal income and wealth, estimates of annual household income for the lower class are $2,000 or less and for the upper class, $60,000 or more; the middle class, obviously, is between these two estimates. Those in the lower class include *campesinos* (peasant farmers) who are landless or have landholdings of less than 10 acres, unskilled and semiskilled workers, and the unemployed. The middle class includes professionals, small business owners, skilled workers, and farmers with land holdings of 10–100 acres. In the upper class are landowners of 300 acres or more, owners of large businesses, senior managers in large businesses, the upper level of government officials, and those with inherited assets. (These estimates were provided by U.S. embassy officials in El Salvador and Dr. Rafael Guido Béjar, a Salvadoran sociologist who has taught at Universidad Centroamericana and one of whose areas of expertise is the social class structure in El Salvador.)
3.   To ensure the subjects' anonymity, we have changed the names of all three families as well as the first names of all family members. All other data and descriptions are, to the best of our knowledge, accurate.
4.   Daphne Patai, *Brazilian Women Speak* (New Brunswick: Rutgers University Press, 1988), 4.
5.   Judith Stacey, "Can There Be a Feminist Ethnography?" in *Women's Words: The Feminist Practice of Oral History,* ed. Sherna Gluck and Daphne Patai (New York: Routledge, 1991), 112.
6.   In 1980 five revolutionary-military organizations formed the FMLN, and—as the text explains below—it now functions as a legal political party.
7.   Between 1980 and 1992, the United States provided $4.2 billion in eco-

nomic and military aid to El Salvador, making it the third largest recipient of U.S. bilateral aid—after Israel and Egypt—during that period (these estimates are from the U.S. Embassy in El Salvador).

8.   Part of the peace accords involved the redistribution of 134,000 manzanas to landless and land-poor families, the vast majority of whom were former combatants on both sides of the war (see Ministerio de Agricultura y Ganadería, *Tercer Censo agropecuario del Programa de Transferencia de Tierras* [San Salvador, 1997], ix, xii). This redistribution, combined with the redistribution of 413,000 manzanas in the land reform laws of 1980, means that approximately 19 percent of El Salvador's total land has been redistributed. Thus El Salvador has undergone the most extensive, nonsocialist land reform in Latin America, except for that of Mexico (see Mitchell Seligson, "Thirty Years of Transformation in the Agrarian Structure of El Salvador," Documento de Trabajo de la Fundación Dr. Guillermo Manuel Ungo [San Salvador, 1994], 35).

9.   The literacy estimates come from the third and fifth national census of the Salvadoran population (1961, 1992). It seems likely that the current index of illiteracy is lower than in 1992, since the national illiteracy level has dropped further since the war. The data on university education are from the fifth national census in 1992.

10.   Brenda Carter et al., eds., *A Dream Compels Us* (Boston: South End Press, 1989), is a compilation of short oral accounts by Salvadoran women activists and provides an interesting perspective on how women's groups proliferated during the war.

11.   Women head approximately 30 percent of the households in El Salvador (Dirección general de Estadística y Censos, Ministerio de Economia, 1997).

12.   In both El Salvador and Palestine, the sense of an "I-self" is greater among younger women than among their mothers and grandmothers. But for comparably aged women, the "we-self" is greater in Palestine than in El Salvador.

13.   For a good exposition of this perspective see James Clifford and George E. Marcus, eds., *Writing Culture: The Poetics and Politics of Ethnography* (Berkeley: University of California Press, 1986).

14.   Dennis Tedlock, "Questions Concerning Dialogical Anthropology," *Journal of Anthropological Research* 43 (1987): 325–37.

15.   Daphne Patai, "U.S. Academics and Third World Women: Is Ethical Research Possible?" in *Women's Words: The Feminist Practice of Oral History*, 137–53.

16.   Paul Thompson, *The Voice of the Past: Oral History*, rev. ed. (New York: Oxford University Press, 1988), 150–65.

La Familia Nuñez

Niña Cecilia

At sixty-seven years (as she claimed), or perhaps seventy-four (as we reckoned), Cecilia de Nuñez has the manicured and matronly look of a Salvadoran older woman of means. She is short and plumpish but carries herself with the slow, quiet grace of one whose place in the world is secure and respected. Having spent her childhood on her parents' *finca* (farm) 35 kilometers west of San Salvador, she now lives with her husband in a four-bedroom house in one of the capital's attractive old neighborhoods. However, it was not there but at her daughter's even more fashionable residence that we first met and subsequently interviewed her.

Cecilia de Nuñez, or Niña Cecilia as we respectfully addressed her, appears here as our first subject. In fact, she was the first person, along with her daughter, Monica, whom we interviewed. With an enthusiasm that surprised us, Niña Cecilia immediately agreed to participate in our study. She is an avid reader, even a writer of poetry, and the project intrigued her. Yet once the interviewing got under way, she proved at times to be an elusive subject—less open than her daughter and grand-daughter.

Now and then Niña Cecilia would bring to the interviews short state-ments that she had prepared for us, and on occasion she read us a poem of hers. Soft-spoken and articulate, she is a person of staunch convictions that generally reflect the conservative views of El Salvador's upper class. The twelve years of civil war and its difficult aftermath have marked her. And yet as a person who, as she says, "always adapts to whatever fate brings," she continues to go about life these days—teas with friends, family visits, trips abroad—with an outward calm and even cheerful-ness.

On occasion we were invited to meet socially with Niña Cecilia and her family—for example, for the *fiesta de elote* (feast of the first corn) prepared at their finca (and of course, we did not take a tape recorder). On this particular visit, her husband offered a tour around the finca, lovingly pointing out some of the thick-trunked trees and whitewashed adobe dwellings that had somehow survived this century's slings and arrows, as he and his wife had. Out of tact or lack of interest, he did not refer to the interviews we were conducting with his wife, daughter, and granddaughter, although we knew from Niña Cecilia that he was fully aware of the project.

In all, we had seven interviews with Niña Cecilia over a period of about a year. As she recalled the events of her long life, at times her memory would fail her. Precisely then, it seemed, her daughter would appear from out of the kitchen or an upstairs bedroom to refresh her mother's memory. Far from being disconcerted by these sudden daugh-terly embellishments, Niña Cecilia would smile benignly and then pro-ceed with the tale as she remembered it. Below, then, are some of Niña Cecilia's recollections from her sixty-seven—or seventy-four—years as one of El Salvador's well-to-do and, in her view, "most fortunate of people."

I come from a large family, eight children in all, and I was the only sister. I was right in the middle, the fifth child. To me this was wonderful. Think of it, just one girl with all those brothers surrounding me. I was pampered by everyone—by my mother, father, grandparents, by everyone. They all doted on me, and I had this feeling, always, of being special.

We lived out in the countryside of Sonsonate [a department in western El Salvador], on a beautiful finca. It wasn't as large as some other fincas in the area, maybe 10 manzanas or so, but oh, what a place! Several kilometers away was the Izalco volcano. Here, I brought you this . . . [Niña Cecilia hands us a colored postcard of a huge volcano hovering over a lush valley, with a sombrero-wearing peasant walking beside a wooden oxcart in the foreground]. That's how it looked. Izalco was still active back then. Today it's dormant, a tourist attraction. And that oxcart, that's how the peasants would haul the sugarcane from the fields. Sometimes, when I was a child, you'd hear this sudden "Brrrrr!" And then the whole earth would shake, and Izalco would light up like a Christmas tree. Red-hot lava would come flying out of it and flow down its steep side. A magnificent thing to see, I tell you, especially if it happened at night. No, no, it wasn't dangerous; we were too far off. You just jumped a little at the first rumble. But really, it wasn't frightening. You had a feeling—how can I describe it?—a feeling you were living in a magical place, a place with a mysterious force around it.

That whole area where we lived was fertile land, good for growing anything you wanted. The finca belonged to my grandfather, and some of my aunts and cousins were living there too, along with our family. We all lived in this enormous house with all these corridors, and many rooms. How my grandfather came to own this place I can't really tell you. I never looked into it. All I know is that he was some high army officer, a close friend of General Martínez, the one who crushed that Communist-run peasant rebellion in the area in the '30s. He was a fine man, my grandfather. He adored me, I remember that. But more than that, where his people came from, I don't know. I guess they came from Spain, maybe sometime in the nineteenth century. I'm only guessing, though, because I know my mother's people came from Madrid about a hundred fifty years ago. Why they came, how they made their money and got their lands, I don't really know. I was never curious about these things. For me, it was enough that we had such a magical place. For a child that's all that matters, right? And to me, that spot we had way out in the countryside was a place as close to heaven as you're going to see in this life.

You'd wake up in the morning with the roosters and robins singing to you, and the cows mooing just outside in the corral where they'd be for the morning milking. I'd look out the window to see the whole world glistening. The nights were cool, so in the mornings all would be covered with dew—coffee bushes, sugarcane, and fruit trees. The scent of my mother's rose bushes, planted near my room, would waft through the window. And the peasants who gathered at dawn just outside the house, would be waiting there for the *mandador* [work boss] to assign them their tasks for the day. Sowing, weeding, harvesting, depending on the season.

We grew everything. Some was for our own use and some we'd market. *Maíz* [corn] and *frijol* [beans], of course, and all kinds of fruits—oranges, bananas, avocados, mangos, coconuts. And we had a bit of sugarcane we'd grow for our own use, squeezing it in a *trapiche* [wooden press], and then filling bamboo molds with the honeylike boiled juice that would harden later, and then you'd chip it off and put it in your coffee or just eat it. Delicious! Real sugar, that was. Like everything else back then, it had real taste. Chickens, like the ones we raised on our farm, they had a rich chicken taste, not like the stuff you get in the supermarket these days. And fresh milk and cottage cheese, which we made on the farm. Even fish—we had a manmade pond, maybe the size of this huge living room we're sitting in—and we raised freshwater fish. What a taste! In soups or just fried up, they were wonderful. *Everything* was wonderful! Life itself was like magic. As God is my judge, it was really like that.

Back then, living deep in the countryside was a calmer life, not so much agitation as this city life of ours. To me it was better. Maybe I say this because for a child everything is wonderful. Later the problems come, right? You can't avoid that. You have to cope as best you can. But when I was a small child, life was carefree. Just perfect.

❧

How did I spend my days as a child? Well I didn't have to work, cleaning my room or sweeping up or in the kitchen. We had *muchachas* [girls, i.e., servant girls] who did all that. My mother supervised them. She was a strong woman and she was in charge of the house. She could cook herself, sure she could. Christmas time, *Semana Santa* [Holy Week, before Easter], or special days like the local saint's day, it was she who took over in the kitchen making her specialties—stuffed fish, roast turkey, or her special *tortas* [cakes]. What a fine cook she was! She taught me when I got older. "Someday you'll need to know," she told me. "The servants may be sick, or who knows what? So watch me and learn!" So I watched and learned, and I can cook. And my daughter knows too. Only my granddaughter, Paulina, hasn't learned. A shame, really. A girl should learn these things, don't you think?

Anyway, where was I? My days at the finca, yes. *Bueno* [good, well], when I was small what I did was play with my cousins. Girl cousins, I mean. I didn't play with the boys, my brothers. "They're too tough for you," my mother told me. "You're going to get hit and hurt. No, no, you stay away from them!" That's what she told me. So I played with my girl cousins. Especially with this one cousin, Veronica. She was a beautiful girl, still is. She lives in the United States now, an old woman now, but still a great beauty. She and I would play together. We'd plan out these plays, with singing and dancing and acting. At first we used dolls, but later we started playing the parts ourselves, along with our other cousins. Me, I was thin as a noodle back then—not the way I am today. So I'd stuff my dress with pillows to play the lady roles, and I'd sing. I had a good voice too, not like today with this raspy sound, right? We'd entertain ourselves for hours like that, day after day. Or we'd sit and chat, chat, chat. That's how I remember it.

And school, certainly, I went to school. I wanted to learn, and my mother and father too, may God bless them, they supported me in that just as they supported my brothers. Even before I was old enough to go to school, I started learning to read. I was four years old and I went to my mother and aunts, and I told them I wanted to learn to read. "You're awfully young for that," they told me. "But if you want to try we'll get you a tutor." I didn't want some stranger coming to teach me. So I insisted—you see, I was a determined little girl—I insisted, "No! *You* are going to teach me!" And that's what happened. They bought this book, a beginner's book, and sitting there in my little rocking chair in the garden, I started learning the alphabet. What I wasn't aware of was that sitting there in the tree above was the green parrot my aunts owned, and he was learning right along with me. He didn't say anything for about a month, he just sat there quietly. Then one day, when I finally had mastered the whole alphabet and was proudly reciting it to my aunts, I hear this *a-b-c-d* coming from above me, and in *my* own voice. It scared me at first, but then I started laughing and laughing. My aunts told me the parrot would practice while I wasn't around, and sure enough, he'd got it all memorized just like me. Can you imagine it?

From then on, I started learning words, and by the time I was five years old, I was reading. I read books for small children—don't ask me to remember. I read anything they brought me. My mother said I was really smart. I don't know, maybe she was right, I guess she was. She had the opinion that a girl had to know how to fend for herself and that education was the way to do that. She herself didn't have much schooling, but she was determined that I'd go. As it was, in the town of Armenia, which was the biggest town around, the schools weren't so advanced then. I went to some small school there for a couple of years or so, yet the only way you could really learn something was to go away to boarding school. One of my brothers was going to a boarding school in Santa Tecla, near the capital. So my mother decided to send me away too. And I went, gladly. I wanted to learn.

It was a two-hour train ride to get to Santa Tecla, even though it wasn't much more than 30 kilometers away. The roads were no good then. So you went by one train to San Salvador, and then took another to Santa Tecla. Beautiful trains. I think they came from England. They had steam engines, fed by firewood. On the outside they were all shiny and on the inside they were so comfortable. In the first-class section there were these cushioned seats, as in a living room. The second-class section had wooden benches, but I don't remember sitting there. I'd go first class, with my brother or my mother accompanying me. I never was allowed to go alone.

I went to this boarding school in Santa Tecla for eight years, from the time I was ten years old till I was seventeen. Santa Inés was the name of it. It was a place run by French nuns, just for girls. My brother went to a boarding school nearby run by priests. I got a good education there, I think. It was the best there was in El Salvador at the time. And I enjoyed it. I had good friends there, girls from some of the best Salvadoran families. We were very close. We spent all those years together, studying and living together. In the summers, of course, or on Christmas and Easter, we'd go our separate ways. I'd go back home and always my mother would treat me like a princess, making me my favorite dishes and spoiling me in her way. That's the way she was with me, softer than she was with my brothers. With them she was firmer. I guess she felt she had to be, especially after my father died and she had to be both mother and father to us all.

My father died when I was ten. It happened while I was at boarding school. I knew he was ill, some kind of kidney infection, but I figured it would pass. Then one day I get this telegram at school. My father had died, it said. I couldn't believe it. He was this strong man, always riding around the finca on his horse. A hard worker, my father was. A good man. And now, gone, just like that. How could that be?

So I took the train home to be with my family. My father was there in the house, laid out in his coffin, and people were already there for the wake. My mother and brothers were in shock, just like me. Nobody could accept it. We didn't talk much, we just sat there all night, with people from all over the area coming in and out to pay their condolences. The next day we took him to the cemetery in Armenia and buried him. In twenty-four hours, he was gone and buried.

Today it's done differently, right? Today, here in San Salvador, they have these ways of preserving the cadaver, and the family will sit around in the funeral parlor—as in La Auxiliadora, that's the best one—and they'll stay there for days before they bury the person. But back then it was done quickly, in one day. The way we did it. After the burial, our family went home and we stayed together for the *novenario* [nine days of prayer or mourning]. We built a small altar in the house with flowers on it. That was the custom then in the villages and towns. You'd recite the rosary and other prayers, and on the last day you'd hand out to guests some coffee, *tamales* [cornmeal delicacy, usually with chicken or meat] and *quesadillas* [cornmeal pound cake made with cheese], and also a small memento of the deceased, maybe a medallion or photo, or some such thing. And that was it. The family would take up its routine again, as best everyone could.

With us, my mother called us together. She was in terrible grief, you could see. My brothers were grieving too, they felt cheated that our father had been taken away from us. But my mother was a strong woman, I tell you, and she called us together and told us, "We've all got to go on, we've got to overcome our grief." She would take over the reins at the finca, she said, along with the help of some of my older brothers. And those of us who were in school would go back to school. This was our fate, she said, we had to accept it. And so that's what we did. I went back to boarding school, and I had good friends there who helped me. They consoled me and didn't leave me alone. That's how I coped with the situation. Eventually I came back to myself again, though the world I'd known before, our family, was never the same again. How could it be without our papa?

I was seventeen when I graduated from Santa Inés. I was given a cer- tificate, not a title like those the Ministry of Education gives these days, like "Secretary," "Office Worker," and so on. Did I think of study- ing more? No, not really. In those days there were no opportunities for women to go to university in El Salvador and become doctors and law- yers, as they can today. The only way you could pursue a university education was to go abroad. That wasn't something I even thought of doing. I wanted to go back home, be with my mother and help her out.

By then Mama was in full control, running the farm just as my father had done, and taking care of the house too. She was a good manager, and the farm kept turning a profit. Enough so that my brothers all got their high school education, and one even went on to university and studied law. Mama was a clever and active woman. I can still see her in my mind, riding her horse around the farm, wearing one of those skirts that open in the middle so you can mount the horse. She didn't wear makeup. Only on fiestas, she'd put on powder, talc, and lipstick. Did she think of marrying again? Oh no, not her. There was nobody after my father. She stayed alone. That was her fate and she accepted it with dignity.

For me, those years after I finished school and before I got married were good years, easy years. I helped my mother with the house, with my younger brothers, but I also had fun. Fiestas, dances, parties—oh yes, we had them. My mother kept her eye on me, mind you, she was very strict. Still, she was also good to me and pampered me. I remember this one time, I was about eighteen. A girlfriend of mine, Yolanda, came by the house with a new hairdo, a *permanente* she called it. It was lovely. My hair was straight, and for months I'd been trying to make it curly, tying it up at night with ribbons and cloth in what you call "anchovies." It didn't really work. So when I saw Yolanda's hairdo, I asked how she did it. She told me she had it done at a beauty parlor in the capital, a place called La Rustó. But it cost a small fortune, something like 200 *colones*, which was like 2,000 colones in today's money.* I told my mother, and she said without a moment's hesitation, "Go tomorrow if you like. Never mind the cost." So the next day, with a *muchacha* accompanying me, I went by train to San Salvador and managed to find La Rustó. And I got my *permanente*. You had to pay before the beautician did it, just in case you didn't like it, I guess. I loved it, though. And Mama, she loved it too. I walked into the house and she said, "Oh my daughter, how beautiful you are!" I swear, it was worth every colón. The beautician taught me how to take care of my *permanente* with castor oil and some red lotion called Bayrom, but no shampoo or soap. Imagine, I still remember the names of those lotions. And you know, it worked. My hair stayed curly from then on, as you see me today. The truth is, I

---

* As of 1998, the exchange rate was $1.00 = 8.75 colones.

wish I could make it straight again, but it's no longer possible. My hair stays as curly as it was when I came back from La Rustó, though everything else about me has changed since then, right?

Back then I was—at least people said so—I was a fine looking young woman. Sure, the boys took notice. I had my share of *admiradores* [admirers], you could say. A girl from my setting didn't have *novios* [boyfriends] until she was older, say, twenty. Up to that time it was just *admiradores*. They'd come by the finca or we'd meet at fiestas. But, as I say, my mother would take note of it and the next thing I'd hear was, "You know this fellow who's coming around to see you a lot, well, I don't think much of him!" She didn't think much of anyone—they all had defects as far as she was concerned. She'd say to me, "Why are you wasting your time with so-and-so? When your time comes to get married, you'll have someone who suits you." My brothers were the same as my mother, always finding something wrong with whoever it was I seemed to like. I think they didn't want me ever to get married. Maybe they figured I'd spend the rest of my life with them. Well, I could see the way things were going I might wind up a nun. I knew sooner or later I'd have to take a stand.

And that's what happened. The way it worked out was that living on a finca not far from ours was a woman my mother had once known as a girl, though at the time they were not in much contact. Señora Erlinda de Nuñez was her name. She was married to a physician and they had an enormous place, hundreds of manzanas. They also had several sons. So one day the doctor comes by our farm and introduces himself as the husband of Erlinda de Nuñez. My mother and he chatted awhile, and then a few days later the doctor comes back with his son—his youngest son, as it turns out. That's how I met Alberto. He was tall, elegant, and well spoken, a truly handsome man. He talked a bit with me, and I knew right then, that very day, that this was the man for me. Later I found out that for Alberto too, it had been love at first sight. But I had to be careful, very careful, pretending I wasn't that interested. Otherwise, my mother would have stopped things before they even started. Eventually, of course, she felt something serious was going on, as Alberto kept dropping by to see me. By then, though, it was too late. I wasn't going to let anyone stop me from marrying this man. I was twenty-one years old and I figured I could decide for myself. When my mother and brothers began to come up with their usual criticisms, I said, "Look, Alberto is a fine man from a good family, one you know. Besides, I love him. If he proposes to me, I shall not, I absolutely will not, refuse him!"

That was not a usual thing for a girl of my background to say, not to her parents or older brothers. A girl was expected to be modest, respectful. She didn't have to marry someone she did *not* want just because her parents said so. No, no, that custom—among people I knew, anyway—was from the previous century. Yet neither was she free to put up strong resistance to her parents' wishes. She wasn't expected to dig in her heels as I did. At first, my mother was taken aback by my determination. But once she saw I was serious she decided not to oppose me. My brothers were a little slower, as I remember.

[*At this point Niña Cecilia pauses, and Monica emerges from the kitchen, saying to her mother, "Miguel. Tell them what your brother Miguelito did to Papa. Remember?"*]

Oh yes, Miguelito—that rascal. *Bueno*, in all families there are some good ones and some bad ones. My oldest brother, Miguel, was one of the latter—a hard-drinking man. So what does he do to Alberto? He comes to him half-drunk one night and tells him to get up and accompany him by horseback through the hills. "Some important business," Miguel insisted. "You're coming, right?" It wasn't important at all, of course. Just some girlfriend in a village Miguel wanted to visit. Actually, the real reason was to test out Alberto, to see if he was tough enough to ride horseback through that cold, damp night. Alberto was tough, though, and took up the challenge. That man, he's never been afraid of anything. Alberto rode all night with my brother, and in the end I guess he passed the test. Miguel decided Alberto was good enough for me. And my other brothers did too. Alberto was smart, he knew how to win their confidence. By the time we got married, which was two years later, they completely accepted him. My mama, too. They could see he was right for me.

Our wedding was done the way they used to do weddings back then in the towns. You would have two ceremonies, one civil and the other religious. The civil ceremony was on the first day, with the mayor reading the matrimonial statutes. They used the same words then that they do today, with the mayor finally pronouncing, "In the name of El Salvador you are now solemnly united in matrimony and are obligated to remain mutually loyal in all of life's circumstances." This civil ceremony was held in the morning, and depending on the couple, they might have a small party, some food and some marimba music. That's what we did, a small party for the guests, about seventy-five of them. But the big party came the next day, after the religious ceremony. That's the real party, the one the bride's parents put on and paid for.

For me, that was a wonderful day. I worked it out so that it was exactly on my birthday, March 8th. A good thing too, I've never forgotten my anniversary because of this—not once. I tell you, I was a little nervous that day. For months, I'd been making preparations. A special seamstress made me this flowing white wedding dress, with a trail of 3 meters. She kept coming to the house until she had it just right. I wore a special veil and a crown, and beautiful white gloves. Another lady, a specialist in setting hair, did mine perfectly and put on the makeup just so. Alberto did not get to see me done up like this until I arrived at the church, and my oldest brother—yes, Miguel—led me to him. It was considered a bad omen if the groom saw the bride in her wedding outfit before that very moment. Then the priest conducted the ceremony. Alberto gave me a beautiful gold ring—though, God knows, I've since managed to lose it. And after that, as was the custom, he gave me the *arras*.* We made our religious vows one to the other, and that was it.

From the church to my family's house was a short walk, and so my señor and I led the way there. Then the party began. What a bash it was. It went on all afternoon. The food, which my mother had prepared, was delicious. Roast turkey, and rice with seafood—my favorite—and champagne, and a delicious three-tier wedding cake. And dancing, dancing, to the marimba band. I can still see us there now, Alberto and I, dancing

---

*The bridegroom gives the bride 13 coins that make up the *arras* (pledge, security).

that first waltz out in front of everyone. "The Blue Danube"—da, da, da, dum—and my señor and I, just the two of us, waltzing away. Who can forget a moment like that? Happy, happy, I was. And then everyone else joined in the dancing, which went on all afternoon. Lovely, lovely. Every bride should have it like that, really.

From the party we left immediately on our honeymoon. I got out of my wedding dress, put on something more comfortable, and we went by train to Lake Coatepeque. We didn't bother to open any wedding presents. The custom then was to wait until you got back from the honeymoon. Altogether, we were at Hotel Lago Coatepeque for six days. A beautiful place—maybe you know it? It's still there, a grand wooden hotel in the old style. How was it for me? Fine, lovely—what else can I say? Well, yes, I was a little nervous, certainly. No, my mother didn't tell me anything about what to expect. She figured I was twenty-four, I must know what to expect. More or less, I did know. I mean, it wasn't like today where the girls know everything at fourteen or fifteen because they teach them in school. But I had close friends, and they instructed me. So I knew [*she laughs*]. It was fine, normal. Look, you can adapt yourself. The adaptation, the change, is swift. But you have to know how to adapt yourself to others. That's life, right? The day after you're married everything's changed. If you're intelligent you know how to adjust. That's how I see it. What more can I say?

◦❧

Anyway, with the honeymoon over, we went home. To Alberto's parents' house, that's where we lived. No, not at their finca, that's where we went for weekends and holidays. They had another home, an enormous place in San Salvador. It was big enough for two families, with plenty of privacy for everyone. They wanted us there with them, and later, after my two children were born, they insisted we stay.

We lived in our part of the house with our *muchacha*, and they lived in theirs. You see, one of the gifts I got for my wedding—the best gift— was our *muchacha*, Virginia. My mother gave her to me shortly after I got married. "You're going to need someone, especially when you have

children," she said. "This girl is a good one. You take her." Virginia was
only a little older than me at the time—a fine woman, a native, but very
intelligent and loyal. We hit it off right from the start, and you know,
she stayed with me all these years. Almost fifty years she was with us.
Only last year, when her legs were failing her, I told her it was enough,
she should go back to her house in Armenia and rest. Now, every month,
on the fourth exactly, I send her a pension check. She deserves it. She
worked like a slave for us all those years. Today, you can't get *muchachas*
like her, no more loyalty as in the old days. The servants these days
come and go. But Virginia, God bless her, was like one of our family.
She helped me in the house, she helped raise our children from the time
I brought them home from the hospital. I can't imagine what I would
have done without her.

In the beginning, those first years after I got married, Alberto didn't
work much at all. He wasn't accustomed to working regularly, and really
he preferred to go about with his friends, or visit the finca, or go hunting.
Well, yes, that was alright with me. If that's what my señor wanted to
do, that was quite alright. We had no financial problems. With all their
properties, his parents were well-off, and Alberto's father was a respected physician. We had all we needed. Later, about five years after
we were married and I'd had the children, Alberto's brother brought
him into business with him. His brother was in the import business,
representing some fine European companies, and he told Alberto there
was good money to be made there. And he was right. Alberto took to
this easily, he was good at making contacts with people, and that's the
line of work he stayed in for many years. He got paid in dollars. He put
a lot of it away in banks in the United States, in Miami. He's still got
that money there if we ever need it.

As for running the finca, that job eventually fell to me. Alberto helped
some, but I did most of the work. This was after his parents had died,
and Alberto inherited the 75 manzanas, which we have today. His brothers got a sizable part of the original property, but Alberto—he was his
mother's favorite—he got the biggest share. His mother also made him
sole inheritor of all the family's stocks, bank accounts, and other properties. All of that is what provides our income today. With the finca, I'm

the one who took over its management. I had seen how my mother did it. She ran her finca alone all those years after my father died. I'd learned from her about sowing, fertilizing, harvesting—when and how to do it. I had a *mandador* to help manage the workers and the daily tasks. For years we've raised mostly sugarcane on the finca. It's a reliable crop that provides a good, steady income, and you don't have to be out there all the time keeping your eye on things.

So I worked—yes, more than many women of my background. And I was active at home too, I took good care of my señor and my children. Of course, I had Virginia with me, and she helped me with the children, day and night. Felipe, my son, was easy from the start. Monica was a little more difficult. She had a bad spell in the beginning, crying every night for months shortly after she was born. The doctor said she was completely healthy. To this day I don't know what could have been bothering her. There was nothing like that with my older child, Felipe. Truth was, everyone adored him—his father, my in-laws, Virginia— everyone. Me, I had no favorites. I adored them both. I felt bad for Monica. Children are very sensitive, they feel these things, so I tried to bend over backward to shower her with attention. I think it helped. You see her today and she's just fine—a wonderful wife, mother, and person. She developed extremely well. What helped a lot, I think, was that I sent her away to boarding school when she was thirteen. To Mexico. They had a much better school there, and I wanted her to get a good education. I also knew she was too tied to me. That was not good for her, she had to get away and become more independent. My son—God rest his soul—he didn't have that problem. Felipe didn't really have any problems at all. Only one problem, I guess you could say. He was adored by everyone, his father's pride and joy. And if you ask me, I think because of that, because he was adored too much, God called him away so soon, so early in his life. "Come with me," God said to him. And my son went.

For years I couldn't talk about this without weeping. Now I can. I've come to see it as God's will, and we must accept His will, however

painful at times. This is what I believe. Actually, when it happened—
this was in '73—I had a certain feeling, a premonition you could say.
My mother, God rest her soul, had died three weeks before. I was still
in deep mourning for her. But she had led a full life, a rich life. She was
eighty-five, at that age you expect death to come. My son, he was only
twenty-six. He had just finished his university studies as an agricultural
engineer. You don't expect death then, not at that age. Still, I had a very
bad feeling the day he told me that he and his friend Juan were going
out to a fiesta in San Miguel. It's a three-hour drive out there along a
road with treacherous curves. I pleaded with Felipe, "My son, at least
go in the daytime!" I had this horrible feeling something might happen.
So what do Felipe and Juan do? They go at night. Juan was driving.
About halfway there, along one of those curves, Juan didn't follow the
road and went right into a tree. Juan survived it. My son, God rest his
soul, was killed on the spot.

My husband and I were out at the finca when we got the news. We
rushed all the way to San Miguel, where they had taken him. I was
weeping the whole way, uncontrollably. Alberto, though, was in control—not a tear. And that's how Alberto stayed. When we saw Felipe's
body, when we sat through the wake at the funeral home, when we
buried our son, Alberto didn't break down. He supported me. Because,
you see, I collapsed. Today I can talk to you about this. Back then, no. I
felt as if the life had been drained out of me. I couldn't eat or sleep, I
just wept. For weeks, months, it went on. It's a feeling that has no name.
I just wanted to die. Even on my worst enemy, I swear, I wouldn't wish
such a thing. I hadn't been so close to God before that time, but I got
closer during those months, and I'm convinced that's what brought me
back. My belief in Nuestro Señor and in the Holy Mother, that's what
saved me [Niña Cecilia pauses to read us a poem in Spanish—part of which
is translated here]. This is something I wrote shortly after my son's death.
It's called "The Passing of My Son Felipe."

> . . . I never thought of losing one
> So loved so soon: a sun,
> Now set. My Lord who gave one day,
> Now takes the light away.
> His will be done.

I ask you, Jesus, Blessed Son—
Who heard your Mother's misery
When on the cross you made your plea:
Father, do not abandon me—
My Jesus, now I ask:
Do not abandon me. My task
Now with your help align
My heart to thank you, God of mine.

I wrote a lot of poetry in those months after my son died. It was a kind of therapy for me. I needed some way of expressing what I felt, and poetry gave me that. It helped me deal with the grief.

And bless him, my dear husband, he helped me too. We talked constantly, we each knew how the other was feeling. I remember this one time, we were out at the finca. All during that day I had been thinking about our son, how I wished he were still with us, even in a wheelchair. And I was thinking of Juan, how he was alive even though he was the one who'd caused the accident. That night I went to sleep and I had a dream. In the dream my son came to me and I asked him, "Son, what was the crash like?" He answered, "Look, Mama, it was just a few thousandths of a second. I felt no pain from it, and no pain when I realized I was on the other side already. I'm fine, Mama, don't worry about me. And don't do anything to Juan, don't say anything. Let it be." Well, that dream was like a cure for me. Truly I did blame Juan. We had the means of doing something with the authorities, but we decided against it even though he caused us all this pain. The dream gave me a sense that I had to resign myself to what had happened, that it had been our son's fate, it was written that way. I told all this to Alberto, discussed it with him. But he couldn't feel it that way. He couldn't see it as our son's fate. Still, no. For him time has not eased the pain. For me, yes. I've managed to go on.

One of the things that helped renew my wish to live was that in the years after Felipe's death, my husband and I started to travel. "Let's see some new things, maybe that will help," we said to each other. And so we began to go abroad. To Mexico, to the United States, to Europe—Spain, France, Germany. We started traveling three to four times a year. We saw all these places we'd only read about or seen on television. It was good for us. Also we went on cruises, especially those cruise ships that had casinos. I developed this—how shall I call it?—this "passion" for gambling. I'd always been free with money, buying whatever I wanted. It's outrageous, I have closets full of dresses and shoes that I haven't even worn once. And I give money away all the time in charity. A poor person knocks at the door to my house, I hear their story, and I give them something for this reason or that. That's my nature. Money for me is a thing to spend, give away. When you die they bury you in one suit or dress—not even your best one, usually—so why hold onto money? I like to spend it, I admit. So you see, once I began going to casinos, I quickly got this passion for gambling. The beautiful plush casinos in the Bahamas, and in Europe too, I loved going to them, though I never hit the jackpot. Alberto, he had more luck and he was cleverer than I was. One time in Paris, he watched this man play one of those slot machines. The man played for an hour without winning a franc. As soon as he left, Alberto went over to the same machine, and on the fifth try, pum! pum! pum!, he hit the jackpot, maybe 10,000 francs in coins. He stuffed as many as he could into the pockets of the new suit he'd bought in Vienna and then called me over and I stuffed the rest into my pockets and purse. Our plane was leaving that night, so in the next few hours we spent it all. We went to one of the best restaurants in Paris, had the best meal and wine, and then we bought all kinds of things. It was outrageous but great fun. Even Alberto was able to enjoy himself to the hilt then, the way he'd always done before. It was good to see him like that again. But unfortunately, it didn't last. Not more than that trip, unfortunately.

I think it was six years after Felipe died, something like that, when the war started here—this war that brought so much suffering to El Salvador and brought nothing good to our people. Thousands on thousands of people died, many of them young people, young men. People were shot down in their homes or in the street or just disappeared with no trace. When that began to happen, in the beginning of the '80s it was, I said to myself, "Better that Nuestro Señor should call our son to him as he did than to have him be suddenly machine-gunned down or, worse, disappear without our ever knowing what happened to him." Isn't that so? So many families lost their sons, fathers, sisters, and mothers in this terrible war. Here, let me read something I began to write for you. I put it down on paper so I won't forget . . . [*Niña Cecilia shuffles through some papers she has brought and begins to read*]. "Death, and especially the death of young people, became our daily portion in this cruelest of wars. And why was there such a war? In my opinion, it came about through the selfish interests of Communist leaders—*comandantes*, they called themselves. These leaders of the FMLN claimed they were patriots, but what they perpetrated was not patriotic. They set the country back fifty years. If the Communist leaders had taken on themselves the task of organizing people to improve their lives, to promote education and campaign for better wages, there would have been no war. Instead, these *comandantes* used the peasants' hardships as a means of improving their *own* lives. Who benefited from this war? Guerrilla leaders. They were poor men before the war and now own mansions in San Salvador and have money hidden away in Swiss banks. The country has paid a terrible price for this fratricidal war they brought on us. Every last family suffered from it, and to what end? No, I say, this war was not necessary!" [*At this point Niña Cecilia puts away the statement and continues to speak.*]

Look what happened in this war. *Look* at all the dead. Pure madness, I say. My husband's brother got murdered by the guerrillas for nothing. He was an innocent man. His only sin was that he was married to the sister of a former president of El Salvador. For this, the guerrillas killed him. And a cousin of mine got killed by the army. Because he was a leftist? No, far from it. Some army officer wanted to settle a score with him. This cousin unfortunately was having relations with a woman, relations outside his marriage. Without his knowing about it, this same woman was also involved with the army officer. So out of jealousy, the officer sent some of his soldiers to my cousin's house and they killed him. That's how things happen in a war, anything goes then. The rich and the humble, innocent and sinners perish alike.

If you ask me, it's as I said, the only real victors were the guerrilla leaders. They exploited the misery of some of our peasants and used them to fight this war. I'm not saying the peasants had no legitimate grievances. Some of them did. There *were* and still *are* landowners that treat them unfairly. Not my husband and I. I feel we've always been fair. We paid a fair wage before the war, and now—since the war the daily wage has been raised—we pay it too. If one of our workers needs medical attention or a loan to get some *maíz* or beans, we lend them what they need. We always have. And we've always treated our peas-ants with courtesy. Not all landowners have been like that. Some of the wealthiest people here, some of those from the so-called fourteen fami-lies* here, are known to have cheated their peasants. Or when they walk by them, they don't even say *Buenos días* [Good morning]. They treat the peasants with contempt.

[margin note: paternalism]

But is this what caused the war nobody benefited from? No! And what would have happened if the FMLN had won the war? It would have been like Nicaragua, with the Sandinistas. I know people there who had to board up their houses and go away empty-handed. The laws of the Communists made them leave with nothing. The same would have happened here. Mind you, a lot of people here—some of the biggest landowners—*did* have property taken away from them after the war. Only now, the government has paid them for it. But if the FMLN had been victorious and defeated the army, the whole country would have fallen into their hands. We—my husband and I, Monica's family—we would have been ruined. God knows what those Communists would have done to this place. Ruined it, just as in Cuba, I'm sure. Ruined it completely.

As it is, the country is in a terrible state as a result of the war. Rich and poor alike have no security. At the end of the war they dissolved the Guardia, the forces that used to watch over the countryside and the peasants. When we had the Guardia, there wasn't much crime. Now all we have is this new *policía civil* and they can't cope with the mass of criminals, gangs, we have now. We still go to the finca, but Alberto takes his pistol with him when we go out there, and we go only in the daytime.

---

*The "fourteen families" are an economic elite who established their fortunes princi-pally in the nineteenth century and still have much power and influence in El Salvador.

At night, even here in San Salvador, we hesitate to go out. If we're invited to a party or wedding these days, we don't go if it means traveling at night because anything can happen to you in the streets now. So more and more, we stay at home. That's how it's been since the war. The country has been set back. El Salvador is no longer the place it was before.

◆

How do I spend my time these days? *Bueno*, I go on, I enjoy myself as best I can. I'm at home a good deal of the time, reading and watching television. I love to read, always have—ever since I learned the alphabet together with the parrot. I read magazines, novels, the Bible, poetry. I'm not writing much poetry these days. Most of what I wrote came in the period after Felipe died. Nowadays, I seem to have less need to write. But I read a lot of poetry. Pablo Neruda is my favorite. His *Veinte poemas de amor y una canción desesperada* [Twenty love poems and a song of desperation] is marvelous, isn't it? Yes, I know they say he was a Communist, but I pay no attention to that. His ideology doesn't interest me, only his poetry, which is beautiful, eloquent.

Besides this, I watch television a lot. It may surprise you, but one of the things I like watching is soccer. I wouldn't think of going to the stadium—too much noise and rowdiness—but on television it's great fun to watch. Especially when our national team plays, or some of those fine European and South American teams, then I love to watch. I watch alone because my husband doesn't care much for soccer. What he'll watch together with me are some of the soap operas. We get some of the good soaps from the United States. Today, for example, I'm going to see *Bendita mentira* [Blessed lie] and *Te sigo amando* [Can't stop loving you]. My husband likes the *Te sigo amando* one, and we watch it together. We don't like the soaps with all the violence and that kind of thing. We turn the television off then and do something else.

I still like to get out and see women friends. We have tea together—you know, at someone's house or at one of the pleasant cafés here. Or Alberto and I will join another couple for lunch, try some new restaurant, even if it means driving an hour or two out of the city. And of course I spend time with Monica and her family. On Sundays we usually join them for lunch, and maybe once during the week Monica will bring me over—I don't drive, never have—and she and I will chat. Paulina and I chat too, quite a bit. Paulina comes to me for advice and I advise her the best I can. Her life and times are so different from when I was growing up—the things they know already, and what they're exposed to, like drugs. But evidently she feels she can trust me. I'm more likely to stay calm, maybe, than her mother. Paulina is a sensitive child, she gets upset over things that seem like nonsense, though for her they're not nonsense at all. I listen to her, reassure her, and if she asks my advice I give it to her. I think it would have been good for her if she had gone to boarding school, it might have made her more independent. I told Monica that, but it's too late now. Paulina is about to finish up high school this year at the British School here. Anyway, Paulina is a fine person, really. I've got great faith in her. She'll do just fine, I'm sure. Just like her mother.

I hope I live long enough to see Paulina move on with her life. A university education, that's what she wants. Fine, I say. Women should get as much education as they can. And after that, get married. I'd love to see that, and be a great-grandmother—wouldn't that be wonderful? But who knows? Only God knows what is in store for us, how much time each of us has.

Death comes, sometimes when you least expect it. Me, I feel healthy and strong, more or less, yet you never know. I can tell you this, though, whenever death does come I am prepared. Without any hesitation I can say I do not fear death. I've had a full life. Almost everything I've wanted to do, I've done. Three years ago Alberto and I finally went to the Holy Land. This was one thing I felt I wanted to do before I die. To pray at the holy places, to see where Nuestro Señor was born and crucified, was something I wanted so much to do. I swear, as we traveled through the Holy Land I felt His presence. On the way to Bethlehem from Jerusalem, looking out at the Judaean Hills where He had walked, I suddenly smelled the scent of incense in the taxi. There were no houses or buildings around where that scent could have come from. I felt God was with us then, right there traveling with us.

This closeness to God makes me unafraid of death. I belong to a Bible reading group, and every Wednesday we meet and discuss matters of religion. And I go every Sunday to the eight o'clock mass, I take Holy Communion, and I confess. At night, in my prayers I hand my soul over to God. If I should die in my sleep, I am prepared. My only wish is that it happen quickly, with no lingering or causing problems for my family.

Yes, I believe the soul lives on. It is foolish to think that we are like animals, like some dog that dies and then that's the end. We have souls and when we die our soul joins those of others who have died. In this way, yes, I expect to join my son and others in my family who have died. But that's not the reason I have no fear of death. It's simply that I accept that our time here on earth is a passage. The eminent die along with the humble and simple. We live as long as God wills, and then we pass to the other side. I have been one of the most fortunate of people. My life has been a full one. Whenever God finally says, "Come with me," I am ready to go. No hesitation. I am ready to join Our Lord.

Monica

The Altamira section of San Salvador covers a hillside southwest of the city. It is one of the capital's newest and most elegant neighborhoods, and many of its residences and mansions have a panoramic view of the city below. An armed sentry protects the entrance and massive walls surround most of the homes. Even its recreational park, Bosque Altamira, has a uniformed guard to provide security for the maids or (less often) mothers who bring the nattily dressed children to its comfortable playground.

Monica Nuñez de Solares has been living in Altamira for four years together with her husband and daughter. Her five-bedroom house, with its backyard swimming pool, lies at the end of one of the neighborhood's tree-lined streets. Here, in her well-appointed salon—with its marble floor, plush sofas, and hand-carved European tables and armoires—we interviewed all three women in her family: Niña Cecilia, Paulina, and Monica herself. And here too, as guests, we occasionally spent a social evening with her family and friends.

At forty-seven years Monica is quite as elegant and gracious as the surroundings in which she lives. She still has a youthful appearance, accentuated by the trim skirts, slacks, and blouses that she brings back from her shopping trips to Miami and Paris. Similar to most women of her class, Monica does not work outside her house. Rather, she spends most of her day supervising her household, socializing with friends, and, not least of all, "running errands for my workaholic husband."

Monica speaks fluent and colloquial English, but all eight of our interviews with her were conducted in Spanish. Perhaps more than any other woman in our study, she has a natural gift for spinning a story; and unquestionably she was our most enthusiastic and willing subject. Unlike her mother, who was intrigued most by the literary aspect of what we were doing, Monica seemed to have a personal, even cathartic, need to air her many experiences. Our interviews with her went far longer than they did with either her mother or daughter.

Monica's many reflections about her public and private life—from the war and political situation of the country, to the difficulties of raising her adolescent daughter "in an era of kidnappings and crime"—would fill the better part of a book. We therefore had to prune these recollections and, at her request, showed her the final version (no other woman suggested this possibility, nor did we offer it). What follows here is a condensed and (almost) unexpurgated version of Monica's life story.

I heard a lot of what my mother told you. I'm surprised, she's still got a good memory for someone her age. Though there's one thing she definitely remembered wrong—her age. She's not sixty-seven. Figure it out yourselves, I was born in '50, when she was twenty-seven. Really, she knows that. My mother, she's a bit of a coquette. You won't get her to tell you the truth about her age. As for the rest, she's forgotten some details here and there, at least from how I remember things. That's natural. Everyone remembers things in their own way, everyone has their own perspective, right? I imagine when you talk to my daughter, Paulina, she'll have a different view from mine on some things. No, I don't *imagine*, I'm *sure* of it. You'll see.

I think the way I want to start is to pick up from what my mother was telling you about where our family comes from. The part she left out was about my father's family. I'm no *machista,* really. I'm much closer to my mother, I admire her and adore her—more than my father. But it was with my father's parents, Grandma Erlinda and Grandpa Julio, that I grew up. We lived in their house and spent our vacations at their finca. So naturally, I knew them more than my mama's people. And they *were* an interesting family with an interesting background.

I don't want to bore you with all the details. I could go on for days, but I'll make it short. I'll start with Grandma Erlinda, my father's mother. It's her family who were the wealthy ones. Her ancestors came from Spain, and they acquired an enormous property here. Thousands on thousands of manzanas that stretched from the department of La Libertad to the department of Sonsonate—a whole city in size, or more. This property was split up in all the subsequent inheritances, but still my grandma Erlinda had a good-sized estate. The 75 manzanas that my father inherited from her are only a fragment of the original land. But Grandma Erlinda never had anything to do with managing her finca. She was a pampered woman, religious and kind, but a woman who never lifted her finger to do any work. She wasn't at all like my mother's mother, who ran a finca by herself. Oh no, not Grandma Erlinda. In all those years I lived with her, I don't think I ever saw her cook a meal. Grandpa Julio liked it that way. "Now, Linda," he'd say—that's what he called her—"now don't you step foot in the kitchen, Linda. I want a wife, not a cook with garlic smelling in her hair!" And she listened to him.

The one who managed things was my grandpa Julio. He was a physician, a tall and handsome man, and a paterfamilias type. He was many years older than my grandma, and he was the boss. Grandpa Julio came from a fine family, though not one that was wealthy like his wife's. He was one of fifteen children. His father, Don Pedro, was a lawyer and judge, one of the men who signed the Salvadoran constitution [in 1885]. Don Pedro was married to Miri. That's what they called her—I think it came from Miriam. She's a story by herself. Miri was a Sephardic Jew. She came to El Salvador from Spain with her parents. I mean, they were Catholics—very devout too—but they had converted back when they were in Spain. Miri, they say, was a great beauty. When she was only fifteen years old she got married to the judge, Don Pedro, who'd fallen madly in love with her. They had all these children, fourteen boys and a girl—including my grandpa Julio—and most of them wound up living here in the capital. Sometimes I think I'm related to half the people in this city. Seriously. They all had big families, and one way or the other I think most of the people in the capital must be cousins of mine!

Actually, a few of these cousins I knew very well. This was because every summer I'd go out to Grandpa Julio and Grandma Erlinda's finca for the summer vacation. Some of them would come visit us there. It would be me, my brothers and sisters, their parents, and some of my father's five brothers and sisters, their children, other cousins, and friends. A real crowd, like a summer camp! That's how my grandparents liked it—lots of people. At dinnertime, Grandpa Julio would sit at the head of this long, long wooden table, like a king sitting over his court. There were lots of little cozy bedrooms for everyone to sleep in, and hammocks hanging here and there if you preferred that. I tell you, I had some of the best times of my life out there in the summer. You've seen the finca, haven't you? It's a little run-down now, but what a place it was then!

Back when I was a kid, my grandparents' finca was several hundred manzanas in size. You could get on a horse and ride an hour or so, and still you wouldn't see it all. Rolling hills, with sugarcane planted all over, and coffee bushes, and lots of little houses where the peasants lived. My grandfather was an enterprising man, and he'd fixed the place up beautifully. There was a stream that ran through the property, near the main house. In one place where the stream was wide, Grandpa Julio had the area enlarged and enclosed with rock walls, so that you had a kind of natural swimming pool with the stream flowing through it. There were fifty-foot-high bamboo stalks growing over the area and trees with long vines hanging from them. My cousins and I would play Tarzan, swinging on the vines and leaping into the pool. What fun that was!

Another thing we'd do is go "sleigh riding." Of course, not on snow—

on this slick grassy hill. When they'd prune the coconut trees, the branches with their wide, smooth leaves made great sleds. You could go whipping down the hill very fast. It was a little dangerous, with the rocks around. Our parents didn't know we were doing it. They'd just see one or two of us come back with a scrape or cut. But they never stopped us, never said anything.

We were free back in those days! It wasn't like today, when parents are afraid, and wouldn't let kids like us, the landowner's kids, go roaming off through the hills. Anything can happen today, kidnapping or God knows what. Back then the countryside was safe. You could roam around all day and nobody would harm you. The only way you could get harmed was if you did something stupid to yourselves—like sometimes my cousins and I did. This one time, you know what we did? We found this dead horse out in the hills. One of my older cousins told us he'd eaten horse meat and it was delicious. I must have been about seven at the time. I was the youngest of the bunch. We all stood around fascinated as this older cousin pulled out his jackknife and cut up strips of horse meat. We gave it to the cook and told her to make us horse meat for lunch. She had the good sense, fortunately, to get my grandpa's approval. The next thing you knew, he came storming out at us. "What do you think you're doing?" he screamed. He was a doctor and he knew about the risks of eating the dead horse. "Don't you know how dangerous this is? Do you want to catch what the *horse* died from?" And he sent us all off to be showered and disinfected. Never in my life did I see him so mad.

Usually, Grandpa Julio was relaxed with us out at the finca, not too strict. He was a sociable man, he loved to have parties and see people having fun. In fact, he was known throughout the whole area for one fiesta that he used to put on every year—every June 13th, in honor of San Antonio. That was some party! And the way it got started, I mean the reason he used to have this fiesta, is sort of interesting. You want to hear it? Alright, here's what happened, the way I heard it. Back when my grandpa Julio was about twenty, he'd gone hunting one time out in the mountains. He got lost, and he'd run out of ammunition. Night began to fall and he heard the baying of wolves and coyotes, and he figured to himself, "This is it, I'm finished. I'm going to be eaten." Then he remembered that his mother—right, Miri—she had told him San Antonio was the protector of lost souls, those who had lost their way. On the spot, he began to pray to San Antonio. Soon after, he felt a hand on his shoulder and someone said to him, "What's happened to you, son? Why are you weeping?" It was a tiny bald man who was talking to him. My grandpa said, "I'm lost. Please get me out of here!" And the little man said, "Of course, follow me." And he led my grandpa out of the mountains and back to the main road. My grandfather began to run, overjoyed at still being alive. Then he stopped and said to himself, "My God, I didn't even thank that señor." But when he turned to thank him, the man was gone, nobody was there. Now my grandfather was a medical student then, a man of science, but he was convinced he'd been saved by a miracle. He had figured he was finished, he'd about given up hope. So in gratitude for this miracle, he later erected a shrine to San Antonio at the finca, and on the saint's day, June 13th, Grandpa Julio would throw a party.

At first it wasn't such a big party, it was only for the family. They'd have a small dinner and say a rosary together. But as the years passed, the little party became bigger and bigger, until it became *the* fiesta of the entire area. That's the way it was when I was a child. Peasants from our finca and others from all over the area would come. Grandpa Julio would have a bull slaughtered, along with a couple of pigs, maybe five turkeys, and two dozen chickens. He'd bring in maybe twenty cooks to prepare the feast. And he'd hire a marimba band that would play all night, with everyone dancing to the music. My grandpa had one rule, though—no liquor. Not a drop of alcohol was served nor could it be brought in. He had to have that rule because, frankly, our peasants don't know how to handle alcohol. They start drinking and then they get euphoric or sad or violent. That's the way it is today too. In every town whenever there's a fiesta, there's lots of problems, people getting killed. So my grandpa had the rule, no alcohol for anyone. And he hired four or five pairs of rural police, the Guardia, to enforce the rule. When the peasants came in they had to hand over their machetes, and at the entrance there was an indescribable heap of machetes with the Guardia watching over them. Inside, there was absolute calm, people gorging themselves and dancing away. Never was there a bad incident. Grandpa Julio, as always, presided over the whole thing. I can still see him, like a king, going about the fiesta happy and proud and, yes, always grateful and always going off to the shrine to say a rosary in honor of his mother's patron saint, San Antonio, who had brought him that miracle in the mountains.

You see, it was my grandpa Julio who was the true head of our household when I was growing up. At the finca, and in the house in San Salvador where we lived, he was the dominant one. Was my father bothered by that? Oh no, not at all. He liked it that way. He liked having his father manage things. My father was really like another kid in the house. That's the way I see it. There was me, Felipe, and then my father, who was like the oldest son. My father used to love spending long weekends at the finca hunting. And as soon as my brother was old enough—maybe seven—he started to take Felipe with him to hunt ducks and deer. That was my father's passion. I tell you, he was like a big kid. The truth is, my grandma Felicia—my *mother's* mother—didn't want my mother to marry him. Grandma Felicia was a widow, who'd raised eight children by herself, run a finca by herself. She knew how to judge people. My father's a year younger than my mother, and Grandma Felicia saw how immature he was. She tried to oppose him, but my mother wouldn't listen. She'd made up her mind, and that was it. Later, after they'd married, Grandma Felicia developed a true affection for my father. He's a kid, but a good one, and she came to love him as one of her own.

As for my mother, she's happy with my father. She loves him, no doubt about it. And I think she has liked having the responsibility for the finca mostly on her shoulders. Just like Grandma Felicia, my mother knows how to run things. In the house, she had the support of my grandparents, and she also had Virginia. So my mother had plenty of help. Especially from Virginia. Virginia's been with our family from the time I was born. Only this year, my mother retired her. Virginia was like a second mother to me and Felipe—our strict mother, you could say, because my mother was a soft touch. Not Virginia, no way! She used to make sure each morning that I was dressed very neatly, my clothes all white and pressed, my shoes shining, neat, neat. If you were sick she'd call you over and, poummmm!, she'd force the medicine down your mouth. That was her way, very strict. She was devoted to us, though, and especially to my mother. She and my mother really loved each other, still do. Back when I was growing up, she'd defend my mother against anyone. Just let my father criticize her, saying to her, "Cecilia, this food tastes bad, it isn't worth eating!" My mother wouldn't say anything, but Virginia later would say, "How dare he talk to Niña Cecilia like that?" Virginia would even go to my father and tell him he had no right to talk to her that way, and then for weeks she'd stay mad at him, ignore him. If you ask me, Virginia got too involved in things. But that was her way. The only other person she was devoted to in that way was Felipe. He could do no wrong in her eyes—she adored him too. But there was nothing unusual in that. Everyone adored my brother—he was the favorite of everyone.

How was that for me? Well, it wasn't easy, not at all. Maybe it was because he was older, or because he was a boy. Here, boys are favored, right? My father, for sure, preferred boys. Once my mother told me—I think it slipped out—that when I was born he was disappointed. He had wanted another son. "Ugh! She's got the face of a virgin!" my father said when he first saw me. Whatever that means! I had this pretty little mouth, so maybe I looked like the Virgin Mary. Who knows? Anyway, my father had a clear preference for my brother. My grandparents, too.

Felipe had this charm about him. He was a prankster, and he had a way of pulling off his tricks without getting anyone angry with him. He knew how to win people over. Everyone adored him. Me, too. If he was given a new toy and I was given nothing, he'd come over to me and whisper, "Don't worry, I'll let you share it." And he *was* given everything. All Felipe had to say is that he wanted something, and it was his. I'll give you an example. Grandma Erlinda used to get this Sears and Roebuck mail-order catalogue. She'd come to my brother—never to me—and tell him to order what he wanted. Then the boxes would arrive with shoes, a jacket, vest, pants, everything. He'd be so excited. And me, I'd just sit there feeling, you know, terrible. It wasn't Felipe's fault, really, that he got special treatment. What was he supposed to do, refuse it?

Fortunately, thank God for her, my mama saw all this and she tried to compensate for it. She'd take me by the hand and say, "Look, since Felipe's got some new clothes already, that leaves me with extra money for you. Let's go to the department store here, and you can choose whatever you like." That's how she'd handle it. She bent over backward to make me not feel this preference. For her, I really believe there was no preference. She's the only one. She loved us both the same. I've always felt that. Really, if it hadn't been for her way of dealing with things, I don't know how I would have grown up. Probably bitter and resentful. She saved me from that, and now that I'm a mother myself I can see how clever and wise she was.

The thing my mother didn't spare me from was boarding school. I was very angry with her when she sent me off. Actually, I thought it was my father's idea. I was thirteen at the time, about a year or so before my grandpa Julio died. My brother was going to high school here in San Salvador, and I had just finished ninth grade here. I was a smart child, but I had some problems with the teachers, and I just managed to get by that year. My father came to me one day and said, "Monica, it will be a good idea for you to go off to boarding school. Here you have no sisters, and there you'll be in a school, a fine school, with all these girls. We've checked it out and there's a good place in Mexico." I was in shock when I heard this. Mexico! I felt he was punishing me, sending me so far away. I went to my mother, pleaded with her not to let Papa do that, but *she* was in agreement with him. "It's for your own good, you'll see," she said. I saw I was lost, there was nothing I could do. _They_ had decided, and that was it. In those days—it wasn't like today—you couldn't argue, I mean *really* argue, with your parents. You had to do what they told you to do.

So I went. Expecting the worst, I went. And I was right. It *was* terrible.

Those first few weeks, months were awful. The British nuns who ran this school in Mexico City were strict, terribly strict. All my life my mother was kind to me. She had done everything for me. I didn't know how to do a thing for myself. And what happens? As soon as I get to the school these nuns tell me, "*You* make your own bed. *You* wash your socks and underwear. *You* iron your uniform." I saw girls eight and nine years old doing this, but I had no idea how to do it. I felt like the most useless person in the world. And the food, ugh! I was used to fine food, my mother's and Virginia's cooking. In this school, you could hardly eat what they served you. Everything was with chile. That's the way Mexicans like their food. One time shortly after I arrived, I told the nun that I couldn't eat this chicken with all the chile on it. You know what she did? She took it to the kitchen and ran cold water over the chicken to wash off the chile. Do you know what it tastes like to eat washed cooked chicken? Tears were running down my cheeks as I ate it, but I had to sit there and finish the whole thing. Awful, horrible!

Each week we had to write home to our parents—that's what they told us. "Good, that's my salvation," I said to myself. I decided to tell my parents what the place they sent me to was like. "They're too strict on us," I wrote. "The nuns make us do everything on time—wash up in three minutes, breakfast in seven minutes. The discipline is frightening, the food is awful, the place is like a prison." Surely if my parents heard this, I figured, they'd bring me home. But of course, they never got the letter. The nuns made you give the letters in an open envelope, and they read every word. And that was it for me! "So we don't know how to teach discipline?" the nuns said to me. "Well, from now on, no Sundays off for you. Not until you learn to write your parents the truth! Tell them you don't know how to make your bed or wash your clothes because nobody ever taught you how. Tell them the truth!"

I got the message. I saw there was no way out. I sat through my month with no Sundays off, no going to the movies, nothing. From then on, I gave the nuns letters telling my parents how wonderful the place was and how I loved it. I realized I had to fall into line. Fortunately, the other girls in the boarding school liked me, and they helped me out. One of these girls was the niece of the director of the boarding school, Sister

Mary's niece. On Sundays she got to go all over the city in a chauffeured car, and since I was her friend, Sister Mary wasn't about to stop me from joining her. And another close friend was the daughter of an important Mexican politician. They lived in this fantastic house, and I got to visit them many Sundays too. This girl didn't sleep at the school, she only came to classes there. So she started bringing me lunch from her house, delicious stuff. She also took my letters, the true ones, and sent them to my parents. That's what saved me at boarding school—these friends. I knew how to make good friends, and these connections were what helped me in the first year or two when I was suffering so much.

Eventually, though, what happened is that I began to like being there. By my third year—I was there five years altogether—I started to enjoy myself. My friends became like sisters to me. That one whose father was a politician is still a friend of mine today. I see her whenever I go to Mexico City. And, *bueno*, in the third year I began to have privileges as an older student. *I* got to monitor the three minutes in the bathroom. If any girl crossed me, it was two minutes! Me, I got a full ten minutes alone to myself—what a luxury! Yes, things were a lot easier by the third year. I even began talking of "my Mexico." When I went back to El Salvador for summer vacations I was no longer complaining. My father told me that at the end of my third year I could stop going if I wanted. But by then I wanted to stay. I had come to like the place.

The truth is, my parents were right to send me. I could already see that by the time I graduated. I tell you, I wish I could have sent Paulina to boarding school—now it's too late—but I wish we could have sent her. She wouldn't have agreed, and besides there're no longer many good boarding schools available. Still, it's a good thing, I'm convinced. I was too tied to my mother before they sent me, I couldn't do anything for myself. My mother saw all that, I'm sure. She just couldn't stop it, especially since she was my only real support in the house. It took five years away at boarding school to help me grow up, become independent. And, of course, I got an excellent education there, much better than if I had stayed in El Salvador. I was able to study many languages—French, Italian, and English. Also, business management and accounting. And then these other things they considered we should know—etiquette, cooking, and all that. It was a complete education. I feel it prepared me for life. To this day, I'm grateful my parents sent me. Though in the beginning, God knows, I resented them bitterly for it.

~&

When I came back from boarding school I was seventeen, seventeen plus. I lived again with my parents. That's what you did. You didn't go off and find a place of your own. I had this title I'd earned at the school. "Bilingual, parliamentary executive secretary, private accountant and archivist"—that's what it was called. I had no idea what I wanted to do, though I did want to work. Then my father came to me one day and said he had an idea. He had a friend who was president of the Banco Central de Reserva. They had nobody there who knew how *connections* to order things, how to keep archives. So I got the job. Can you imagine it? I wasn't even eighteen yet, and I was receiving all this confidential material about the balances of the Central Bank of El Salvador. It was an important job. Still, I didn't like it. Boring, boring! After six months I was going out of my mind.

What I really wanted to do was to travel, see some of the world, and be more on my own. The job I decided I wanted—can you believe this?— was to be an airline stewardess. I knew my parents wouldn't go for the idea, certainly not my father. So I went to my brother and asked him what he thought. "Fine idea," Felipe told me. "If that's what you want, then try to do it!" He really encouraged me. He agreed to go to my mother and try to persuade her. Meanwhile, I went to our airline here, TACA, and applied. I had an aunt who was a friend of the head of the airline. That helped, of course. Before I knew it, I was offered the job. My father, as expected, was completely opposed. But Felipe and my mother were on my side. And besides, I was able to show my father that there were other girls from good families who were stewardesses. In my time, some of those girls were from known families. Once my father saw that, he relaxed a bit. He no longer opposed me.

For the next six years, then, that's what I did. I went all over— throughout Central America, Mexico, many cities in the United States. I even got to go to places in Europe. Every six months we were given free tickets to use on other airlines, and so off we went. Two or three other girls and I, we got to be close friends, and we'd travel together. My father sort of kept looking over my shoulder, inspecting who I was going with, but eventually these other girls became like part of my family and he accepted them as if they were his own daughters.

That was a truly fun period of my life, those years as a stewardess. But great though it was, something horrible happened then. Felipe. He died in an automobile accident. My mother must have told you about it, didn't she? I tell you, it destroyed us, our family. That's what I think. Until then we were a fairly happy family. Since then, no, you can't say that.

I was here in El Salvador when it happened. I was off duty, not flying that week. My parents were out in Armenia visiting relatives when they got the first news. They had been at their finca and then went to visit these relatives. On the way there, my mother later told me, they had passed an area where she smelled the scent of cypress trees. That scent is associated with death because people put wreaths of cypress on the grave when someone is buried. My mother said to my father, "Alberto, I'm smelling cypress, it's very strong!" Since it was late November, my father said, "It's the time people are beginning to cut cypress trees for Christmas, that's why you smell it." People use the cypress as little Christmas trees, so he figured that was it. Then they arrive at my mother's cousin's house, and she's told, "Look, there's some very bad news. Felipe's been in an accident. Out toward San Miguel."

Well, from that moment on, my mother began sobbing. And when they got out there, she collapsed in grief. My father had to support her. He was amazing then. He stayed under control through the whole thing, looking after others, making sure they were alright. But we could see then, and even later, that he was too much in control. Not my mother, she went on sobbing. You could talk to her, but she was always weeping. I remember this period really well. I was thinking, "My poor mama. She who has been happy her whole life, always laughing, is never going to laugh again. She'll never wear her red dress again, I'll never see her smile again. Never." And me, too, I was in great sorrow. Felipe had been such a support to me—encouraging me to take the job at TACA, or helping me with my car, or going to parties with me. I relied on him, much more than on my father. I couldn't imagine life without him.

For months this terrible grief went on. And then I could see that Mama was slowly coming out of it. Me, too. My father, no. Mama had sobbed and sobbed, and she had found her relief. Little by little, she was coming to accept it. But not my father. He had never broken down and found his relief. Instead, he began sinking deeper and deeper into grief. He couldn't talk to anyone, couldn't sleep, couldn't eat. I think it was better to sob and sob as she did rather than to fall into a silent depression as he did, and which he still hasn't come out of. My mama, bless her, has since come back to herself. She laughs, she enjoys herself, and yes, she can wear a red dress again. My papa has not returned to himself. His life collapsed when Felipe died.

It was about two years after Felipe's accident that I met Francisco, my husband. I was still working at TACA and he was just getting started in his business. Don't print exactly which business, alright? It will be too easy to identify him. But he was in a business that caused him to fly a lot and to be associated with TACA. I had seen him around, but I didn't know him. Then one day he comes to me at the airport and asks me if I'd do him the favor of driving him to the garage where his car is being fixed. I was a bit taken aback, but I agreed. On the way, he starts talking about the classical music on the radio. It turns out that he plays the piano. Bach, Mozart, Chopin—he knows about all this—but not about the Supremes or any of the popular groups then. "An interesting guy, not the usual type," I thought to myself. Anyway, I drop him off at the garage. "Thank you, thank you very much," he says, and I figure that's it.

But the next thing I know, Francisco is calling me up at home. He says he wants to visit me. At the time I had a boyfriend, and actually he had a girlfriend too. But what's the harm, I figured. I told him he could visit me. *Bueno*, from then on he began visiting me often. For the next few months, in fact, he came around every day, whenever he had a spare hour. And we were going out too. My parents got along well with him, especially my father. With Francisco, Papa talked. Francisco loves to talk and can talk to anyone, everyone. So they hit it off. Mama, too, she seemed to like Francisco. The more she knew him, the more she liked him. In any case, when I finally told her and my father that Francisco and I were thinking of getting married—this was six months or so after we met—they both agreed.

Francisco's parents were also very accepting of me. He's their only son, and they took me in like a daughter. They are, were, very warm people—they're both gone now. They were fine people. They had a huge house in Santa Tecla. Francisco's mother came from the L—— family. Yes, one of the "fourteen families." Her family never accepted Francisco's father, although he was an outstanding person, and had his own modest properties. To this day, Francisco resents the L—— family for having rejected his father. Though the funny thing is, my daughter is proud to go around saying she is one of the L—— line. Sometimes she signs her name by adding the L—— family name. Francisco doesn't like this, but what can you do?

Anyway, I'm getting ahead of myself. Let me tell you about our wedding. Well, in a word, it was just the way I wanted it! My parents gave us the money and told us to do as we liked. For months we planned it— the arrangements at the church, the list of invitations, the party at the hotel. We wanted it to be perfect, with fine food, liquor, and beautiful table settings. And it *was* perfect. I wore a fine white satin wedding dress as I'd always dreamed, and Francisco wore this tuxedo with tails as *he'd* always dreamed. You see, Francisco had played piano and he always dreamed of dressing up like the great pianists and conductors. His wedding was his first chance. You should have seen him. Happy, happy. He kept going around from table to table, dancing with all the women guests. He was a happy groom, like one you sometimes see, dancing and dancing. I was really happy too. We both were, like a couple in love with life. The party was in the evening, like they do it these days, and it went on till two in the morning. We didn't leave early the way some couples do. We stayed till the end, till the cutting of the cake. Then some friends drove us to a hotel here, Hotel El Salvador, where we spent the first night.

How did that go? *Bueno*, if you want to know I'll tell you. It was sort of amusing. Because what happened is that when we got to our room, Francisco realized he could hardly stand up. He had bought these new patent leather shoes for the wedding and they were too tight on him. He hadn't noticed it at the party, he was having too much fun dancing. But when he went to take off his shoes, both his feet were two huge blisters. He couldn't walk a step. So the first few hours of our wedding night we spent taking care of his blistered feet [*Monica laughs*]. It wasn't until dawn, some time around then, that anything else happened.

How was it for me? Well, it was the first time, yes. I more or less knew what to expect. I was twenty-five then and I'd heard from others. The close friend who took us to Hotel El Salvador had explained everything, or almost everything, to me. My mother, no. She hadn't said anything except *Que te vaya bien* [May it go well with you]. I think when Paulina gets married I'm going to prepare her. I think that's the way to do it. But anyway, this friend had talked to me just as if she were my mother, and she'd even said to Francisco, joking, "Now treat her right, you hear? Don't be too crude!" Francisco laughed when he heard this, he took it in the right spirit.

If you ask me, though, I think it takes time for a couple to get used to each other. Some weeks, anyway. At least that's my experience. We went off on our honeymoon and I developed, well, this kind of discomfort women sometimes get on their honeymoon. Nobody had told me about that. What pain! I didn't say anything to Francisco, I didn't want to spoil his fun. But as we were going around from place to place, I was suffering from this. And Francisco, he's a great sightseer. We went to New Orleans for a few days and then to Miami. In Miami, he had this wish—maybe he had it from his childhood when he was there, who knows?—but he wanted to see all these places I'd never heard of before. Monkey Jungle, Parrot Jungle, and Alligator Land. We saw them all, with Francisco happy as a kid, filming everything. We've got these honeymoon films, me with parrots and all the animals. But really I enjoyed it too. I mean, even with my problem, I enjoyed being there with him,

seeing him so happy. That's Francisco. He's a person who gets real enthusiastic about things. It's something I liked about him when I first met
him, and it's something I still like about him. He's got real enthusiasm.
Almost like a kid.

After the honeymoon we went to live with Francisco's parents in
Santa Tecla. Our house, which we were building next to theirs,
wasn't quite finished, so we lived for awhile with them. I was still working at TACA, though I stopped within a year. And Francisco was busy
with his work, though at the time he wasn't making much money. The
truth is, we didn't have so much then. If we went out we'd go to Don
Pedro's, a sort of diner. No fancy places for us then.

But Francisco was, still is, a hard worker, always thinking of how to
move forward. He didn't finish college, yet the man has a knack for
business. He knows how to smell an opportunity and how to take
chances. Before we got married, he had invested in coffee land. His aunt
lent him some money and he won the lottery once. He used this money
to buy 50 manzanas located about 20 kilometers from here, and since
then he's built it into a very profitable coffee plantation. But that was
only a sideline for him, a kind of hobby. Where he's really made out
well is in this business he's been building all these years. He's got a
couple of partners, and at this point he's the main shareholder and president. It's a multimillion-dollar enterprise now, and we're doing really
well. No complaints, none at all.

Right after we got married, though, we had nothing like what we
have today. I mean, we had fun but we didn't have the luxuries we have
today. It was a good time, though. We were a young couple, free as
birds, and life was good. The idea of having children was far from us.
Francisco wasn't thinking about having children, and really neither was
I. Maybe some day, I figured, but I wasn't eager for it. Francisco and I
were happy as we were.

And then a strange thing happened. I don't know if you'll believe it,
but I'll tell you anyway. It happened as Francisco and I were on a trip

to Miami. Our plane had stopped over in Guatemala and there was a delay. It turned out that in the VIP room of the airline we were traveling on there was a special guest—Mother Teresa. She was on her way to Panama, and she too had a layover. Someone came up to us and offered to introduce us. Francisco at first said, "No, what have I got to do with nuns?" But I pushed him, I wanted to meet this woman. She was just sitting there off to the side with other nuns, all of them in their white Indian saris with the blue stripe. The only luggage she had was this little cloth bag. And tiny, she was so tiny. I figured we'd just say "hello" and "good-bye." But no. Francisco, who didn't want to go over, starts talking to her, and he couldn't stop. I expected her to be a real serious type, and in the beginning she *was* serious. The war here had just started—this was in '80—and Monseñor Romero had just been killed. Mother Teresa asked, "Why did they kill him? Why so much bloodshed in El Salvador now?" She said she was praying all the time because she feared that the killing of a priest was going to bring tragic consequences to El Salvador. I'll never forget how she said that. It was like a judgment. Well, we went on talking, not just about this, but on lighter subjects. Francisco and she were actually joking around. She had a real sense of humor, a real spark. It went on like that for an hour and a half, until it came time for us to board our plane. As we got up to leave, Mother Teresa asked us, "You don't have any children?" Francisco said, "No," and then added, "And we don't want any either." She looked at us with those eyes of hers that seemed as if they could see into your soul, and she said, "Children are a blessing, gifts from God. Soon you are going to have one. I'm going to pray for this." I'll never forget that moment, her pointing her finger at us and signaling that it would happen. Francisco, not taking it seriously, said to her, "Alright, one only. No more than that." And with that, we said good-bye and left. For me, it was as if she had blessed us. We'd been married four years then and I'd not gotten pregnant, but who knew?

I thought no more about it, until six months later when one night I started getting this nauseous feeling. It didn't go away, so finally I went to the laboratory and took a test. Sure enough, I was pregnant. "Me, a mother?" I thought. "Am I ready for this?" And our friends—we'd told some of them about the incident with Mother Teresa—they started saying to us, "Mother Teresa! It was her. She did it!" I was glad, though. It felt like a blessing to me. And Francisco got used to the idea too. He may not have wanted a child at first, but once it was on the way, he got used to the idea.

The problem was that just then the war was going badly here. Lots of killing everywhere. My gynecologist suggested that if we could manage it, maybe it would be best for me to go to Miami and give birth there. You see, I have this rare blood type, and the doctor told me there was no reserve of my type of blood here in El Salvador. Those who might have been able to donate blood, some of them had fled the country. So even though the pregnancy was going normally, he told me it would be wisest to go to the United States.

And that's what we did. I spent the last two and a half months of my pregnancy in Miami, in a rented apartment. We had friends there and I wasn't alone. Francisco visited me every weekend, flying up from El Salvador. It was fine, and I felt fine. In the end, there were no complications, it was a normal birth. I had contractions for fourteen hours, but look, it's the kind of pain any woman can bear. I had taken the Lamaze lessons before in El Salvador and that helped. The main thing was, my daughter was normal, completely normal, and everything was alright. The next day at the hospital the staff put on a champagne dinner for us. I was in my bathrobe, and Francisco was enjoying it all, saying, "What fine champagne, really good stuff!" Of course it all was on the bill, right? All this special treatment you had to pay for.

Anyway, the next day we took Paulina back to our apartment in Miami. I was a little scared with no nurses around, but I also felt how nice it was to be there with my cute little girl, in her cute little cradle. How beautiful and perfect! And then, seven o'clock that night, she started crying. Crying, crying, without a letup. I rocked her, Francisco rocked her, and he kept saying to her, "Be quiet! I tell you, you're going to quiet down now!" As if she could understand, right! This went on till one in the morning. Then she was fine. I fed her, breast or bottle every hour or so, and she was calm until exactly seven o'clock the next night. Then she started right up again for hours on end. This is the way it went for months, maybe six months. Back in El Salvador, it was the same thing.

Paulina was a colicky baby, and the truth is, she about drove us out of our minds for six months. Until suddenly, one day it stopped. She's been healthy since then, a fairly healthy child, I'd say. Yet my God, those first months were tough on us. Francisco wasn't exactly thinking about Mother Teresa's "gift" with much gratitude back in those days.

[*Throughout our interviews with Monica—and for that matter, with Niña Cecilia and Paulina too—we often had a coffee break. A uniformed maid would come from the kitchen with a tray of biscuits, muffins, and local coffee, sometimes coffee from Francisco's coffee plantation. At one of our meetings—the one below—it was Monica herself who went off and did the preparation and serving, and thus she began with some reflections on this departure in the routine.*]

I just got rid of the maid last week, so excuse me, I'm doing the serving around here myself these days. What happened? Well, I found out she was carrying on with one of the construction workers next door. She's a married woman. "What's Paulina going to think?" I wondered. Besides, I don't want strangers in this house. You never know what can happen. We could be robbed, or who knows what? So I got rid of her. I've got to find a replacement. Meanwhile, Francisco and Paulina and I are doing the work around here. They say they like it this way. More privacy. I like that part too. Francisco does the laundry. Paulina does some of the cooking. What a mess she makes of the kitchen! It's good for her, I know, but I can't go on like this. I can't run this place without a *muchacha* or two. Next time you come, I'll have someone. So excuse the place for being a little out of order this time, alright?

Anyway, last time you said you wanted to know about the war here, what happened to us and all that. I've been thinking about what I wanted to say. I talked with Francisco and he told me to say what I think. He's open that way. Not all people here are so free. Politics can get you into trouble. But Francisco is open this way, he told me to tell you things the way I see them. So I will.

The way I see it—and I hope you're not going to be offended, Mike—

my view is that the Americans were the ones who really stirred things up here. They played a big role in causing our civil war. That Jimmy Carter of yours and his foolish advisers were behind a lot of things here. You see, after Vietnam they had this idea about land reform. They thought the way to head off revolutions was to redistribute lands in certain countries. They took a look at Nicaragua and decided to throw out Somoza and bring about land reform. As a result the Sandinistas took over there. Carter was behind all that, for sure. And then they turned next door, to us, and sponsored a *golpe de estado* [coup], and they brought in a junta with Duarte as head of our country. You remember all that, don't you? It was in '80. And with Duarte, we had all these land reform laws passed. Carter figured that was the way to head off a revolution here. But in the end, the land reform laws he and his advisers pushed on us led to our civil war. We paid for Carter's experiments. We were his guinea pigs. That's the way I see it, anyway. You see, once they started with this *reforma agraria* [agrarian land reform], the leftists here gained strength. The FMLN began to grow. Their leaders had studied in Russia and Cuba. And what they did is form cells in the universities. Then they sent organizers around to the peasants and told them they needed to fight and take over the country. Remember their slogan—*La tierra es de los que la trabajan* [The land belongs to those who work it]? The next thing you knew, the peasants were joining them. Not all, but many of them. Their minds had been poisoned with all this propaganda. Peasants who had never thought in terms of taking their owners' land began to feel, "Yes, that's right, the landowner is my enemy!"

Look, when I was growing up, a peasant was a simple person, and content with being part of the finca. There was no venom toward the landowner. The landowner was like a father to them, a patron who looked after them. Sure, there was a certain paternalism in this, but there was also a personal involvement. I can remember this one peasant, Rodrigo. His father had worked for my great-grandparents. Rodrigo was a good worker, but he liked to drink and chase women. When this happened, his wife would come complaining to my grandfather, and Grandpa Julio would call in Rodrigo and give him a tongue-lashing just as if he were one of his own sons. And you know, Rodrigo wouldn't be *he wouldn't have told you otherwise.*

offended. The opposite. He'd feel grateful that my grandfather was helping him out with a family problem. Really, that's the way it was. There
was this relationship—a good one, the way I see it—but now it's gone.
The FMLN, the civil war, ruined all that.

Many landowners lost properties during those early years of land
reform in '80, and others lost properties in the settlement after the war
ended in '92. Did we? No, but we were lucky. With those land reforms
in '80, my parents just about lost their 75 manzanas. The infamous Decree no. 207 almost finished them. The way it worked was that if the
landowner had accepted rent or had a sharecropping arrangement with
the peasants, then the peasants could claim the right to own that land.
Thank God, my parents hadn't done that. They gave their workers a
manzana or two to use however they wanted, and in exchange the peasants worked on the finca. Some tried to claim they were renting and
tried to trick my father into signing a paper saying so. But my father was
wise to them. He contacted his lawyer, found out what this Decree no.
207 was all about, and refused to sign. Then all those who had tried to
trick him, he threw off the finca. But other landowners we know, they
lost lots of their properties. Francisco, no. He never had rented out his
land either. He paid his workers a wage, a fair wage. He wasn't subject
to Decree no. 207. We were lucky. We still have everything we had before
the war started.

During the civil war, though, you didn't know what was going to
happen. Francisco kept going out to our coffee finca during the war,
making sure that production went on. Sometimes the peasants who were
working for him would come to him—I think it was a way of threatening
him—they'd come and say, "*They* have been asking about you, Don
Francisco. *They* have you on their list." Or some anonymous note would
arrive saying that they were going to kill him, and all that. But Francisco
ignored the threats, he just went right on going to the finca. He went
armed with his pistol, the one you've seen him with, right? And nothing
happened to him, though I was very worried every time he'd go out
there.

Actually, the toughest time for us during the war was not something
the guerrillas did to us. It was something else, something a government

person, a *militar* [military man], did to us. I'll tell you who it was, but you can't print his name. Francisco doesn't want me to use his name. The man still has influence here. But I'll tell you the incident and what almost happened to us. This *militar* came one day to our house in Santa Tecla. This was sometime in the middle of the war—in '86, I think it was. It was on a Sunday. Santa Tecla is one of those little places where everyone knows everyone else, and people linger at their doorways saying hello and good-bye, and cars and people are all going by, very busy. That afternoon it was about six o'clock. There was this commotion in the street, people ogling this *militar* as he strolled up to our door with four bodyguards, all armed to the teeth. Francisco let him in, not knowing why the man was coming to visit. And Paulina, who was five or six years old then and a very social child, immediately ran up to her room after refusing to even politely say hello. Me, I stood there trying to smile as this *militar* came over and gave me a kiss on the cheek, the way people do here, but I felt something dirty in it.

Bueno, the guy sits down with his bodyguards. Francisco offers him something to drink, and he takes half a glass of vodka. There's some chitchat, friendlylike, and then the *militar* begins to talk to Francisco about his business operations. And, my God, he knew everything, all the details of Francisco's business—more than I did. Then wasting no more time, he says to Francisco, "I'm going to make you a proposal." Francisco looks at him warily and asks, "And what's that?" And the *militar* answers, "You are going to have some new partners in your business. Me, and others too. Your old partners are leaving, they're out." Francisco looks at this guy with four bodyguards next to him and tells him straight to his face there's no way he can do that and betray his partners. The *militar* looks straight back at him and shouts, "Look here! I'm not *asking* you, I'm *telling* you! Do you hear me?" And Francisco, calmly but in control—I don't know how—tells the *militar* that nobody shouts at him in his house. "I'm the one who gives the orders here," Francisco says. "If it doesn't seem that way to you, the door is right over there." The *militar* glares at him, stands up with his bodyguards, and heads for the door, saying as he walks out, "*This* you will not forget! I'm going to break you!"

Me, I was scared to hell. I'd been listening to the whole exchange from the kitchen, and I was trembling. I knew this man's power and I knew that if he wanted to kill us, he could arrange it anytime. Paulina came down from her room right after and went to Francisco, asking, "Papa, what does that mean, 'I'm going to break you!' " I don't remember what Francisco answered. I just remember he and I immediately decided we had to contact everyone we knew—his partners, our friends, anyone we knew who had any power here. Fortunately, Francisco knew some important politicians and he let them know his head was about to be on the platter. The next thing we knew, a day or so later, this *militar* passed the word through a friend that Francisco had completely misunderstood him. "There were no threats, no problems," the *militar* lied. He said he had only meant to pay a friendly visit, and evidently Francisco was nervous these days and going around chattering like a *vieja de pueblo* [old village gossip]. And you know, that was the end of it. No more threats, nothing. The whole thing blew over. But I'll tell you, for weeks after I was still shaking. I thought we were going to wind up shot in our house, or in the street—just like so many others in this war.

It was very easy to die in this war. Everyone living here knows people who died in one way or another. Every family lost someone. We were lucky. All of our immediate family survived it. But look, my father's brother got machine-gunned down in front of his house, and one of my cousins got killed too. My mother told you about this, I think. And many of our friends got killed too. People were getting killed all the time, sometimes pure accident, or sometimes just a matter of someone taking revenge. Oh yes, it was very easy to die during the war.

Many of our friends left the country during the war, and lots still haven't returned. Francisco calls it a "war psychosis." People couldn't tolerate the tension, they were nervous all the time. All they thought about was the war and that they were going to get killed. Better to get out, they figured. Truth is, we thought about leaving too. In the beginning of the war we were living with our suitcases packed. And again, during the final offensive, when the guerrillas attacked the capital, we did leave for a few weeks, we went to Miami where Francisco had some business to take care of. All the rest of the time, twelve years, we were here. In a way, Francisco and I are optimists. We always believed it would work out alright. And it did.

In the end, the United States brought about a settlement. The U.S. was involved in our war from start to finish. Their misconceived ideas about land reform caused the war to start. Then they saw they'd brought about a disaster here and in Nicaragua too. So they provided arms to overthrow the Sandinistas there, and they provided our government with arms to fight the FMLN. And then in the end the United States put up hundreds of millions of dollars to buy off the top military people here and the top FMLN people too. Then they brokered a peace agreement, with the FMLN becoming a legal political party, just the same as all the other political parties of the right and center. That's the way things stand today. You've got the right, left, and center all represented in the legislature. Only God knows how things are eventually going to work out. I'm no leftist, I guess that's obvious. But it's not so easy to believe in ARENA* these days either. My mother, she's still a staunch supporter of ARENA. Francisco and I, we're skeptical. Too much crookedness and greed among *all* politicians—that's the way I see it. I don't trust any of them. Maybe we need a new political party, a clean bunch. Who knows? As I say, though, Francisco and I are optimists. We're hoping for the best.

A little before the peace agreement was signed in '92 we started building our new house here in Altamira. Our friends told us we were crazy. They said, "The situation is too unstable! How can you put your money into a new house now?" But we decided to take the chance, and nowadays we're glad we did it. We love all this space and the beautiful view from our house, and the air up here is really fresh, not polluted like down below. And the neighborhood is fairly secure now. I mean, for El Salvador these days, this area with its armed guards is not too

*ARENA, or Alianza Republicana Nacionalista [national republican alliance], has since 1981 been the leading right-wing political party in El Salvador.

bad. Right, every time you come into the neighborhood the guard checks where you're going and takes down the license plate of your car? He's supposed to, anyway. We've had to beef up security here because things were pretty bad for awhile. There were a few kidnappings here. People were snatched right off the street and held for a few days, until their families came up with a ransom. Nobody was killed, but it scared all of us. We've added extra protection in the neighborhood, and lately things have been fine.

I'm not so worried about Paulina having anything happen to her when she's in the neighborhood. If she walks over to a friend's house here, fine. It's when she goes out, especially to parties on weekends with her friends—then I'm scared. Look, one of the boys from her school was kidnapped and held for almost a year. It was a big thing here because he came from a wealthy family, friends of former president Cristiani. It was a sophisticated operation. The people who are doing the kidnapping, some of them, are former *militares*. Everyone knows that. So if you have money you're a ready target. And besides all this kidnapping, you've got crime—much more than before the war. Lots of delinquents looking for someone to rob or beat up. Paulina knows this. But she's young, and when you're young you never think it can happen to you. If I voice any objection to her going out at night, say to some party, she tells me, "You're treating me like crystal. Everyone else is going, and *you* want me to stay home!" She and her friends have no fear. *I* do. For awhile we had terrible arguments. I took her to a psychologist, and the psychologist said to me, "Her generation is different from yours. They go out to parties, you have to accept that. You can't overprotect them." So what can I do? I don't want to start World War III in our house. When she's invited to a party these days I just sit around silently hoping it will be called off, or some obstacle or other will come up.

I can remember when I was young, Paulina's age. Goodness, it seems like just yesterday. Well, we had parties too. But in my time, adults would also be part of it. For us that was fine, natural. The adults would be in one part of the room and we'd be in another part. It was warmer that way, more homey. Nowadays, Paulina and her friends don't want adults to come within kilometers of their party. If I showed up, or any other adult, they'd feel a ghost had entered the room. Not because they're up to something bad, I don't think so. It's simply the way things are now. In one generation it's all changed, completely.

Actually, Paulina and her friends—most of them, I mean, because there are always a few bad apples—they're good kids. They have good morals, they've been raised right. They don't get drunk or take drugs, and they have the right ideas about, you know, about sex. Paulina, she's got some of these feminist ideas about how she has a right to be boss just as much as any man. I tell her things don't work that way. "And why not?" she says. I tell her that for centuries, since the time of the cavemen, I think, the man has been head of the house, and it's not possible in ten or fifteen years to change all that. Frankly, I don't think it *should* change. In my experience, I've seen that things work better if the man gives the orders in the house. "No way," Paulina tells me. "I want to be equal with the man." She and I don't see eye to eye on that at all. Where she's in agreement with me—I think so anyway, though I've never sat down and discussed it with her—is the area of sex. Look, I went to a Catholic boarding school, and I believe girls should stay virgins until they marry. Besides, this is a Latin country. No matter what he may say, no man really wants a woman who's passed through the hands of another. If the girl thinks she can behave like a man, have sex with this one and that one, she's going to lose out. There're exceptions I know of, but almost always it's hard to marry well if you're a girl who's played around. I tell you, because of this it would have been easier if we'd had a son and not a daughter. I'd rest easier these days. Still, I'm quite sure Paulina sees it the way I do. I don't tell her what to do. I don't say, "Look, Paulina, you have to stay a virgin until your wedding night." If a mother insists on this, these days a girl might decide out of spite to do the opposite in a weak moment. So I keep quiet, and I hope she's picked up the right morals and doesn't do anything she'll regret.

I trust her in this, really I do. She's a fine girl, and I think she sees things clearly. She knows she's got her whole life ahead of her. There's a right time for everything. My mother has told her the same thing. Meanwhile she's doing very well in school, the British School here. She's planning on going to university next year. Some days she talks of study-

ing law and other days business administration. She wants to be in an
area where she can make lots of money. And she wants a family too—
a big one. Once it was five kids she was going to have, now it's down
to three. I think she'll settle for two. She says she doesn't want to have
only one child as we did. Though, really, I think she has liked being the
only one. She hasn't minded that at all, I think. Even these days, even
with her being a teenager, she likes going away on vacation with Francisco and me. We almost always take her.

On weekends we often go to friends' houses at the lake or the sea,
and she'll usually come with us. We used to have our own place at the
sea, but we neglected it and it's in ruins now. Maybe we'll rebuild there,
I don't know. So now we just visit. That's on the weekends. Francisco
works awfully hard, he's a workaholic. I've got to get him to relax on
the weekends or he'll work himself to death. What we like to do to take
a real break from things is to go abroad. Usually to the United States or
Europe, and usually three times a year—Christmas, Easter, and in July.
If we want to do some quick shopping, it's Miami. To relax and eat good
food, it's San Francisco. To have it all, restaurants and shopping and
culture, then it's Europe. Francisco loves to eat in fine restaurants where
the service is just so and the food just so. That's his way of enjoying
himself. And Paulina, now that she's older, she wants to visit Europe.
Before, no. She'd put up a big fuss, she didn't want to go there. But just
the other day while we were talking at lunch, she said, "Mama, let's go
to Europe next vacation. I *love* Europe!" That's the way it is with her
now, every couple of months she changes her mind. So I suppose the
next vacation we'll be off to Europe.

If Paulina had her way she'd go off next year to study in England. Or
maybe the United States. Francisco and I won't let her—no way. She'll
only be seventeen, she's not ready to live on her own. She's going to
university here in El Salvador. For graduate school, yes, she can go
wherever she wants. When she's twenty-one, or twenty-two, yes. Not
now. She's my only one. And for the time being, she's staying here with
me, with us. She may not like that, but that's the way it's going to be.
That's for sure. What else can I say?

Paulina

We first met Paulina in September 1996, on the same afternoon we met her grandmother and mother. Having discussed our project for an hour or so with Niña Cecilia and Monica, we then asked to meet Paulina. Monica went off to fetch her from the upstairs bedroom where she was doing homework, and in moments Paulina was standing before us: a thin, sad-eyed girl with her long black hair pulled back, still dressed in her school uniform of blue skirt and starched white blouse. She attempted to be polite and acquiescent, but it was apparent that she was not there—not that day—with the same willingness, let alone enthusiasm, of her grandmother and mother.

"I couldn't imagine why you wanted to know about *my* life," Paulina admitted some months later, when the interviewing was comfortably under way. " 'Oh, how boring!' I thought. 'And psychologists too!' I didn't want to do it, but there was my mother telling me to go along. And my granny too—I always trust her. So I said, 'Alright, I'll try it, okay.' "

As it turned out, Paulina was the most frank and open of the three women. Her initial shyness soon gave way to a rush of heartfelt opinions—on politics, religion, sex, and not least of all, her parents and *their* views. Occasionally Monica would be within earshot (her daughter, cat-like, somehow knew exactly when), and at those times Paulina would lower her voice to a whisper, and she would avoid saying what was on her mind. But otherwise, she was free with her views and feelings, especially when talking alone with Marta, who did most of the six interviews with her.

Born in 1981, shortly after the outbreak of the Salvadoran civil war, Paulina was a child during the war. Her teen years are now being spent in the war's painful aftermath. Like all those of her generation, she has been inescapably influenced by this national trauma; and as the daughter of upper-class parents, her views have been shaped by the threat the war and its aftermath represent for her and her future. And yet, despite this raucous political background, what seems to come through loud and clear (at least to our psychological "third ears") is the story of a sixteen-year-old, looking backward a bit, but mostly forward, and trying to negotiate the troubled waters with her parents and peers. A wealthy sixteen-year-old, to be sure, but above all, a teenager with her own sure-eyed slant on the world.

Hence, "my life so far," as told by Paulina Solares Nuñez—or, as she sometimes prefers, Paulina Solares Nuñez L——.

I'm sure my mother has told you the story about Mother Teresa, hasn't she? She likes that story. She tells it to everyone. I've heard it several times, but I can't say I remember all the details, even though it's about how I was born. I think what happened is that my parents accidentally met Mother Teresa in an airport. In Guatemala, I think it was. She asked them if they had any children, and they said, "No," and Mother Teresa said something like, "You can't go on like this forever, you have to think of having children. Children are a wonderful thing." And my mother thought to herself, "You know, that's right. If I go on like this I'll get to be sixty without a daughter." I think Mother Teresa's words got her motivated. For us Catholics, Mother Teresa was like a saint—not really a saint, but like one—and it was her words that got them thinking. Up until then, my parents weren't thinking of having a child. The way my mother told me, they were like still on their honeymoon, traveling all over the world, the United States and Europe, and all that. If they had a baby, it wouldn't be the same. They'd have to take care of it. You know, really tiring for them. But after that meeting with Mother Teresa they got motivated. And a year or so later, I was born.

That's the way I heard it from my mother. The part I remember, though, happened about six or seven years later when Mother Teresa came for a visit to El Salvador. I say six or seven because that's how old I was at the time. My mother had already told me the story about Mother Teresa many times, and she insisted we go to the airport and join the crowd that was going to welcome her. I didn't want to go. I mean, what a pain standing in a crowd for an hour just to wave to someone. But of course, I got dragged along. On the way, as we were heading out of the city there was this boy selling flowers on the street—the way they do here, right? Yellow roses. My mother bought some so we could wave them in the crowd. Then when we got to the airport a lady came up to my mother and said the reception committee had forgotten to bring flowers for Mother Teresa. "Would it be possible," she asked, "if your little girl comes along and presents the yellow roses to Mother Teresa when she arrives?" And my mother, well, she was like, "Oh yes, sure. Of course." And me, I'm like thinking, "No way. I want no part of this!"

I'm sure my mother's shown you the photographs of all that, no? She's got a scrapbook with all the newspaper photographs. In a way, it's nice—now, I mean, looking at them now. Back then when it happened it was a pain. I got pushed to the front, and when Mother Teresa came down the stairs I handed her the flowers and she gave me a kiss. Then she said to my mother—I don't remember this, but my mother told me— Mother Teresa said, "And this is the child I prayed for?" My mother couldn't believe it. After all those years, Mother Teresa still remembered. "Take care of her," Mother Teresa said, "because she is a gift of God." Or something like that is what she said. My mother was in shock, she couldn't believe it. Ask her. She'll show you the pictures, if she hasn't already.

Unfortunately, after me my parents didn't have another child. I'm the only one. It's boring that way. I'll never do that. I'm going to have more than one, that's for sure. These days, alright, I'm used to it more or less. When I was little, it was terrible. I never had any kids in the house to play with. No sisters or brothers or cousins. It was boring and lonely lots of the time. If you ask me, my parents should have had at least one more—a sister, preferably. But they didn't want more. My father was against having more children. He had no patience for babies, and all the crying. I was a baby who cried a lot—so they told me. A colicky baby. I was up all night crying, sleeping in the day and crying at night for three months. My father was afraid of having another one like that. He said, "What, have one crying all night and another bothering me in the day?" So for that reason it was no more children, my mother says. Though I would really like to have had a sister or brother. Because, come to think of it, if she—my sister—were older, then she'd have gone through adolescence first, all the stuff I go through now with my parents. They'd be used to having an adolescent. Life would be a lot easier for me, I think, if they'd learned on someone first before I came along. And I would have had the benefit of having this older sister, or even a brother. Oh God, I wish it had happened that way!

As it was, I grew up alone. In Santa Tecla. That's where we lived until we came to Altamira four years ago. We lived in a house on the same property as my grandparents—my father's parents. Our house was just a few feet from theirs, only a door separated them. It was a big place and we had a big garden. There were lemon trees and pomegranate bushes, and also some orange trees with very sour oranges that I like. And we had lots of baby roses, which I used to cut even though I wasn't supposed to. I can remember playing out there a lot, usually by myself but sometimes with my grandpa. We'd play tag together. He'd be wearing his khaki pants and a funny cap, a pilot's cap. That's how he usually went around. You see, he was an amateur pilot, one of the first in El Salvador. He was the one who welcomed Charles Lindbergh when he visited here, and Grandpa Alfonso and some others made the first flight to Guatemala. My father's really proud of him. He keeps his picture around in his office.

The person I spent the most time with was my grandma Emilia. We used to spend hours every afternoon watching soap operas. She was addicted to them. I'd go over after school with my dog—I still have him—and he'd sit at the foot of her rocking chair and she'd pet him. We'd all watch together. Then sometimes, if there was nothing we were watching on TV, I'd make up my own plays. I'd have my grandparents sit down, and I'd also bring in the *muchachas* and sit them down in my theater. I'd then put on a play. Or sometimes I'd say to my grandma, "Now, you're going to be the queen," and I'd turn to my grandpa and I'd say, "And you're the king." Then I'd tell them what to do, to kiss or something like that. I used to love doing that, getting them to act. I'd sit there and applaud for them and we'd all laugh. I guess they liked doing it too. I was their only granddaughter, so they went along with everything. They liked playing with me.

But then they died. First it was Grandpa Alfonso, and then three or four years later I lost my grandma too. I can still remember the day Grandpa Alfonso died. I was like six years old then. I was putting on my clothes to go out—a sky blue dress and my patent leather shoes. I was just tying the laces when my father came into the room and said to me, "Look, Paulinita, your grandpa Alfonso isn't going to be here anymore because, you see, because he went to a place where he is going to be better off, where his parents are, and he's going to be very happy there, and ——." I interrupted and said, "Papa, are you telling me Grandpa is dead?" And my father began to cry, "Yes, yes, that's it." That night they had the wake. Usually kids go. I was real sad, but I was curious to see what a dead person looked like. There was a little window on the coffin, so I looked. It was very, very ugly. He was all dry like that, not at all like my grandpa when he was alive. Maybe I shouldn't have looked, I don't know.

I know that when my grandma died a few years later, I didn't look. I didn't do anything. No wake, no mass, nothing. I couldn't go. I was too upset. I knew she was going to die. She had been in the hospital for a week in the intensive care unit. They told me I couldn't see her because they had a rule that nobody under twelve years old could enter. So I made up a story about having to rush to the bathroom, and then I sneaked into her room. She was lying there, hardly able to breathe. She didn't even know I was there. That was the last time I saw her. Even though I knew she was going to die, I couldn't get over it. I kept crying and crying. To this day, yes, even this minute, I'm beginning to . . . I still can't accept she's gone. I loved her so much. She was always so good to me. I wish she were still here, I really do.

After both my grandparents were gone, the house seemed so empty. Just my parents, my dog, and me. Alone there in the house. Actually, during the day I would be out. I was going to the British School. I still am. Every day my mother would drive me back and forth—just like today. I started kindergarten there, and next year I'm finally going to graduate.

The kids in my class at the British School, many of them, I've known almost all my life. No, they're not just kids from wealthy families. There are also some kids whose parents don't have much money at all. How do I know? Well, you can tell. We all wear the same uniforms, yes, and the school has a rule that you can't wear any jewelry. But some kids, like some of my friends, come in big cars driven by a chauffeur. Other kids come by bus. And the poorer kids might have frayed collars on their blouses, or their skirts are a faded color, and if we go out at night they wear the same shoes they wear to school. Things like that. But it's ugly to talk about this, because really we don't treat each other differently. We're accustomed to seeing each other equally, and whether a student is good or bad doesn't have anything to do with how rich they are. I've had friends from poorer families too. All through my time there, all twelve years. We've been through a lot together. Really we have, if you think of it.

The whole time the war was going on, I was going to school there. In the early years, the teachers didn't talk to us much about it. They didn't want to get into it. I don't know why. But we all knew about the war, of course. I can remember in the early grades we used to have to store some things in our lockers just in case something happened and maybe we couldn't leave the school overnight. We had to have a sheet there, and some tins of food—each one of us. Though as far as I can remember, we never had to use any of these things. I don't think the school even shut down for one day because of the war. The only time it closed down was because of something else.

Yes, in '86. The school closed down for four months because of the earthquake here. The whole city was a mess then, right? So much damage and so many people killed. The part I remember is the moment it happened. I was in kindergarten then. I remember this very well. Our teacher was reading us *Alice in Wonderland*, and right at that moment she was at the part where Alice was about to fall into the giant hole. Our classroom started trembling. I thought, "Wow, that's really cool!" I was thinking the trembling was part of the story and I got real excited, until a few moments later I realized, "No, it's not part of the story, it's really going on outside." Then I started crying. Other kids were crying too. I wanted my mama right then. All the mothers came to get their children—all except mine. She didn't arrive till later. When I saw she was alive, and she told me my father was alive too, I felt alright. But was I scared! I thought I was never going to see them again.

Right about this time another thing happened that also scared me very much. I suppose my mother has told you about it. That time when a *militar* came to our house with all his bodyguards, and he was about to kill my father. I was up in my bedroom when the whole thing happened. I was too young to understand it all, but I heard a lot of shouting going on and the sounds of some pushing and shoving. Then I heard my mother say—trying to calm things down—she wanted to introduce her daughter. So she came and brought me downstairs, and, and this I'll never forget. This *militar* who had all these guys with guns on them, this guy wanted to touch me. I squirmed away. I was real unsociable, surly, but he started to touch me anyway, and I said, "Leave me alone, let me go." I ran back up to my room. And then there were more curse words, more threats, and I heard my father say, *Mirá, ¡mi cabeza la tenés en una bandeja!* [Look, you've got my head on a platter]. I was so scared, thinking, "Oh no, they're going to kill my papa!" And I was thinking, "What's so important about a company, or whatever it is they want? I just want my papa to stay alive!"

When that *militar* finally left with all the others, I came down from my room. I asked my mama what it was all about, why they had been cursing and shoving Papa around. She said, "Oh, they were just playing around. It wasn't for real. It was nothing." I guess she didn't want me to worry, so that's what she said. It was a few years later that she told me what had happened. Or really, she didn't tell me—I overheard her telling friends about it. By then I was eleven or twelve. I had stopped thinking about the whole thing. I couldn't believe what my father had been through, that he'd been sitting around for a long while after that day, never knowing if this *militar* was going to take revenge on him or not. And me, I had never known. I'd calmed down and didn't realize he was still in danger.

This was the worst thing I can remember from the war period. Our family was very lucky, not like some others. We lost nobody. Most of the time during the war I was too young to understand much. My parents protected me from things. Here, in San Salvador and Santa Tecla, there wasn't much shooting or bombing going on. It wasn't like hearing gunfire day and night. Only at the end of the war was it like that—the "final offensive," they called it. I remember it well because it took place around Christmas. That's my favorite holiday. I always feel great then. But that year, because of the final offensive there was a curfew. Except for Christmas day itself, you couldn't go out of your house. And they didn't allow anyone to shoot firecrackers, like we always do on Christmas. So it was a boring Christmas. I mean, it wasn't fun. But it wasn't quiet-boring. There was a lot of noise, a lot of shooting going on during that time. Machine guns and bombs. One night during that period, in the middle of the night, there was a ringing at the door of our house in Santa Tecla. The bell rang and rang, but my parents didn't answer it. What my mama told me is that the next day there was this guerrilla lying dead near our house. God knows what would have happened to us if we'd let him in!

And, oh yes, during that same period the army's planes were flying overhead, right over our house. You could hear them whizzing by. My father is a little *loco* about airplanes. So he had to go see them. He got up on the roof of our house and he called the rest of us to come up to join him. Can you imagine it? The war is going on, planes are flying around on bombing missions, or who knows what. And we're up on the roof watching them with my father because he loves planes.

But shortly after that, the war was over. There was a cease-fire and then they began negotiating the peace agreement. This I remember clearly. My parents talked about it at home. And in school some teachers also discussed things with us, though they were careful about what they said. They didn't want to offend anyone. Maybe some teachers had tendencies to support the FMLN, or they might have just been critical of the government and army. But look, we've got students in the British School whose fathers were officers in the army fighting the FMLN. If the teachers were to talk against these people, the fathers would pull their kids out of the school. The British School doesn't want that. So the teachers have had to measure their words. But still, they do say some things, and there have been discussions in class. Little by little, I've begun to understand what the war was about. Or at least I feel I do—now. I don't think my views are exactly like my parents'. Mostly, yes. But not exactly.

The way I see it now, our civil war came about because of the differences between the rich and the poor. The injustices, I mean. I'm not an FMLN supporter, no way. I don't support what the guerrillas did. Yet I think it's true there were—still are—a lot of injustices here in El Salvador. To me, that's sort of the way of the world. The rich are always going to take advantage—not every rich person, but in general. So naturally the poor rebel. It's normal. Anyone in their place might think of rebelling, no?

Here in El Salvador, unfortunately, the Church got involved in it. I was only a baby then, but I've heard how Monseñor Romero used to

give speeches in church that fired up poor people against the government. He'd give a sermon saying, "Imagine, my brothers and sisters,
how *they*"—and by "they" he meant the government and army—"Imagine how *they* took away so-and-so, and the others, and they've disappeared except for an arm or leg showing up here and there!" I don't
think he should have been talking that way in church. People go to
church to feel good and to feel love of God, supposedly, and not for one   *hmmm...*
part of the people to be set off against another part. These sermons by
Monseñor Romero and those other priests that followed him were a way
of adding fuel to the fire, and setting the poor against the rich. And all
this contributed to the civil war here.

What I want to say is that I understand why it happened, but I wish
it hadn't happened. And I pray it won't happen again. Thank God, the
FMLN didn't win the war. Me, my parents, we all agree about that. If
the FMLN had won, they probably would have done like in Cuba. You
know, take away our properties. They would have said we could have
only one house, and maybe only 15 manzanas. The rest would have been
given to the poor. They would have expropriated factories and businesses from people and had the government run them—just like in
Cuba. I'm not against more equality, really. But I think there's always
going to be some inequality, and if you start taking away all the properties of the rich, the country will break down. Factories and companies
won't work well. The banks won't work well. The rich will leave the
country and then what will you have? It'll be worse for everyone.

So I'm glad the FMLN didn't win the war. The United States brought
about a peace settlement. The U.S., with all its power, decided how it
would work out. That's how things happen in El Salvador. The U.S. is
in charge here. Take a look at the U.S. embassy building. It's the biggest
building in the country. That's because the U.S. is the boss here. We rely
on their aid and they direct everything that happens here, including
what the government does. The U.S. wanted a settlement negotiated
between the government and the FMLN, so that's what happened. The
FMLN is in the legislature now, and their power is growing. The new
mayor of San Salvador is from the FMLN, and some people say he'll be
the next president.

Does that worry me? Well, no, not really. Even if the president is from the FMLN, I don't think they'll go to extremes. The poor will get some more power, but I don't think the properties of the rich will be taken away. My parents and I talk about it sometimes. They vote with ARENA, though they don't like them so much. Me, I don't support any political party. My father says, "We've got to wait and see, and hope for the best." Really, though, I don't think our family will lose much. The rich here won't allow their properties to be taken away. And the U.S. is not going to allow El Salvador to be turned into a Cuba. No, no way I can see that happening. For the time being, I'm not too worried. I think it'll work out here alright for my family and me.

The thing that worries me right now is all the bad stuff that's happened since the war. All the delinquency and the kidnappings. My parents say it's because after the war all the guys who were fighting in the army and with the guerrillas, well, these guys no longer had anything to do. So some became criminals. Maybe that's the reason. Whatever. The thing is, it's not very safe here in El Salvador. If you go anywhere, especially at night, you've got to be careful. I know that. And my parents, my God, they're always reminding me. They won't even let me take driving lessons, like my friends do. Maybe it's because I'm their only daughter, and if something happens to me they'll have nobody. I don't know. But I *do* see why they're worried. I mean, I try to play things down, not get them too excited, but we all know some terrible things are happening.

Look what happened to Andrés Suster, who was kidnapped for over a year. He's in the British School, so all of us were really involved in a personal way. He got kidnapped, you know, while his chauffeur was driving him to school. We didn't know about it until three days later. His family was keeping it a secret while they were negotiating with the kidnappers. But when he wasn't released, they made it known publicly. The way I first heard about it was in school at the Monday morning assembly. The principal told us, and we all sat there in shock. Then the principal suggested that we pray together for Andrés—something that became a habit for us at the school. Every Monday we prayed for Andrés. And for months we couldn't get it out of our minds. We talked about him a lot. Andrés was a super bright student, the very top of his class, brilliant, and sort of a prankster. He knew how to say nasty things, but he did it in a way that somehow got you to laugh. He was super popular.

After about six months, even though we prayed regularly for him, it was no longer on our minds in the same way. The truth is, we thought he must have been killed. We figured we weren't going to see him again. Then some months later—this was almost a year after he'd been kidnapped—there was word in the newspapers and people were saying that he was still alive and maybe they were going to release him. All of us at the school, and really all around the country, everyone began putting up yellow ribbons. On our lockers, on trees, on buildings—all over. Andrés became like a national cause. And then it happened. He was freed. The kidnappers got a ransom and Andrés was let go.

When I saw his picture in the newspaper I couldn't believe it was the same Andrés. He was a well-groomed boy, with tanned skin and freckles. In the newspapers, he had this shoulder-length hair, and he was emaciated, and even his freckles were gone. Apparently, he had been held—God, I can't imagine it—he had been in a small hole, a cistern, for the whole year with his feet tied together. He hadn't seen a ray of sun the whole year. How horrible! I don't know how he lived through it. If he cried, nobody came to him. A whole year without talking to anyone, thinking all the time you could die at any moment, and you would never see your family and friends again. It must have been pure hell. And then suddenly he was released, and all the TV cameras and newspaper reporters wanting to talk to him. I don't know how he managed it.

About a month or so later, he finally came back to school. He had put on some weight, his freckles were back, but he walks with a limp now. I haven't talked with him about what happened. He has just started going out now with a girlfriend of mine, and I understand he doesn't like to say much about what it was like for him. That's natural, I guess. He wants to put the whole thing behind him. I think he's amazing to have adjusted the way he did. You see him in the corridor and he's like, "Hey, Paulina, how's it going? What's up?" Friendlylike. He's a little more serious now than before, not the same prankster as before. Going through what he did, I guess it's a trauma you can never forget. Still, I think he's handled it all amazingly well. To be kidnapped like that and lying in a cistern for a year—it gives me the shivers just to think of it!

Do I worry about that happening to me? Of course, yes I think of it. Especially after Andrés. I wonder how it would have been if that had happened to me. Still, I don't want to stop living because of what happened to Andrés, and stay shut up here in the house just thinking. As it is, I spend almost every day of the week stuck in the house doing homework. The British School is a hard place. Everything is taught in English, and they load you up with homework. Just now in literature class we're reading *Animal Farm* and *Lord of the Flies*, and we have to write reports in English. I'm doing homework for hours every day. So hey, when the weekend comes I want to get out, even if it *is* a bit dangerous to be out at night. The way I look at it, we all have our fate and if it's my fate to be kidnapped then it'll happen even if I'm at home. Thinking this way doesn't make me stop being afraid, but it lets me go on living.

Comes Friday night, and especially Saturday night, I want to go out with my friends. We go to parties, or out to eat, or to the *Zona Rosa,** and we have fun. But we don't hang out until one in the morning. If we're in the *Zona Rosa,* we only stay till ten o'clock or so. I don't go there with lots of jewelry, gold earrings, rings. I like jewelry, but you don't want to flash it around these days. Some gang can come by and try to rob you, and if you put up any resistance, damn, you can get shot. So you have to use good sense, keep your eyes open, and not wander off alone onto side streets. I know that. I've discussed it with my parents—over and over. I know they're worried. My mother probably would keep me shut inside our house if she could. But she knows she can't. What I do is try not to talk about these things, like saying, "Look, Mama and Papa, look what happened to so-and-so the other night." If I start talking like that it only makes them uptight, so I prefer to avoid topics that can get them worked up.

---

*The *Zona Rosa* (pink zone) is a popular area in San Salvador with many restaurants, bars, and discotheques.

❧

The situation here in El Salvador *is* dangerous. Okay, we all know that. But I tell you, even if it weren't dangerous, I would still be having problems with my parents about what I do and who I do it with. I'm sure of it. Maybe if I'd had an older sister it would have been easier for me. I don't know. Because some of the things they do, I mean, really they make no sense.

Alright, so they won't let me take driving lessons. But you know what, they won't give me an allowance either. Can you believe that? I've discussed it with them again and again, and always it's No! My friends all get allowances—1,000 colones or more a month. They buy things for themselves and they save some money too. That's what I would do. I'd like to have a bank account. It teaches you how to manage money. I explain this to my parents, but always it's No, no! I mean, they buy me what I want, all the clothes I want—and I love clothes—but they refuse to let me have my own money. It's embarrassing. Every time I go out, even to Burger King or Pizza Hut, my mother has to pay. I don't like it, but what can I do? That's the way they are. I've given up trying to convince them.

For awhile, a couple of years ago, things were so bad between us that I went to talk to a psychologist. Two of them really. A man, and then a woman. I went for a few months and I liked it, sort of. The problem was, the psychologists were telling my parents *they* had to change too. My generation is not like their generation—that's what the psychologists explained to my mother. She didn't want to hear it. I was willing to change my attitude, to stop shouting and screaming at them. But my mother had her ideas about when I could go out, or sometimes even who my friends should be, and she didn't want to change her attitudes. So I stopped going to psychologists.

Just recently I had another flare-up with her about a friend of mine. Margarita. Oh damn, it makes me so mad! Margarita was my best friend. Actually, we were four friends, always hanging around together. I was closest, though, to Margarita. We were like sisters. Whatever she suffered, I suffered too. It was like we were one person. My mother didn't like her. She said she was not a good person, not warm and nice, and all that. Margarita is the quiet type, true—if you don't talk to her she doesn't talk to you. And my mother hardly talked to her. My mother, if she doesn't like someone, it's written all over her face. And Margarita knew my mother didn't like her. Then what happened is that Margarita got involved with Carolina's boyfriend. Maybe it wasn't so nice on Margarita's part, but I wasn't about to split with her over that. For my mother, though, that was proof positive that Margarita was no good, untrustworthy. She kept telling me I should split from her, and when I refused finally my mother prohibited my seeing her. Can you imagine it? I didn't know what to do. I went to my father, and he said he'd speak to her and straighten it out. But she was adamant. To this day, she refuses to let me see Margarita. I tell you, it depresses me. It makes me think that if I get close to someone again, my mother could do the same. Like, I'm not free to choose my friends according to *my* taste! *She* has to approve of them.

And, you know, it's not like I'm hanging around with a bunch of alcoholics and drug addicts. My friends are clean. They're like me, they don't go for that stuff. When we go to the *Zona Rosa*, we don't smoke marijuana, not even cigarettes either, and nobody drinks. Some of the guys we're with do drink, and once in awhile they get soaked, but then we stay away from them. Bad things can happen if you hang around guys who are drunk. I'm not naive, so I stay away from guys who are drinking.

Right now, none of my friends really have boyfriends. Wait, yes, Suzanna has a guy—someone she's been with for a couple of years, since she was fourteen. He's a good type, clean, into religion and all that. But all the rest of us don't have any guys right now. Me, I've had a boyfriend or two in the past. Nothing serious. My parents knew these guys and they didn't say anything. It was alright with them—they knew nothing was really going on between us. Like, we'd do homework together sometimes, or we'd go to parties together, but it wasn't anything heavy. You know what I mean, right?

Sex, right. I mean, none of us—all my friends think alike about this—we're not into having sex, I mean, having everything before marriage. It's not like the United States here. Yes, I know how it is in the U.S. I've got some relatives who live in San Francisco, and we've visited them. My cousin—a distant cousin—she's my age and she's got all this freedom. She does whatever she wants. She hangs out in bars till two in the morning, she goes camping overnight with a group of boys and girls. Her parents don't say anything. Can you imagine me getting away with that? No way! Really, I think it's too much freedom, too liberal. Maybe if I were born there I'd think like they do. But I was raised here, so my way of thinking is like the people from here.

And let's face it, this is a *machista* country. Like it or not, that's the way it is. It's very easy to get a bad reputation if you're not careful. This is a small country. Everyone knows everyone. You do something stupid, everyone knows about it. Like, if you're in the *Zona Rosa*, and a girl is brushing up against some guy, or kissing him—you know, passionate kisses—the next thing you know everyone is talking about her. She gets a reputation. The guys who go out with her, *even* if nothing happens, they tell their friends they made it with her. They don't want anyone to think *they* didn't succeed with her. That's the way guys are, right? And girls too, they gossip too. We tell each other that so-and-so is a *zorra* [slut] if she's openly going around making it with a guy, or if we know she's slept with him. Some of the older girls at the British School are known to be sleeping with guys, and none of us, my friends and I, none of us go along with that.

This is a Latin country and you want to be real careful about your reputation. To stay a virgin until you marry, that's the best. I never really discussed this with my mother, yet I know how she feels about it. Of course I do. Only one time did she ever say anything directly to me. I asked her once if she was a virgin before she got married. I knew she had had a few boyfriends before she got married, that she'd gone out with them in a childish way, I imagine. So I figured she was a virgin, but I thought I'd ask her. "Yes," she said, "I was." Nothing more than that. You could see she didn't want to talk about it, except she said, "Go ask your father, if you want to know." And I did, and he said, "Yes, yes, she was." That was all he said, nothing more. I can't talk about sex with either of them. My mother, she's real uncomfortable about it. Anything to do with sex, she won't talk about it.

I can remember getting my period. Oh God, that was awful! I knew nothing. Wait, I knew one thing. I knew something was going to happen. This was when I was eleven or so. I remember telling my mother, "Mama, my body is beginning to change, I'm beginning to develop." She said, "Ah hah, don't worry about it. It's normal." And then she said that one of these months or years I'd get a "period," and she said, "Your body cleans itself out this way." Nothing more. Nothing about reproduction or anything like that. And then when it happened one day, I was in the bathroom and I began to shout. She came running in and just stood there laughing. I was so scared, but she didn't explain anything more to me. "Your body is cleaning itself out," is all she repeated. Only later, when I told a friend of mine, she explained it had to do with reproduction and all that. And a year or so later, at the end of sixth grade or the beginning of seventh, I forget which, they explained it in school. About the menstrual cycle, how babies are conceived, the birth process, everything. And now in biology class we're learning more—about masturbation, about how homosexuals have sex, everything. All the details. I mean, I want to know these things, but sometimes the details are a bit, well, a bit embarrassing. Thank God, they're not showing us videos yet! Because some of the kids in our class, they ask all these questions. Like, "What happens if the man is too big and the woman is too small?" Or, "What happens if at the time of giving birth the woman pushes so hard she shits?" Like, it's a class on perversion or something! I don't know, maybe I'm too shy about these things. Maybe I am. Maybe because I couldn't ever talk about these things at home, I'm too shy now, I don't know.

I know when I go to the beach—it's embarrassing to admit—but I don't feel comfortable showing my body. I never wear one of those shirts that come right below the bust, or a bikini. I always go with a one-piece bathing suit and cover myself with a shirt or something. Actually, I love bikinis and I'd like to buy some, but always when I'm about to buy one I stop, I can't go through with it. It's embarrassing because all my friends except for the *gorditas* [fat girls] are wearing bikinis. I think this is because when my friends were young their mothers dressed them in bikinis. Mine—never! My friends sometimes say to me, "Come on, girl, get a

little tan! The boys aren't going to come near. Your belly is too white!"
But I just can't do it. I don't know, I think I'm too shy about these things.

The truth is, sex and all that is not something I'm really comfortable
with. It scares me to death just thinking about kissing a guy, really kissing, I mean, because once you get started it could happen, you could
sleep with him. And then if you slept with him but didn't marry him,
maybe the man I wound up marrying would have a different image of
me. And me too, maybe I couldn't forget the first one. Oh no, I don't
want that! I tell you, I try not to even think about kissing a guy because
then it all might happen. And say my mother were to discover I'd slept
with someone. Oh God, she'd go crazy, ranting and raving. I'd get the
sermon of the year. Only, maybe, if I get to be fifty and haven't married,
then she might figure, "Well, why say anything to her?" But at sixteen
or seventeen—oh no, she'd go nuts. It would be all over for me.

Actually, the one adult I can talk to about these things is my grandmother. She's cool. She's sort of modern. She's not like my mother,
so conservative about everything. My grandmother is relaxed, easy. I've
asked her whether she was a virgin when she got married, and she said
yes. But she didn't stop there and refuse to answer any other questions.
She told me how she felt, how it was for her. She told me in a real way,
not like my mother. *Abe*—that's what I call her instead of *abuelita*
[grandma]—she's like a friend to me. Sex, boyfriends, love, you name
it, and I can talk to her about it. No embarrassment, not at all. I think
she's the only one in the family who really understands me.

If I'm having some problem, I pick up the phone and call Abe. Sometimes, like when I'm very depressed about something or real confused,
I'll call her four or five times a day. She always has time to chat with
me. I'll ask her for advice and she gives it to me. Say my mother is
against my going in a car with some guys, I'll ask Abe and she'll say,
"Well, why not go with them, but with another girlfriend or two?" Or
if I'm all upset about some fight I've had with a girlfriend, and my
mother is telling me she thinks the friendship is over, Abe will reassure

me, saying, "It'll all sort itself out in a few days or weeks, you'll see."
And she's almost always right. She's a calm person, not like my mother,
who's always got to be moving around, arranging something, doing
something. I'm like my mother. But Abe, she's always calm. She's on the
phone with my mother once, twice a day too. They're very close. Abe
has always got a kind word, a word of reassurance for everyone. And
when you think about it, it's amazing. When you think about what she
went through, losing her son like that in an automobile accident, I'm
amazed how she is like she is. I've talked to her about it. I'm the curious
type. Even though I could see it wasn't easy for her, I insisted on talking
about Felipe. I asked, "How did you find him? What happened when
you saw him?" All that. And she told me. One time she read me the
poem she wrote about him. It made me so sad to hear her read it. I could
feel what she must have gone through. I started crying and crying. Then
she told me, "Felipe would have understood you, he had your same
character. You would have got on well together. And you would have
had cousins." And so on. It was very sad for both of us. But she's amazing. She lived through this, and she's a calm person today, an easy person. She's really special.

Maybe what helped her—I think so, really—is that she believes so
much in God. Abe is very religious. She belongs to a group of women
who're always doing things for the Church. She says the rosary every
day, I think three times a day. She's more religious than my mother
or me. I mean, my mother and I go to mass every Sunday. Not my
father, he stays at home. But we go. We're observant, believing Catholics.
Abe, though, she's the most observant of all. I think that's part of what
gives her her strength and has helped her live through the hard things
in her life.

I'd like to be strong like her. And like I say, I do believe in God and
the Virgin Mary, and I go to mass and confession. But I have certain
doubts about things. Abe and my mother, they believe that everything
happens according to God's will. Now, I've thought a lot about it, and
I just can't see things that way. It makes me feel guilty criticizing, but I
have these doubts. The Catholic Church wants us to believe that everything that happens is due to *la voluntad de Dios* [God's will]. If bad things

happen, you're supposed to resign yourself because it's God's will. I think we can accomplish things if we have faith in God, yes, but also in ourselves, and in our own potential. If you are in a bad situation, sick or poor, you don't have to resign yourself. You must use your faith to overcome the situation. I've read a lot of books about this, books on what's called "metaphysics." And I believe our minds, if set in the right direction, and with great faith, can help us to accomplish what we want. The priest I talked to about this doesn't agree with me, and I'm not sure Abe or my mother does either. Still, this is the way I see things. I have great faith in God, and I also believe it's up to me to accomplish things for myself, not just go along with this or that.

What do I want to accomplish? Well, I don't know. I'm not completely sure yet. I just have some ideas, general ideas. Nothing definite. I know I want to get married someday and have children, and I know I want to have a career. I want both. I don't want to be like my mother, just a housewife. I'd go nuts just staying in the house, cleaning and cooking and planting all these little plants in the yard the way she does. Oh no, that's not for me. I'm going to have a career, a profession, that's for sure.

Right now I'm thinking about business administration or law, or maybe combining the two, studying mercantile law. I want to be a success, to make a lot of money. Sometimes I think I'll go work with my father. He'd like me to do that. He's always telling me to visit the coffee finca with him, and in the summer I worked a little in his business. Once in awhile I make out the payroll for him, and he pays me for doing that. But I don't know. My father—you've met him, so I suppose you know— he's a perfectionist. If things aren't just so, he gets angry, loses his temper. I mean, I get along with him—now more than ever. Yet to work with him, that could be a different story. I couldn't take it if he started yelling at me, insulting me. And let's face it, he's fifty now, there's no way I'm going to change *him*. So I don't know. I'll have to see.

The one thing I'm sure about, though, is that I *am* going to have a

career. A woman has to be able to support herself, especially these days
with all the divorces. You have to be able to take care of yourself. So for
me, there's no way I'd get married before finishing university. Only,
maybe, the last year when I'm sure of getting my degree. Maybe then.
And my husband will have to be the type who accepts me as a profes-
sional. I'm not about to marry one of these *machista* types who expects
me to stay at home. Uh, uh! I'm not saying I'm a feminist. I mean, I don't
go on demonstrations or carry placards. But I don't go along with that
stuff my mother says about the man being the boss in the house. For me,
it's two bosses, both of us equal. Otherwise, I swear, I'd get rid of the
guy, divorce him. Nobody is going to be my boss in the house. No way.
And these days there *are* some guys who understand that. It's not the
way it was in Abe's time, or even my mother's time. Things have
changed some.

And yes, I'm going to have children too. Maybe three, or at least two.
My mother knows a little about reading palms, and she showed me on
my hand—you see these lines here?—there's two, or maybe with this
little line, maybe three. I don't want just one child, the way my parents
did it. Boring, boring. It's much better to have a house full of commotion,
with the television and CD player blaring away. Boom, boom! That's the
way I want it. Listen now, here in this house you don't hear any noise,
just a little construction work going on outside. It's boring, lonely. I want
my house to have music and noise, and to have kids' things lying
around, not just older people's things. And I want to have a Christmas
tree full of decorations made just by kids. That's cool! That's the way I
want it when I get married.

And I think I'll have what I want. It's possible, I mean. Like I was
saying, if I put my mind to it, I believe I can accomplish what I want. I
want the best. Career, husband, children, a fine house, everything. I believe I can have it all. It's up to me. That's the way I see it.

La Familia García

María

On January 16, 1992, after twelve years of civil war, the government of El Salvador and the FMLN guerrilla organization signed a peace agreement. As part of the settlement the government agreed to redistribute some 134,000 manzanas of land to landless and land-poor families. The government also gave these people loans to pay for the land (and has since pardoned almost all the loans) and compensated landowners for the expropriations. Of the 33,600 recipients of this land, the vast majority were former combatants, either government soldiers or guerrillas. In general, each person received about 4 manzanas of land that adjoined other such plots to form new *comunidades* [communities].*

Henríquez is one such community. And for the past five years it has been home to our next trio of women—María, Lupe, and Niña Dolores—who all participated in the FMLN guerrilla organization. Twenty-six

---

*The data presented here come from Ministerio de Agricultura y Ganadería, *Tercer Censo agropecuario del Programa de Transferencia de Tierra* (San Salvador, 1997), ix, xii.

93

families live in Henríquez, and its lush 65 manzanas were once part of an estate owned by a prominent local family. Situated 35 kilometers north of San Salvador, Henríquez is an isolated place. It rests snugly in the foothills of Mount Guazapa, about a kilometer off the main road to Suchitoto. A dirt road leads from the main road to the community's health clinic, one-room primary school, and small grocery store. But from there to the houses, it is a half-kilometer walk on a lane that cuts through sugarcane fields, a cow pasture (on Sundays it serves as a well fertilized soccer field), and back and forth across a gully that in the rainy season is negotiable only for those who intimately know its contours. In both rainy and dry seasons, the entire area is awash with vegetation, and on the walk to the residential area you are accompanied by birds and bugs whose chirping and buzzing is all you hear. As you approach the houses, these sounds give way to those of dogs, roosters, and children, and the earth smell of the fields fades into the even earthier smells of the 128 people living there. The houses—a few still made of wood planks and tinplate, the rest newer concrete block structures with tile roofs—have one large room apiece, with a cooking area attached to the side of the house. In front of each house is a small, perhaps quarter-acre, plot of land where the family grows crops or raises animals (its principal plot [*milpa*] is located outside the residential area).

María Morales García's home sits in the middle of the residential area, about 75 meters from that of her mother and that of her grandmother. She now lives there with her five children and her husband, Antonio. Both María and Antonio were guerrillas in the civil war. Antonio spends most of his days in the fields or attending to community affairs (he has been *presidente* of Henríquez for three years), and María is almost always at home caring for their small children, cleaning, or making tortillas. "This is my life these days," she says in her matter-of-fact manner, "and it's fine with me. No complaints."

At twenty-nine years, María was the most active fighter of the women (or men) in her family. From the age of thirteen until she was twenty-two, she was in the mountains with the FMLN. She seems to have come through those years unscathed, either physically or emotionally. She almost always dresses in a simple skirt and blouse ("I stopped wearing pants when the war was over and I came down from the *monte*," she says). She smiles easily and her face is attractive, with high cheekbones and light brown eyes. No matter what she is discussing, her voice has no sadness, no hint of self-pity or even self-congratulation about what she feels are the FMLN's successes in the war. In a word, she has a humility and unflappability that, in light of what she has lived through, seem to an outside observer rather remarkable.

We interviewed María nine times over a year. All four of us usually sat in rickety wooden or plastic chairs on the concrete patio of her house, around a metal table that seemed on its last legs. There were frequent interruptions during the interviews as one or another of her children called or ran up to whisper to her, or as a neighbor or relative dropped by. Antonio occasionally was there, but he obligingly moved off to the side to eat his lunch of tortillas and beans or went into the house to lie in a hammock. In the midst of this flow of traffic, María continued to tell her tale, or tales, unfazed and undistracted—to the amazement and gratitude of her three interviewers.

Below is María's story.

&

I've been here in Henríquez since '92, and it looks like we're here to stay. Good land, here. You toss down some seeds and they sprout. *Maíz, frijol*, bananas, papaya—it all grows here. You can make a life here. I believe we're staying now. If you asked me back then, back in '92, I wasn't sure. I didn't know how it would work out. I wasn't sure the war was really over. They'd signed the peace, yes, but that didn't mean the whole thing wasn't going to start up again. At least that's how I looked at it.

I'd been demobilized for about two years. I was living over in Santa Marta, in Chalatenango, with my family—my grandparents, parents, and my two children. It's a few hours' bus ride from here, Santa Marta is. An ugly place. The houses are bunched up one next to the other. You hardly see the sun. That place was a community controlled by the FMLN too. But unpleasant, ugly. Then we got word they were looking to populate over here in Henríquez. The FMLN had this community here, but they only had twelve families. They needed more people, they said. An uncle of mine who'd been with the FMLN came over and had a look. "Good place," he told us. "We ought to go there quickly while they still have openings." So I came too, along with my grandparents—my father's parents. They're the ones I was living with, along with my two kids. The FMLN brought us in a truck. Safer that way. You still had government soldiers going around and occasionally messing with people they thought were ex-guerrillas. So we came and we got our place here. And then a month or so later my parents came with some of my brothers and sisters. And then my grandmother, Dolores, came too. We all got registered here. All of us had been with the guerrillas—me, my mother, my grandmother too. And that was it. We settled in here.

Not like we are now, though. In the beginning we were all living over in that place you pass on your way here. Right, the place where the clinic and school and store are. Over there is where the owners of this estate had their house. We lived there in the beginning, and then we moved out here. Then for three years, we all had these houses made of metal sheeting and wood. You had plastic on the roof and the side to help keep out the rain. And the floors were just earth, stomped down earth. My grandmother's place—you've seen it, no?—it's still like the original houses. They haven't fixed up her place yet. Most houses, like ours, are new. Real comfortable now. Big—maybe 10 meters by 3 meters—and room enough for a few beds and hammocks. Like the way we have it, real nice now. The first year here I lived with my grandma Flora and grandpa Santos, and my two children. No, I wasn't married. The children's father is a man I met in the guerrillas. He's with some other woman now. He doesn't have anything to do with us. I was raising the kids myself, living with my grandma and grandpa. They're like parents to me. I grew up with them. They're old folks now—he's about seventy-five and she's sixty-eight, maybe. They live just below, down the lane a bit. I was living there with them in the beginning. Then Antonio started coming around. He was *presidente* of the community, so he'd stop by and chat with us. And he kept coming and coming. And soon it was obvious he really was looking after me. I wasn't interested at first—not at all. But he kept all this coming around, and after awhile I felt I couldn't refuse him. I had gotten to like him. So we got *ajuntados*. It'll be four years this Christmas that we've been together.

With Antonio, I've had three more children, counting this last girl I just had. I've got five now. Enough, don't you think? My oldest, Dora, is eight and Luis is five. Dora's in school and Luis starts next year. Dora is real smart, they tell me. Soon as she started first grade—it must have been a month later—she was already reading. She caught on real fast, so they put her right into second grade. She likes school, the way I did when I was her age. Except she's going to get a chance to go on through. I tell her, "Dora, you go on and be what you want in life, but I want you staying in school." That's what I tell her. Antonio too. He encourages the kids to go to school. He didn't have a chance to learn and it embarrasses him. He can only sign his name—he taught himself—but that's about it. Me, I can read and write a little, but not so much. I'm hoping my kids do better. Here in Henríquez now, I think they will.

I grew up in the department of Cabañas in a village right near the Lempa River. I lived there nine years, something like that. As far as I can remember, I've always lived in the house of Grandma Flora and Grandpa Santos. My parents and my brothers and sisters lived near us in a separate house.

Why was that? *Bueno*, the way I heard it from my mother is that soon after I was born my grandma said she wanted to have me. You know, raise me in her house. My mother didn't like the idea so much, maybe since I was her first. But my father said that was the way it was going to be. My grandma didn't have a daughter left in the house, only one son. Her daughter had married and gone off. So she wanted me. Later, when my mother had my brothers and sisters, I just stayed living with my grandparents. I'd go over sometimes and be with the others during the day, but I lived in my grandparents' place. It was okay that way with me. I didn't mind at all.

My father and grandfather have always worked together in the fields. They had their *milpa* they owned, and all the time I was growing up they worked it together. Me, I mostly stayed in the house with my grandma Flora. To this day, I'm still close to her. These days, if I've got a little time at night, I'll go over there to her house and chat—"telling tales," we call it—with her and my two sisters who live here in Henríquez. We gather there, not at my mother's house where she's still got young kids. Grandma Flora is good to be around. You know, easy and good-natured. I love her. Always have.

My other grandmother, Dolores, I can't say the same about her. Truth is, I don't like her very much. My sisters and brothers either. When I was growing up she lived nearby, and she was always nasty to us. "You're a bunch of lazy good-for-nothings," she'd say to me and my sisters and brothers. Or other nasty stuff. That's her way, always talking foul-mouthed.

How was my grandfather—Dolores's husband, you mean? Well, he wasn't around when I was growing up. He died when I was nine days old, or maybe it was nine months. That's the way I heard it from my mother. The way I heard it, he was killed by the Guardia. He had a liquor still. No, he wasn't making his living that way. He was a farmer, he had some land. He just had the liquor still for his own use. It was forbidden. He knew that, and he knew the Guardia might come after him some day. And one morning, as he was hanging around the house all drunk, sure enough he heard the Guardia was coming his way. He tried to escape, all drunk like he was. He made it to the river, tried to swim across to the other side, but they nailed him. Uh huh, they shot him dead right there in the river. My grandmother had six children then, maybe more. She was left a widow, nobody to look after her support. Except she had her mother living in the same village. My great-grandmother, she's the one who was making a living selling her home-made liquor. Over at her place she had a still, and there was always a bunch of bolos [drunks] over there lapping it up. I knew about it, sure. Though I can't say I went over there much at all. She was as nasty as Grandma Dolores, even nastier. She'd start swinging at us if we came over to her house. You know, kids see something and immediately they start talking about it. She didn't want that, so she was cursing us and swinging at us if we went near her.

But I don't remember ever spending any time there with her, or at Grandma Dolores's house either. I never had a meal there, I don't think.

I stayed with Grandma Flora, or over at my mother's house. More with Grandma Flora, especially when I was small. We had a nice house, one with a kitchen and patio. Grandma would let me sleep late in the morning, until eight or so. She herself would be up at dawn grinding the *maíz* and making tortillas. That's what we'd have for meals—tortillas. Also beans. And coffee in the mornings and evenings. Sometimes we'd have some eggs and cheese, because we had chickens and cows. And sometimes Grandma Flora would make her *quesadillas*. Delicious. She knew how to make them taste good, put lots of cheese in them. On those days we didn't think of eating tortillas.

Grandma Flora did the cooking. I didn't start helping to make tortillas until I was seven or eight. She told me, "I'm the one who takes care of the house, but these things you've got to learn how to do, and the only way you'll learn is doing it." Besides this, I did a little work in the house to help out. A little sweeping up sometimes. Or I'd go fetch firewood— that was easy because there were lots of pine trees around us. And I'd let the cows out after the morning milking, and I'd bring them back in the evening. And I'd go bring jars of water from the river, and I'd go down there with Grandma Flora when she washed the clothes. I didn't help much. I just sat there in the shallow water playing around while she did the washing. I liked that, just sitting there in the cool little pools of water. Like I say, she was good to me and let me enjoy myself.

School? No, there wasn't any school near where we lived. The closest one was a long walk up through the hills. I was the only one of my brothers and sisters who really wanted to learn. I went for a few months along with one of my brothers. The place wasn't a schoolroom, it was more like a little pen where you'd sit with the others. We didn't learn anything. I was eight, I wanted to learn to read and write. All we did, though, was sing songs and make these stupid paper flowers. And this woman teacher was always yelling at us. Little by little, the kids stopped coming. My brother stopped too. And me, I was scared to walk all the way up there by myself. It was just forest and hills, and who knew what could happen? So I stopped going, even though I still was hoping someday I'd learn to read and write.

❧

A couple of years later, I did get to go to school again. This time, to a fine place. In San Vicente, after we'd moved from where we were in Cabañas. We moved because there was some kind of family problem, a dispute, and my father and grandfather decided we'd move over to San Vicente. They bought a little land, and we moved into a small house there in the town of San Vicente. The house wasn't too nice, but it was right on a street that had electricity, so at night you had the street lamps throwing strong light into your house so you could see. And just down the road was this huge school. I got my grandparents to send me there. In the morning I'd get up early and bring my grandfather and father their breakfast out in the fields. Then running all the way, I'd make it to school just in time.

I was ten and I started in first grade, learning to read and write. This place was a real school. You know, with writing desks and a blackboard. I had to buy pencils and notebooks, but they were cheap. My teacher was a kind lady, not like that angry one I had in the other place. This one liked us. In the breaks, we'd go out to this yard and play ball—the boys playing soccer and the girls baseball. But that wasn't the part I liked about school. I liked the learning we did. I would have liked to go there for years, to learn a lot. As it was, I only went two years, through second grade. Then it all stopped.

The reason the school stopped was that the director got killed. I think this was in '80. People were being killed a lot then. You'd wake up in the morning and somebody would be dead in the street. You see, around this time the guerrilla movement was just getting strong. Where we were in San Vicente was one of the places the guerrillas were starting to organize. The guerrillas would paint their initials in red letters on houses. Then the army would come by and see it, and they'd start watching those houses, figuring maybe the people inside were with the guerrillas. If they thought so, they'd drag the person away for investigation or they'd just shoot him in the street.

That's what happened to our school director. It was on a Sunday morning, I remember. There was suddenly a lot of commotion near our house. People said the school director had been shot there, he'd just been carried off. The next day we went to school like usual, but nobody was there. No teachers came. Not the next day, and no time after that. The school closed down. Nobody talked about it. Better not to talk. If someone went around saying what they thought had happened, well, soon they'd be dead too.

I can't say I knew all of what was happening back then. But kids are curious, right? Nobody in my family said anything to us. I knew the men were going off to some kind of meetings, and I knew—I mean, it was obvious—my grandfather and father weren't sleeping in the house anymore at night. I imagined they were sleeping somewhere out in the fields. My grandfather told me, "If the soldiers come by, tell them I'm not here. That's all." More than that he didn't say. And I knew well enough not to ask, and do as I was told. I didn't go outside much after the school closed down. I was scared the soldiers might come and ask me something, but nothing ever happened. As far as I know, nothing ever happened to kids or women. Only the men were hauled off, or killed. An uncle of mine got hauled off for investigation, though in the end they let him go. He was lucky, I think. My father and grandfather too were lucky. Nothing happened to them.

Because of all this, my family decided we had to get out of San Vicente. Sooner or later, they figured, something might happen to one of us. We just didn't have any place to go. We took off one day—we left the houses and the land—and took off for Chalatenango. Many people were running then, refugees like us. Our family wound up in Nombre de Jesús, a town on the border near Honduras. Turned out that wasn't a safe place either. We headed off across the border, but the Honduran soldiers were cooperating with the Salvadoran army, and they messed with us too. The only safe place to go was this refugee center further up in Honduras. It was a place called Mesa Grande. Some international people—I don't know exactly who they were, maybe the United Nations—had set up a group of refugee camps there. We all went. Must have been a few thousand people there in a bunch of camps all next to each other. Places with wire fencing around them that were guarded by Honduran soldiers. That's where we wound up living.

To me it was like jail. The international people gave us everything.

You didn't have to work. They just gave you things. We had all the food we needed—*maíz, frijol,* rice. And they gave us clothes, shoes, soap, medicines. We had everything. But you couldn't go anywhere. There were Honduran soldiers guarding us day and night, and we weren't allowed to leave. Boring, real boring.

What happened is that people from FMLN came to the camp. Yes, guerrillas. They came just like they were refugees. They'd stay awhile, and when they were there they had these meetings. The guerrillas told us about what was happening in El Salvador, why we had to organize and fight for a better life. I went and listened. It made sense to me. I'd seen how the Fuerza Armada treated us, and here we were, my whole family, stuck in a refugee camp in Honduras. Besides, the guerrillas told us it was going to be good, enjoyable, to be with them. We wouldn't be penned up like prisoners the way we were in Mesa Grande. We'd be moving around, free. So I decided, yes, I'm going to join up, get out of the camp.

If you were young like me, the guerrillas went to your family and asked permission to recruit you. Sometimes the family said yes, and sometimes no. If the family said no, well, sometimes the young people would just sneak off anyway. My grandparents said okay, so I didn't have to sneak off. But anyway, I wasn't living with them right then. I'd taken up with this boy. I was with him and his family. Oscar was his name. We got together after I'd been in the camp for almost a year. I was thirteen then. Yes, he was my first. We were *ajuntados,* living like a couple with his parents. But we both hated being in the camp, and we decided we'd go off and join the FMLN.

The way it worked is the FMLN organized our escape. No, no, you couldn't just walk out the gate. You had to escape at night. The FMLN had it all worked out. They knew where the Honduran soldiers were stationed and when they passed certain places on their patrols. There was a large group of us who all escaped that same night. We crawled under the fence, one by one, and then each keeping some distance from the other, we quickly walked off into the forest, following our guides. We walked through the mountains and across the border into El Salvador. It took us three days. Finally we got to this place in Chalatenango where the FMLN had their training camp. And that was it. That's how I got started with the guerrillas.

In the beginning, what they did is give us some basic training. Everyone learned how to use a rifle. The M-16 and the G-3—that's what we had. I think they came from Cuba, by way of Nicaragua. That's what I heard. And some of the arms came from government soldiers who'd been killed on raids. In the beginning, in the '70s—this is what I was told—the guerrillas didn't have more than machetes and sticks. But slowly they started picking up arms on raids, and then from Cuba. By the time I joined up they already had plenty.

I was only thirteen then, a girl. So after basic training I didn't have a rifle anymore. They put me to work as a *molendera* [a grinder who grinds corn to make tortillas]. Me and some other girls and some older women. We did the cooking for the guerrilla camp. Or later, when we went out on raids, like in small groups of twelve people, I'd be the *molendera* of that group. Making tortillas, beans, or whatever. Depended on what you had. Sometimes, especially in the beginning, we didn't have any food. Later, the FMLN had it better organized. We had suppliers, "collaborators," the army called them. They brought us food. My mother and father and grandfather later worked like that, helping supply food to the guerrillas. In the beginning, though, we didn't have this worked out. So sometimes we went hungry. Or we'd steal. Anything we could grab— a few vegetables, or chickens, whatever. We'd steal mostly from families whose sons were with the Fuerza Armada. Some of the guerrillas knew who these families were, and we'd steal from them. That's how we managed in the beginning.

I worked as a *molendera* for about six months. But I didn't like being a cook. To this day, I don't like it. I do it for my family, sure, but cooking is not something I like. Maybe I got that way because of being a *molendera* in the guerrillas, I don't know. Anyway, I was looking for something else to do, and then the FMLN gave me a better job—as a *radista* [a radio operator]. They figured I could do this work and, I guess, they trusted me. They saw I was committed to staying with them. Because what happened is that Oscar took off. After four months, he just went back to Mesa Grande. Never said a word to me or anyone. Just took off. Me, I didn't let it bother me. I figured, "He wants to go back, that's his business. I'm staying."

That was my work for the next five or six years. I operated the radio for whatever group I was with. There were other women who were doing the fighting along with the men. Believe me, some were better shots than the men. And some women were *explosivistas* [mine experts]. That was dangerous work. If you made one mistake, you stayed right where you made the mistake. But I didn't do this type of work. They decided my skill was to operate the radio, to make communications between our unit and others. I could read a little, so I memorized all the codes. There was a whole book of them. The codes were in numbers and letters, and let's say you wanted to indicate your location, then you'd send a coded message—usually three numbers or letters was enough. Or, if you wanted to indicate the time of an operation, you'd use the letters and numbers to signal what you were going to do. And also, I'd have to receive messages from other units and give them to our group. I liked this work. From one place to another in the mountains, I went around as a *radista*.

Once in a while, I got to go on leave. You know, go visit my family who were still up in Mesa Grande. I took my first leave after I'd been in a year or so. I went through the mountains with others. It was no problem getting into the refugee camp. I went for a few weeks. And you know, a funny thing happened. That same guy who I'd gone off with, he was still up there. The first day I was back, he came over to my grandparents' place looking for me. "Are you with the police or something?" I said to him. "Because there're no bad people here. No need for anyone to come searching for anything here." I sent him away. Then about a week later, I was up at the bath house of the camp. And there he was, prowling around. "Look here," I said to him. "You're wasting your time coming around after me. What happened with us, happened. You had your chance and you blew it. Now go on, find another. But stop coming after me!" And that was it. I'm sorry I ever started with that guy. It was a mistake. Falling for someone who goes off to the fighting zone with you and then runs away—what kind of person is that? No, I didn't love him. You can't love someone like that. I know they say the first one you have sex with, he always stays with you, you can't forget him. But I don't believe that. Because for me nothing is left. It's just a stupid thing that happened back then, that's all.

❧

A nyway, after being with my family for awhile, I wanted to go back. I was the first of my brothers or sisters who went with the guerrillas, and my mother wasn't happy to see me go. But that's what I wanted to do, and nobody was about to stop me. So I went back to my unit and stayed there. Until '89. Yes, as a *radista*.

Me, I was lucky. Nothing ever happened to me. Not even wounded. Some of my *compas* [*compañeros*, or comrades] got killed on raids. And some girls I knew got captured by the Fuerza Armada and, you know, raped and tortured. These things happened to some people, sure. But personally, I can say I was lucky. I never got shot or hurt. The only bad thing that happened to me was that I lost my first baby when I was in the guerrillas. That was hard on me. I felt real bad about that.

It happened a year or so after I returned from Mesa Grande. I was sixteen at the time. I had this boyfriend then who was in another unit. Well, originally he was in my unit, then they moved him. He was older than me, twenty-five. We started getting together. Then he got shifted. The FMLN had a rule that if a couple got together, they had to be split up into different units. Before they had this rule, what was sometimes happening is that one partner would get killed, and then the other partner would desert the FMLN. So they made a rule that if a couple was getting together, they'd have to be separated into different units. Actually, we were all told it wasn't a good idea for any couple to get too involved with each other. But naturally, these things happened. So they split you up and then let you visit each other every fifteen days or so. And also, there were *fiestas* sometimes in the towns near where we were. In safe areas, where the FMLN had control. We'd come down from the mountains, go listen to the music and dance, and have a good time. This way a couple could get together for a few days.

So what happened is that I got pregnant. I didn't know it at the time. What do you know at sixteen? All I knew was that I was nauseous and vomiting a lot. And one time when I went to take my food, I just couldn't look at it. My intestines were turning upside down. The *molendera* who was cooking for us—she was an older woman and knew about these things—she said to me, "Perhaps you've got it." I didn't catch on. "Got what?" I asked. *"Bueno,"* she said. "Could be you're pregnant. If these are the only symptoms you have, well, could be you've got it."

I didn't pay much attention to this until a few months later. By then I wasn't nauseous anymore, but I could feel the baby kicking inside me. I can't say I was happy about this, not at all. It was no time to be pregnant. My unit was real active during this time. Running from here to there, making raids and then escaping. Sometimes we'd be stuck in a little cave for days, hiding out and with nothing to eat. And then—I was already in my last month—we got attacked by the Fuerza Armada, helicopters shooting at us, and we had to scatter in all directions. For days we were on the run. No time to eat, and sometimes we had nothing to drink either. And me with my belly like that. It was a bad thing.

Just before I gave birth, my unit told me I should go down to our hospital. We had a small place in Chalatenango, in one of the towns we controlled. It was just a room with some beds made out of planks of wood. Good doctors, though. Some international people, I think they were French. Good equipment too. Giving birth was the easy part. There were some other FMLN women there giving birth too. I watched how they did it. It wasn't too hard. Only three hours of these pains and it was over. Except the bad part was that my baby was born what they call "anemic," something like that. She was sickly, you could see that right away. I didn't have even a drop of milk in me to breast-feed her. I was sick from all the running around we'd done those last months. It was a sad thing. You could see her wasting away. Then she died—fifty days after she was born. Real sad, the whole thing.

I felt bad, but what could I do? I went back into the mountains and rejoined my unit. When I got there, my *compas* told me the man I was with, the baby's father, had been killed. In an ambush, they said. It happened after I'd given birth. That's all they told me. I never received anything of his, no clothes or anything. And nobody told me anything else about it. I found myself wondering if he'd really been killed or, well, if he'd just taken off. I don't know. Not that I loved him. No, it was just one of these—what can I say?—a flash of light, say. But it's strange, I think, that I never did receive a thing of his, and I've never heard another word about him.

After that, I told myself I should be careful, not get involved with anyone and get pregnant again. Not as long as I was with the guerrillas. Wait till it ended, is what I was thinking. But, *bueno*, it didn't work out like that. A couple of years later I was with another boyfriend. Yes, a guy in the FMLN. Again I got pregnant. This time, at least, I knew what it was. I was able to take better care of myself. We had adequate food with us and we had water. I didn't get so worn out like the first time. And this time I didn't lose my baby. She lived. Dora, my eight-year-old. She's real healthy, you can see that.

After I had her, I took a leave from the FMLN. Actually, I figured to get out then. I went to Santa Marta, where my family was. They'd been there for three years, after they left Mesa Grande. I went to stay with my grandparents. This was in '89, around then. But what happened is that I got word from the FMLN that I was still needed. They wanted me to come back. They told me I could bring my daughter. So that's what I did. I went back, but no longer as a *radista*. I couldn't do that with my girl around me all the time. I became a *molendera* again. I can't say I liked it any better the second time than the first. Still, that's what my unit needed, so that's what I did.

Yes, I was still involved with Dora's father. I saw him now and then. And then I got pregnant again. Right, with Luis, my son. I stayed with my unit as long as I could, working as a *molendera*. And then I left again to give birth. Luis was fine too, healthy. But that was it for me. I couldn't go on with my unit. Not with two kids. Besides, by then the negotiations for peace were going on. The war was about to end, that's what some people were saying. I wasn't so sure. Only thing I knew, for me the war was over. I'd been in nine years. I went to Santa Marta again to be with my grandparents. No, my children's father didn't come with us. He didn't want to. I didn't mind that so much, that's a fact. I went and told him, "If you don't want to be with us, then go your own way. Just help me a little with some money for the children." He never did, though. He didn't even come to see Luis—never has. He went to live with his new woman. Me, I stayed a little while in Santa Marta. Then when we got word they were looking to populate here in Henríquez, I came over here. In '92. I've been here since then.

It's worked out real well for us here in Henríquez. Those families who came here and got a place, at least one person in the family had been with the FMLN. And because you'd been with the FMLN, it was arranged that you got some things. *Bueno*, you got the materials to put up your house, and you got some chairs, tables, tools, things like that. You got your land, 3½ manzanas. Or really, the way it worked is that you got a loan to buy the land. But a little while back they gave us all a pardon on that loan. None of us have to pay the money back to the bank. Same thing with a cash loan they gave each one of us. I got 10,000 colones—to buy things like seeds, fertilizer, chickens. And that loan too has been pardoned. So all in all, we did okay. We were able to make a start of things here.

When I first came here, I lived with my grandparents. Me and my two kids. About a year after that I put up my own place and I got my own *milpa*. Did I work it myself? Sure. I'd worked with my grandpa, I knew how to do it. *Maíz, frijol*—I knew how to sow and take care of it. No problem. I did it, sure. Then, like I told you, Antonio started pushing to get together. By the time I was in my own place, I'd already got around to liking him. He was living in his own house then. He'd left his wife and four kids. Too much fighting between him and her—that's what he told me. He wanted to get *ajuntado* with me, and I said yes. He moved in with me. No, not where we are now—in a metal sheeting house I had down below. This place where we're living now is only a year and a half old. We lived in the other place for a couple of years after we got *ajuntados*.

How did his wife take it? Well, truth is, she tried to make some problems for me. She tried to hurt me, work *brujería* [witchcraft] on me. I don't know how she did it. Maybe she paid someone to do it. There're people who know how to do these things. Don't ask me how they do it. I just know that one day as I was preparing lunch, grinding the *maíz*, I suddenly had this terrible fear. I felt someone was grabbing me from behind, I sensed my eyes growing real big, and then a fever came over me and I felt I was going to faint. I was pregnant at the time, but this had never happened before. And this feeling, the fear and sense of being grabbed from behind, it kept coming back day after day. I couldn't get rid of it.

At the time, there was a *curandero* [faith healer] living around here. People told me I should go see *él que cura* [the one who cures]—that's how they call him. So I went. As soon as I saw him and began explaining my symptoms, he said, "Don't go on! I know what it is!" What he said is just what I was thinking. Antonio's wife had worked some *daño* [harm] on me. Antonio went and cursed her out, but she denied she had done anything. To this day, she still denies it. But anyway, *él que cura* told me he could help me. "It'll cost a lot of money," he said. "How much?" I asked. "It's 2,000 colones," he said. It *was* a lot of money—almost half of what we earn each year from selling our harvest, selling what we don't need for ourselves. But I figured I had to do it. I was feeling awful, I couldn't go on like that. So for the next few months he brought me these herbs to bathe in and to drink. And he prayed for me, some Catholic prayers. Little by little, I started feeling better. I can't tell you how these things work, but I know they do. It did with me, that's for sure. By the time I gave birth, I was feeling healthy again. My son was born fine.

Since then there have been no more problems. I've had two more children with Antonio. And his wife hasn't bothered us anymore. Antonio gives her *maíz* and *frijol* from our harvest, and he buys clothes for his other children. She leaves us alone. No problems now. What happened is over. Those fears I had back then never came back.

With this last little girl I just had, I think that's it for me. Antonio agrees. We've both decided we've had enough children. I've got a friend who told me about this "rhythm method" as a way of not getting pregnant. But she says it doesn't work so well. Another friend, who only had three children and then she stopped, told me about some injections. You go to Suchitoto and get them. You can't just administer them yourself—it doesn't work that way. You have to do it according to a plan. When I have a chance I'm going over to Suchitoto to look into it. I don't want to be like my mother, who's had eleven kids. Or my grandma Dolores, who had twelve or thirteen. No, no. For me five is enough. Antonio is with me in this completely. He says if that's how I want it, it's fine with him.

Truth is, Antonio is a good man. He's not someone who tries to tell you what to do or watch over you. You know, be the one who gives the orders around the house. He helps me out around the house when he can. Mostly, the last few years he's been busy outside the house—in the fields, or doing things as president of the community. But when he's here at home, he helps me out. You've seen him here yourselves, no? When he comes in from the fields, he'll put down his machete and take over grinding the *maíz* for tortillas. Or if I need help with some of the kids, he'll take one or the other and rock the child to sleep. In the evening, he likes to lie around in the hammock, rest. The older kids put themselves to sleep. They eat some tortillas and just go off by themselves. It's me who likes to take off at night. I go over to my grandma's house to tell tales with my sisters. That's fine with Antonio. He never questions anything. I'm free to go where I want.

No doubt about it, things have changed a lot in this way. When I was growing up, men worked outside, and when it came to the house they did nothing. And men didn't let women go out—the women were stuck in the house. If a woman had it in her mind to go out, the man would tell her she had to obey or he'd beat her. And he did, sure he did.

Now it's changed. Because of the FMLN and the war. Back in the refugee camp, people from the FMLN used to come and give lectures about men-women relations, about our equality. I was too young to go then, but I know my mother went. My father, too. These days we still have people giving lectures about this. Yes, here in Henríquez. My mother is now one of the people who do some of the talking. All these talks, they've made a change.

These days, if a woman around here wants to go out to work, take some job outside the house, she does it. Men don't oppose it. And men have started helping out with the work around the house. I see my father doing things now he'd never done before. The way he used to be is that he'd go out to work in the fields and wouldn't come back till sundown. He didn't do anything in the house, didn't take care of the kids, or even make food if there was none. Now, if he comes home and there's no food, he says, "Never mind, I'll do it myself." And my brothers who are still at home, the older ones, they help out in the house now. They don't leave it all to my mother. It's good to see. Because, after all, men and women both have hands and both can do that work.

Look at the change in my mother's house. She's out these days almost as much as my father. She's real busy in the community. If you ask me, she's even too busy. She's a coordinator of the *comedor* [dining hall, where the community's children ages 2–12 eat their lunch on weekdays]. She's taking a course at the clinic here on public health. And just now, she got elected to the directorate of the community. I told her, "Mama, don't you think you're taking on too much? You're never going to be home. That's no good for the little ones." She didn't like hearing that from me, no. But look, she's got a couple who are still as small as my kids, and the thing is, her house *is* neglected some. Me, I wouldn't do it her way. Some people wanted to vote me onto the community's directorate. There're nine members, including the president. I said, "No thanks." I didn't even go to the meeting when they had the election. I was afraid they'd try to talk me into it. I've got no time for that now.

Antonio has been doing that work for three years. I know how much time it takes. The people here wanted him to be president again, but he said, "No more. I'll walk out of the meeting if you vote for me." He was president when the community started, and he served two more years after that. People here want him to be president because he knows how to get things done. He has some kind of cleverness that way. He was an officer in the guerrillas, right from the beginning until the end—maybe thirteen years. He knows how to lead people, get them doing things.

And yes, a lot has been accomplished. We've got pipes bringing water now from up in the hills, and we're about to get electricity here. We have a primary school, a *comedor*, and they say we're about to get a kindergarten next year. And we've rebuilt almost all the houses with concrete blocks and red tile roofs. And look out there in the yard—those concrete things, they're new latrines and everyone is getting one. A lot is going on. But getting all this stuff takes lots of time. Meetings and meetings. Antonio's tired of it. He wants to be left alone, he says. Just go back to the *milpa* and spend his days working out there.

For me, it's better if he does this. He'll be around more now. And also, we need to work the *milpa* more, and maybe get a few animals to raise. We need the cash. Being president of the community didn't pay any money. It's a voluntary job. Lots of work, but no cash from it. If he puts more time into farming, it'll work out better for us. We need to buy a new cow or two. We had one who was just about to give birth. But just a month ago some crooks around here came and stole her. They stole ours and my mother's cow too. Now we've got to get another. That's where you can make a little cash—raising animals. So we've got to put our minds to doing that. With five kids now, we've got to think of these things, right?

Besides that business with our cow, I've got no complaints. I like how things are here in Henríquez. Antonio and I sometimes sit around at night and talk about it. He and I, we both feel good about how it's all worked out. All those years we were in the mountains with the FMLN, never knowing how it would end, and now here we are in Henríquez, here together with the kids, and it's all worked out. Sometimes we think that if the FMLN had won the war outright it would be even better. But look, even though we didn't win outright, the way it ended is good enough. If you ask me, I don't expect there'll be another war. I wouldn't want to see that happen. The way things are for us is fine now. No complaints. If you ask me, the future looks okay for me and my family. Our life is good. That's the way I feel.

Lupe

Just a minute's walk up the winding dirt path from María's house is the house of her mother, Lupe. It is the uppermost house in the residential area. Beyond it, the community's *milpas* begin—each one sown with *maíz* or *frijol*, depending on the season. And still farther up the slope is Mount Guazapa, a tree-covered peak that was the site of fierce skirmishes during the civil war.

Around Lupe's house is a small grove of banana trees that grows almost up to the front porch. In size and structure, the house itself is a replica of María's place. But the large single room holds more furniture: the usual cord-strung beds and hammocks, some blue plastic chairs, a huge wooden armoire, and a 12-inch black-and-white TV along with a car battery to power it, sitting on a metal table ("Gives the kids something to do—keeps them out of my hair so much," says Lupe).

Lupe and her husband, Jorge, have ten children, five of them still living at home. Four others, including María, are married and have their houses in Henríquez. At forty-four years, Lupe appears every bit her age, if not older. Her black hair is streaked with gray, and her light brown eyes have a look of fatigue and, quite often, undisguised annoyance. She talks in a quick, impatient manner and from time to time punctuates her points with a range of epithets and curses.

Unlike her daughter or her mother, who were almost always at home when we visited, Lupe was usually outside the house: in the community's health clinic, the *comedor*, or off on some errand to Suchitoto or San Salvador. While her daughter María has become something of a homebody since the war, over the last five years Lupe has grown increasingly active in the community's affairs. Indeed, at this point Lupe *is* without exaggeration the most active woman in Henríquez—as a coordinator of the *comedor* and now *presidente* of Henríquez. "Some of my family think I'm out too much these days," says Lupe, "but it suits *me* fine."

Perhaps her active role in the community is what caused Lupe to interrupt her busy schedule for our interviews. More than her mother and even her daughter, Lupe seems to have an ideological sense about her life. She does not call herself a "feminist" (in fact, she wasn't sure what the word meant) or a "socialist" either. But in her own searching manner she gradually has begun to perceive her life and that of others in these ideological terms. And what is more, she seems willing, even eager, to discuss her thoughts with others, including us, as potential bearers of this message.

In all, we interviewed Lupe eight times over a period of a year. Sometimes we caught her at her mother's or her daughter's house, sometimes at her own place. Inevitably, there were others around listening. If it was her children, she dispersed them with a quick flick of her hand; and if it was her husband, she waited until he drifted away before continuing with her story or message.

What follow, then, are Lupe's story and message: the recollections and reflections, as she might say, of a "changing" *campesina* in El Salvador.

❧

The TV? Oh, we bought it two years back. We run it on that car battery. Every fifteen days or so you've got to recharge it—over at the gas station in Suchitoto. There's one other TV here in Henríquez, that's all. Soon as the community gets electricity, others will be getting them, I'm sure. Gives the kids something to do—keeps them out of my hair so much. They're watching whenever you let them. My husband watches it only a little. The news is what he likes. After he comes in from the fields in the evening, he watches before dozing off. Me, I don't watch. Except for *La María del barrio.* You know that soap opera, don't you? I like that one, but that's about all I watch. No time. At night, I'm too tired. I just want to shut my eyes and get some sleep. Because at dawn, even before, I've got to be up again. Making tortillas, fetching water, doing a wash—and then to my work here in the community. *That's* what I like, working outside the house. María says I'm out too much. But that's her opinion. I like it this way, getting involved in things here in Henríquez. That's my way.

María told you I was just elected to the directorate, did she? Yes, that's right. We just had new elections and we've got a new directorate. Who's president? Look, the way it happened is Antonio said he didn't want it anymore. So they voted for me. Right, I'm the president now. María didn't tell you that? Well, I am. Yes, I'm the first woman.

Thanks for your congratulations. But the truth is, I got elected because hardly anybody else wanted to take the work on their shoulders. I was willing, so they gave it to me. People saw I was someone who likes to work in the community. For awhile now, I've been giving talks here on men-women relations, you know, the equality of the sexes. And now I've just finished the course in the clinic, I'm talking to our women's group about birth control and all that. I like doing this talking. It's a way of learning something and opening people's eyes.

Besides this, I'm busy most days at the *comedor.* We've been running it more than a year now—me and two other women here. It's for kids two to twelve years old. Anyone that age who wants to eat, *bueno,* they come and get a lunch. Vegetables, fruit, rice, meat, chicken. We've got fifty-seven kids coming each day. No, their parents don't pay a *centavo.*

Some organizations, like IMU [Instituto de la Mujer], are picking up the bill. On Sundays, I go to San Salvador and do the buying for the week. Yes, I get paid for this—300 colones a month. It's not like being president of Henríquez, which is something that takes your time, but you get nothing for it. *Nada*, not a centavo. But no matter, I think it's worth doing even if it doesn't bring in money.

What does my husband think? *Bueno*, I'll tell you, but hold on a little ... [*Lupe nods in the direction of the patio hammock, where Jorge, lying down, is chatting with a neighbor. She enters the house and brings out a handful of apples for her guests, saying, "I just got these at the market—they gave them to me when I bought all the other stuff for the* comedor." *Some moments later, when Jorge and his neighbor leave, as if not noticing us, Lupe resumes.*] Look, the truth is, he's not so happy about my becoming president of the community. He told me, "You're going to have all these meetings, and all this work to do. What are you taking on all that for?" I don't answer him. Better that way. He's right about all the extra work. But I know he's not going to stop me. No more. He's accepted that things have changed, it's no longer as it was before.

Little by little, things *have* changed. Through what we call "the struggle of dialogue." You know, explaining and arguing between us—between men and women. With Jorge and me it started back in the beginning of the war. When we were up in the refugee camp in Honduras, we'd have these meetings and talks by people from the FMLN. Jorge and I'd go together. They were saying things we hadn't heard before. About men and women being equal people. Like, God gives both of us hands and heads, not like we're two different kinds of beings. And just as women can carry a rifle alongside men, so men can help women out at home. Pick up a broom, wash the dishes, rock a baby to sleep—both can do it.

Of course, the men didn't go along with this at first. The men would say—even those who married their wives for love would say this— they'd say, "Look, that's why I married a woman, right? To take care of the house, to take care of the kids." Jorge was saying the same. Back then, he'd never do a thing in the house, not even make a fire or make a tortilla. I remember how he was at first. I remember up there in the camp we had this international lady, someone from Spain. She asked me to help out with the public health committee we had there. "Sure," I said. "But my husband isn't going to let me go to meetings at night." She went and spoke to Jorge herself, told him off. *Bueno*, he said I could go. But then as I started going off in the evenings, he'd follow me. He'd be a distance behind—and then he'd stay somewhere nearby. I'd return home from the meeting, and a few seconds later he'd enter too, all jealous like. Still, he didn't say a word. He didn't stop me, because he could see I was never up to anything bad.

These days, there's nothing like that anymore. Through the struggle of dialogue it's changed, with me telling him now and then, "You've got to get rid of this stupid mentality you've got." And, I tell you, it's changed a lot. He does some of the work around the house, he helps me out now. My sons see it, and I tell them too, "You boys, I want you to learn how to do these things too, like your father!" They see and they help too. I'm not sure it's changed like this in all houses. You just don't know what goes on in someone else's house. As the saying goes, *Caras vemos, pero corazones no sabemos* [We see their faces but don't know their hearts]. I know there're many men who still think the way they always have. That's why I go on giving talks. And in our women's group here in the community, we go on talking about this struggle. It takes time to change. But things *do* change. I know for Jorge and me it's no longer like it was in the beginning. We're much more equal now. He goes along with what I do, and I respect what he does. The way it's supposed to be, right?

Jorge is not someone who wants to get involved like me in community business. Jorge is happy in the *milpa*—that's where he likes to be. Always has. And he's good at what he does. He's not lazy, or a *bolo* lapping it up all the time. Not Jorge. He's a good farmer and we're doing fine these days. We get good harvests from our *milpa*, enough for us and enough to sell at the market. Jorge also raises animals. When we got our loans in the beginning—he got 12,000 colones and I got 8,000—we bought some calves and goats, six altogether. He bought the goats for 1,000 colones each, fattened them up, and then sold them for 2,000 colones. He sells the males and breeds the females. He's made good money this way. Enough for us to buy what we need for the house and children.

And with the money Jorge's also bought some more land, just outside the community. He's bought 4 more *manzanas*. Some of it he sows with *maíz* and some of it has coffee on it. That's the only work I do in the fields—pick the coffee. This year we got four *quintales* [400 lbs.]. Not much, but it's something. And now Jorge and his father and our son-in-law, they've bought 6 more *manzanas*. They're just figuring out what they want to do with it. It's got a spring on it, good water. The question is whether to sow it with *maíz* or raise animals. Animals give you the best profit. The problem is, we've got a lot of thieves roaming around these days. If you don't watch carefully, they'll grab your cows and goats. Just a little while back our family lost five animals that way. Grabbed out of the corral at night. We lost a cow and two calves, María lost her cow that was just a little way from giving birth, and another daughter lost her calf. Five animals, gone just like that. You bust your ass getting what you have, and then people go taking it from you. I tell you, it's a big problem these days. Too many people grabbing what isn't theirs, messing you over that way. Not a thing you can do about it either. Just start over again, that's all.

If you ask me, the reason for all this robbery and all these delinquents, it's because of—well, because of a couple of things. After the war there were many people around with rifles. People from the army and from our side too. Some of these people had never worked a day in their lives, and they weren't willing to start either. So they became bandits, going around and grabbing what isn't theirs. Because of that we have a lot of delinquents these days. And also because the parents don't take responsibility for their children. So many women raise children alone, and they can't manage it. Or sometimes the fathers are there, but they've got no work and there's not enough money to support the family. Some of the children get in their minds that the only way to get something is to steal it. It isn't right, but that's how they figure it. You see, even though we had the war, there's still a lot of poor people in this country. People in the *campo* [countryside] and in the cities who don't have anything. They're not like us or some other people. We came out of the war with something to show for it. Our situation is much better now than before, no doubt about it. Look, we've got our land now, our community, and we're managing fine. And the FMLN is in the government now, working for us. Things have changed and they're still changing.

You've got exploitation in the country, the rich exploiting the poor, but in some ways things are better. You know how it was before the war, right? Almost all the land in this country was in the hands of the rich. The "fourteen families" and those other rich ones had the land to themselves. For a *campesino* to buy a small plot was real hard. Even to rent it was hard. Look what was here in Henríquez. This whole property was in the hands of just one landowner. Over where we have the clinic and school, this landowner had his big house. On weekends he'd have his parties there. The ex-president—what's his name?—yes, Duarte, used to come out here with a big crowd, and with a big group of army officers too. They'd slaughter an ox and have a feast. Just them.

And what about the *campesinos* living near them—what did *they* have? Nothing much. These landowners would hire the *campesinos* to harvest their sugarcane or coffee, and pay almost nothing. And they'd mistreat them, not even giving the workers lunch or anything. I know about this, believe me. My husband used to go now and then to cut cane in order to make a few colones. In San Vicente. Me, I'd never do it. But I remember how things were. The poor worked their asses off and the rich made all the money. That's how it was. And it's still bad, I tell you. But not like it was. You get a better wage now cutting cane or picking coffee. That's because of the FMLN. And some people got land. It's better that way, for sure.

And in other ways too, it's better now. It used to be you had to be careful what you said about politics. If you didn't like the president, you had to keep your mouth shut. Now, no. If I think the president is rotten— like this ARENA guy who's in now, Calderón Sol—I can say so. And yes, that *is* what I think. I'm not afraid to tell you that. Or look, the way it used to be you were scared when you went to the mayor's office in town. Say you had to arrange some papers. A birth certificate, an identity card, say. You had to do like this [*Lupe bows her head down*]. And you had to talk in a soft, scared voice. If you didn't carry yourself like that, the official wouldn't like it. He'd be rough with you, ignore you, do whatever the hell he wanted. Now, no. You can speak right up, say what you want. No fear now. With the FMLN in power in so many towns, and with the other side afraid to lose in more places, you get much better treatment.

So if you ask me whether the war was worth it, I say yes. We spilled a lot of blood. Lots of our people died up there in the *monte*. But we got something from the war. My family, for sure. Others, not so much. There's still a lot of exploitation, a lot of poor people, but things did get better. And I'm hoping they'll be better in the future—that the poor will get a better life here in El Salvador.

When I was growing up, if I think back on it, we *were* poor. But we weren't the poorest of the poor, you know, like they say, *comiendo tortilla con sal* [eating tortillas with salt]. My mother, yes. She grew up like that, not having enough to eat. Her family had no land. But she married my father, and he had some land. He inherited it from his father. Ten manzanas or more, that's what he had. Over in a village in the department of Cabañas, on the shores of the Lempa River. That's where I grew up. It's about four hours from here by bus. I was raised there, got married to Jorge there—he's from the same village—and I lived there the first twenty years or so of my life.

There weren't too many houses where we were living. It was an isolated place, a flatland near the river. How was our house? Well, like the others. Made out of wooden poles and mud. You weave the poles together, make a frame out of them, and then pour mud in the center. The same as you see today in many places in the *campo*. One big room for all of us, and a kitchen made out of adobe bricks off to the side. The usual, nothing more.

Altogether living in that house—before I got *ajuntada* with Jorge— maybe there were nine or ten of us. My mother has had, let's see, thirteen children. Eleven with my father, and then two more with two slobs she met after my father died. But when I was still there she had maybe eight. Oh yes, it was crowded. That's for sure.

Me, I'm the oldest. There was one she had before me, a miscarriage. I'm the first one who lived. All the rest, my four brothers and seven sisters, came after me. I can't say it was good being the oldest, or bad either. I think it was the same for all of us. Except that some of my younger brothers and sisters got to go to school more than I did. Some of them got to third grade, or fifth grade even. Me and the others who came right after me, we hardly learned at all. The school was far off, a few kilometers' walk. My father said I could go, and I went for half a year. My mother stopped me. "You're not going anymore," she told me one day. "You're just wasting your time there, becoming a lazy good-for-nothing. Better to learn how to work!" That was her attitude about school. So I only learned how to read later—when I became an adult. I took a course up in the refugee camp and also here in Henríquez. To me it's important to know these things. But to my mother, it was just nonsense. She wanted us home working with her, helping her out.

That's how it was when I was a kid. The boys worked with my father in the *milpa,* and the girls stayed at home working with my mother. A *molendera* is what I was—always grinding *maíz* and making tortillas. Or sweeping up, or going down to the river to wash clothes. My mother worked us hard. And she worked hard too. When she wasn't working with us, she'd be making *petates* [straw or reed sleeping mats, often placed on the cord-strung beds]. I used to admire how fast she did it. In one day she could weave a *petate* 2 meters long and 1 meter wide, or even bigger. The *petates* were for us, or she'd sell them in the market at a good price. She taught me how to make them too, but I can't do it like she can. We still use them today. They're much better than those store-bought mattresses. More natural.

Apart from working, there wasn't much to do. I don't remember playing as a kid. No, not with dolls. And no games. But sometimes I'd go out in our banana grove with Victoria and Oscar, my sister and brother. We'd haul down a bunch of bananas and have ourselves a little feast. Or I'd climb the fruit trees we had, like the *nance* tree [a type of fig]. Ah yes! I could sit up there for hours just dreaming away, not paying attention to anything. This one time I was up there for a few hours, and sure enough, whoosh!, I came falling down. I landed on the back of my head. I was stunned. My mother came out of the house, took one look, and yelled at me, "I didn't send you up there, so you just pick yourself up. I don't care if you've broken every bone in your body, you take care of yourself now!" She was tough like that sometimes. Real stern. That's her manner, always has been.

My father was easier—at least in some things he was. He didn't mind your lazing around, taking it easy. That's what he did too whenever he could. With his *chicha* [alcoholic beverage made of corn and sugar], that's how he'd have himself a good time. He made it himself, from the *maíz* he grew and his sugarcane. You know how to make *chicha*, no? It's easy. You just put some *maíz* in a pitcher of water, and when the kernels swell up you dump the water. Then you toss in some brown sugar, add some more water, let it sit a day or so, and there you have it—*chicha*. Simple as that!

I can remember this one time, me and Victoria and Oscar found him out in the banana grove lazing around. He had this pitcher with him. We were real young then, five or seven. We didn't know what he had there. He called us over. "You kids want a soft drink?" he asked. Then he poured some for each of us. Real sweet stuff. Then I began to feel the world sort of spinning. The others must have felt the same. Like three little drunks, we stumbled back to the house. It must have been some sight. My mother didn't say anything, but she must have known what had happened. She knew how my father was.

He liked his *chicha*, my father did. And he liked brewing it and making *aguardiente* [a stronger liquor made from *chicha*]. That's what cost him his life. I know María told you about this. Right, I was there when she told you about it. That's how he died. The Guardia shot him swimming across the Lempa River. Sons of whores, those Guardia! My mother was left a widow with all the kids to take care of. She was only about thirty-five at the time. It was *real* hard on her, that's for sure. She had to raise the young ones by herself after that. It wasn't easy.

When my father died, I was already *ajuntada* with Jorge. I'd had my first child by then—María. She was nine months old. I was living in the same village with Jorge and his parents. I was sixteen then. Yes, that's all. In the *campo* back then—and still today—you get *ajuntada* real quick. You find someone, or your parents tell you about someone, and that's it. You're hooked up before you know it.

How did it happen for me? Let's see . . . I might as well tell you, it doesn't matter anymore. And it's no secret, not at all. What happened, you see, is Jorge is—well, he wasn't my first, put it that way. There was someone before him. The way it happened is that I had this boyfriend. Or really he was a man, almost thirty. He was a small man with a little body, but I liked him. I was fourteen at the time. This man lived nearby with his mother, in the same village. He started to come by our house chatting with us or, really, chatting with me. I liked talking to him, though I could see my mother didn't like his coming by so much. Then one day, as I was chatting there with him, my mother picked up this huge stick and started whacking me and cursing me. Luis—that's his name—he said to me, "Let's go. Better come with me so your mama doesn't go on smacking you." I agreed. And I told my mother I was leaving. She shouted after me, "Go then, old whore! Run off like a dog!" And I answered her, "All I was doing is talking to him, nothing more. What's wrong with that? You're the one who started cursing and whacking me for nothing. So fuck it all, I'm taking off!" And I went. I didn't take anything with me, not even one rag of a dress. I just went like I was.

Luis's house was near ours, just a few houses down the way. When we got there his mother said, "What are you two doing? Luis, you're bringing her here?" He told his mother yes. *Vaya pues* [fine], she said. "It's alright with me." So that night we spent together, off in a separate room. That was the first time I'd ever been with a man. I had no idea what to expect. But Luis, he was good to me. Affectionate, if you know what I mean. Yes, it was fine. I didn't know anything, but it was fine. I wasn't frightened with him at all.

The frightening part was the next morning. When I got up I didn't want to go out of Luis's house. I didn't want my parents to see me. Then up there at my parents' house I heard my grandmother—my mother's mother—shouting at my father. She'd got up early in the morning and she was already there yelling, "Joaquín, are you going to go get her? If not, I'm handing my skirts to you and I'm going to put on the pants!" My father was drunk and full of courage then, and he came storming down after me. Fortunately, Luis wasn't there right then. God knows what might have happened. Because my father grabbed my arm, hit me twice with the back of his machete, and told me to come back with him. "And don't get any ideas about running," he said. "I've got my pistol here and I'll shoot you!" And that was it. I had no choice. I had to leave Luis.

No, I never went back to Luis's house. And Luis didn't come after me at my house either, thank God. Sure, I saw him in the village after that and we'd chat quickly. I told him, "Don't go around thinking about me anymore, because it's not possible for us to be together." Luis tried to convince me to come back, but I told him, "My father will go wild, that's how he is, and I'm going to get killed. Or you, or both of us. So that's it, I don't exist anymore."

That's how it ended with Luis. About a half-year later, Jorge started showing up at my house. My father came to me and said, "Here's the man I want for you." And my grandmother said, "This Jorge is the kind who can work, he's not some bum like the other one. Jorge's the one to get together with." I just wasn't ready to get together with Jorge then. But what could I do? I decided to go along with it. Except I told Jorge, "I don't want any problems afterward. Better if you know what happened. If you can accept me this way, I'll get together with you, and if not, no." And Jorge said, "Yes, I accept you as you are." You see, my mother had told me that if the woman is not a virgin, the man won't love her so much. I didn't know about these things, I just felt ashamed. I knew Jorge was aware of what had happened. Everyone in the village knew about it. It had been a big scandal. Everybody knew. Still, I wanted to tell him directly by myself. So I did, and he accepted me. Except once in awhile, he'd say, "You preferred that Luis. You didn't really want me." What could I tell him? There's a saying, you know, that you never forget your first love. The first one is the one you go on loving the most. It's true you can't forget, even though you've got to forget these things. But in your mind it comes back, right? You remember your first love.

And I did love Luis. It was only one day, one night really, but you can't forget. Not really.

⁓

Anyway, after I decided to get *ajuntada* with Jorge, I moved into his house. Jorge was living there with his parents. Jorge and his father had their *milpa*. They worked it together. That's how it's always been—Jorge and his father working together. I worked with his mother. House-work, of course.

Then I got pregnant. I was fifteen years old, ignorant. I didn't know what to expect. No, my mother didn't explain anything to me. Nor my mother-in-law. I just kept going about my chores really until the last minute. The day María was born I was working as usual. I got up early to do the grinding for the tortillas, and I milked the cows. We'd been saving the curd for about a week, my mother-in-law and me. That day we were making *quesadillas* to bring to the priest. *Bueno,* in the afternoon, as we were about to go put the batter in the oven, I had to stop. I told my mother-in-law to go to the oven by herself—it was down from our house about 100 meters. I was feeling some pains. Actually, the pains had started in the morning, but I wasn't thinking it was *her* wanting to be born that day. By afternoon, the pains had gotten sharper. I sent Jorge for the *partera* [midwife], an older woman who was known all around the area. Jorge couldn't locate her right away. She was off tending to someone else. So I lay there, and just as María was coming out the *partera* showed up. My mother-in-law too. My mother-in-law took one look and said, *Vaya, una molendera vino ya!* [Well, a grinder just got here].* The *partera* cut the umbilical cord. You know how they do it, right? Tie one knot at the belly and another a little way above, and then with a red-hot machete or a burning corncob you scorch the part between the knots. That's how they do it a lot in the *campo*.

After it's over, the *partera* washes the baby for you and then wraps

---

*Among *campesinos*, when a girl is born people often say, "It's a *molendera*," that is, a potential grinder of *maíz* for tortillas.

her up in some rags that you save for this. She wraps the baby from the top down to the ass. Hands close to the body so the baby can't scratch itself. Some wrap the legs too, but we didn't. We only put some blankets around the legs so they don't get crooked. For about six weeks you do it like that, and it works fine. All mine came out fine that way.

That same *partera* who came when I had María also helped me with four or five others. Because later, when I wound up in the refugee camp in Honduras, she was there too. And when I had two up there, she helped me out. With the others, I had another *partera*, and twice I gave birth in the hospital. The hospital is a good place to go, I think, just in case you have problems with the birth. But usually I was too far from a hospital. The poor creature would get born somewhere in the fields if you tried to make it to the main road and catch a bus. So I used *parteras*. It was fine for me that way. They knew what they were doing. Yes, you paid them something. A couple of colones, I think. I don't know, Jorge paid them. Or you might give her a chicken if you didn't have cash. It was up to you—that's the way it works.

The *partera* didn't come back to help you after the birth. You were on your own. With me, I had my mother-in-law to help me. She showed me how to take care of María. And really, I knew something about how to do it already. I'd helped my mother with some of my brothers and sisters when I was living with her. So I had my own understanding already.

The problem that came up with my mother-in-law wasn't *how* to take care of María. It was something else. Turns out, you see, my mother-in-law wanted to raise her as her own child. A few months after María was born, she told me that since María had been born under their roof, *nació en poder de ellos* [born under their power], she had a right to raise María as her own. I went to Jorge and told him to stop this, not to let his mother have her way. But Jorge opposed me. To this day, I'm not sure why. Maybe if our first had been a son, yes, maybe he'd have figured, "He's one who could help me in the fields." Then he might not have gone along with his mother. But the way it was, her children had all grown up. Her last daughter had married, and she had no one in the house, no daughters. So she wanted María. And me, I couldn't do anything about it. Little by little, those first two years when we lived under their roof, she took over my daughter. We both fed her, dressed her, and all that. Though when it came to telling María what to do, disciplining her, my mother-in-law took over. She made María hers.

I was unhappy with this. And I told Jorge we had to get out of their house. I didn't want my mother-in-law doing that to me again. I wanted to have no more children in their house. And that's the way we did it. We built our own house, not far from theirs. We've always gone on living near them. But apart, you see. I've raised the rest, the ten who came after María, all under my roof. María stayed with them. She's *my* daughter, but they—her grandma and grandpa—are the ones she lived with. No, I still don't accept the way it happened. There's still resentment there. Things happened over the years, things still go on. But look, I don't want to go into this. The less said, the better.

W e went on living up there in Cabañas. I had my first four children there. Jorge and I were in our own house, my in-laws in theirs with María. And my mother, yes, she was here too, raising my younger brothers and sisters by herself. Except she wasn't just by herself all that time. She somehow got hooked up with two different *bolos*, one right after the other, and she had a child with each. What slobs they were! They just came to live there, drink and screw, that's all. Drunken bastards, that's all! Especially the last one. He was about fifteen years younger than my mother.

I tell you, one time I came over to my mother's house and there she was running into her house as this drunken bastard was coming after her to beat her. I started screaming at him, "You drunken slob! Who the hell do you think you are, running after my mother like this? My father is gone, but you're not the boss here. We are! If you don't cut out your shit, me and the rest of us, we're going to throw your ass out of here!" Well, the drunken fool, real brave, picks up his machete and whacks one of my sisters, Isabel. Thank God, he caught her with the reverse side—

that drunken slob! I went running off to get Jorge, but by the time I got him, the whole thing had calmed down. No more beatings that day. But then you know what happened? A few months later, this same slob who beat Isabel, what does he do? He runs off with *her*! She was only fourteen. The bastard took her to San Salvador, to go live with him there. Of course Isabel didn't stay with him. A short while later, she left him and found some work in San Salvador as a maid. I found out because she came back a year later with her new boyfriend. Since then, I haven't seen her. Twenty years ago was the last time I saw her. My mother never said a word about the whole thing. And to this day, I've never said anything to her about it. It's not one of those things a daughter can talk about with her mother. All I can say is, well, at least after that she didn't take up with any more drunken fools. She'd had enough after that slob, I guess.

It was a little while after Isabel showed up with her new boyfriend and then disappeared again that me and Jorge and the rest of us had to leave our village in Cabañas. We got rid of our land there and moved to San Vicente. Why did we move? The plain truth is that in Jorge's family there were also some problems going on at the time. It wasn't safe for us to stay there in Cabañas any longer. Really, it was a stupid thing. Jorge's brother had taken a fancy to a young girl in the village—a girl who was the daughter of a cousin of mine. My cousin didn't want her to get *ajuntada* with Jorge's brother. But you know how it is. A man wants a girl and can't get the parents' consent, so he sometimes takes off with her. And that's what he did. Jorge's father knew there'd be trouble. Because my cousin, the father of that young brat, was a little crazy. He was going around saying he was going to take his machete and hack them to bits. And he probably would have. He was a man who liked to drink, and in some drunken rage he would have killed someone. So we decided to leave. We went to San Vicente. No, not my mother and her kids. She wasn't part of the thing. She didn't have to leave like we did. So she stayed in Cabañas and we moved to San Vicente.

❧

For me, that was the first time I'd moved from our village. I was twenty-two or so then. I'd been my whole life in that one place. So it was hard, yes. You had to get used to a new place. Besides that— though I didn't know it right then—the move to San Vicente was just the beginning of a lot of moving around we had to do. From then on, it's been moving here and moving there, because the war and all that happened then. We've been going from one place to another, trying to find somewhere we could stay.

When we went to San Vicente, you see, it was in the late '70s. We didn't know it when we went there, but San Vicente was one of the places where the guerrillas were just getting started. We were living in a little house right near the main street of the town. Jorge and his father had got some land there, up in the hills outside the town, and they were working it together. Then a little while after we got there, things began to happen. The FMLN started organizing people. They'd have these meetings at night, and some of the *campesinos* started going to hear these talks. Jorge and his father went. Not me. Jorge would come back and tell me some of the points they were making. How we needed to organize for a better life. How the land should belong to those who worked it and not to the rich. This was the first time I'd heard of people talking like that.

What happened is that the Fuerza Armada, the government's army, started showing up. They came to stop the whole thing. Where we were living, just above us, the army put up a kind of barracks. The whole hillside was green with them. That's what they wore, green uniforms. And they'd come down on raids, searching for the people of the FMLN. Jorge and the others kept going to meetings, but they stopped coming home to sleep at night. They had to sleep out in the *campo*. Because the army was going door-to-door looking for FMLN people or sympathizers. And when they found the men at home, they'd haul them off. Or just kill them. Each morning you'd find bodies here and there in the streets. I tell you, it got to be real dangerous.

I remember one time—right about the time they murdered Monseñor Romero in the capital, in '80 I think it was—and we were still in San Vicente. I remember I was waiting for a bus. When it arrived a bunch of soldiers nearby boarded it, began searching the people on it. Then suddenly, I heard three shots inside the bus and one of the soldiers fell. All the other soldiers outside rushed onto the bus, and they dragged out this girl. She was about fifteen. The way I figure it, she must have been with the FMLN, maybe carrying messages for them. There were many people working secretly like that. She had a pistol with her in her bag, and I guess she must have figured they were going to find the pistol anyway and haul her off and do God-knows-what to her, so she might as well shoot one of them first. It was terrible what they did to her. A bunch of them tore off her clothes, raped her right there in the street, and then left her lying there dead with a flashlight stuck in her. Right in her vagina. You couldn't lift a finger to help her, or they'd have killed you too probably. All you could do is stand there helpless.

After that, I knew we had to get out of San Vicente. Sooner or later one of my family would get caught, maybe murdered. The whole situation had become real vicious. Jorge and his father agreed. But we had no place to go. We couldn't go back to our village in Cabañas, and we had no other place either. So we took off north and went first to one place near the Honduras border, and then—because the Fuerza Armada was harassing us there too—we had to cross the border into Honduras. And from there we wound up in Mesa Grande, the big refugee camp in Honduras. We had no choice. We had to flee El Salvador to save ourselves.

Altogether, our family was up there in the refugee camp for almost six years. It was me, Jorge, the kids, and his parents. And, oh yes, my mother and some of my brothers and sisters too. My mother had to flee Cabañas the same as we had to flee San Vicente. The army was going after the *campesinos* there too, murdering whoever they thought was in the FMLN or collaborating with them. And my mother *was* part of the FMLN. She'd joined up with them while we were in San Vicente. Ask her about it. I don't know the details. She was one of the first women in her area who joined up—I think that's what she told me. She was a *mo-*

lendera with them, until she left and ran across the border. She wound up in Mesa Grande like us. There were a few thousand people up there, all of us living in the camp.

When we'd been in Mesa Grande for about a year, one day María came to me and said, "Mama, I'm joining the guerrillas, I'm going off to the *monte*." I didn't want her to go, but I knew I couldn't stop her. She'd got together with some boy who was also going off to the *monte*. They were determined to go. Even though I believed in the FMLN—my whole family was on the side of the guerrillas by then—still I didn't want her going to fight with them. I knew how dangerous it was. The war was at its height then. I wasn't sure I'd ever see her again. Believe me, it was hard to see her go off.

Then maybe a year later, she came back. She had got malaria. I hadn't heard one word from her, and she just showed up sicker than hell. "Look at yourself," I said to her. "Look what's happened to you!" And she answered me, "Mama, I'm sick now but as soon as I get better I'm going back." That's María. She had it in her head to do something and she did. I nursed her for three months. Just like I always did when she was sick. It was always me, not her grandmother, who took care of her then. So this time I took care of her too. And then when she got better, just like she said, she went back to the guerrillas. Me, all I could do is worry about her. At lunch, when I was serving tortillas and beans, I'd be wondering, "My girl, what is she eating? Is she going without anything?" I would get attacks of nerves worrying about María.

And she was only the first one who took off to join the guerrillas. Some of my sons went too. I couldn't stop them either. I tried to explain—it was nothing for boys to get mixed up with. Even grown men could hardly stand it. Again, nobody listened to me. They took off and went to the *monte*. Jorge, too, got involved in it. Though at least he didn't go fight with them. He'd go off for short periods, a few weeks, say, and work with the FMLN. He'd carry messages and food from place to place. Then he'd come back to Honduras, to the camp. It wasn't hard to do this. One of my brothers was a guide with the guerrillas, and he was sneaking people in and out of Honduras all the time. He knew the way to do it. Back and forth, that's how Jorge operated when we were up there in the camp. I suppose you could say we were lucky. My family didn't lose anyone. Jorge and María didn't even get wounded. One of my sons, Jesús, got wounded in his leg, and José came back without his arm, or just a skin flap that's left. But at least we're all alive. Nobody lost, dead, like what happened to so many other families.

All those years when we were in the camp I didn't get involved with the FMLN. I had my hands full taking care of the family. And also doing a few things in the camp. I was working with the public health team there, with this lady from Spain I told you about. That was my first involvement in things outside the house. I liked it. But really, the main thing I did was just take care of the family. Jorge and I got married when we were in the camp. Yes, a church marriage, you could say. We'd already been together for fifteen years and had six, or maybe it was seven, kids by then. We decided when this bishop came to the camp and offered to marry a bunch of couples together, well, we figured we'd do it too. I'm glad we did. No, I didn't get a ring, and I still don't have a ring. I'm glad we did it, though.

While I was up there I had two more children. The same *partera* from Cabañas helped me out. The births were fine. But with one of them, Ricardito, he died before he got through his first year. To this day I don't understand how it happened. He was fine, healthy, up to then. That day we hadn't eaten anything unusual. Then suddenly, he got this high fever, he stopped breast-feeding, and there was like something stuck in his throat. I took him to the infirmary there, where we had some doctors from that group Doctors Without Frontiers, some international people. They couldn't do anything for him. Within a few hours his whole body was hanging like a rag, he couldn't breathe. Then he was gone. Just like that, my son gone. I can't understand it, no, I can't. The only way I can figure it is that somebody up there worked some *daño* on him. Earlier that day some Hondurans had stopped by my house, and I think one of them must have done some *daño* to Ricardito. Because as soon as they left, Ricardito became sick. I tell you, to this day I don't understand it. He's the only child I've lost. All the others are alive. To me it seems like it must have been some witchcraft. Otherwise I can't figure it.

Anyway, some time after Ricardito died we decided the time had come for us to leave the camp in Honduras and go back to El Salvador. We'd been there six years and we'd had enough. This was in '87. We heard about the possibility of returning to El Salvador, to Santa Marta in the department of Chalatenango. The FMLN controlled some of that area, and they were repopulating it. Lots of people in the camp were saying then, "Look, let's go back to our country. Nobody can stop us now." That's the way we felt, Jorge and me. So we packed up the few things we had and took off. None of us had ever seen the place. But at least it was in our own country. And since the FMLN was there, we felt safe enough going there.

It turned out that Santa Marta wasn't a real good place. Where we were it was too crowded. The houses were one next to the other, people heaped up one on the other. Besides that, it wasn't so safe either. Where we were the people supported the FMLN. But now and then the army would come through searching for people. You had to be real careful. Especially since we, our family, decided to go on collaborating with the guerrillas. I got into it too. That was the first time I actively got involved. I decided that since all my family was in it, I couldn't stay apart. I had to contribute too.

What I did was the same as Jorge. I brought things to the guerrillas, whatever was needed—food, batteries, even munitions. As a woman I could get away with carrying large baskets on my head. That's how it is, right? Women always go around carrying large baskets on their heads. So I loaded up with supplies and brought things to the guerrillas. It was dangerous, yes. Because if the army caught you and found out what you were doing, they'd arrest you and sometimes torture you. I heard about women they'd caught and raped, or cut their breasts off. Still, I figured it was my turn to do what I could for the FMLN.

I never did get caught. Only one time, I had a close call. I was carrying some batteries to the guerrillas, the kind they use in flashlights, radios, or in those *minas quita pie* [foot-removing mines]. They're ordinary batteries, the kind you can buy in the store. *Bueno*, I got stopped by some soldiers and they told me, "Don't you know it's prohibited to be going around with batteries?" I played dumb. "Look," I answered, "there's advertisements all over for these batteries. They're in all the stores. How should I know they're not allowed?" The soldiers didn't do anything to me. They just confiscated the batteries and told me I could get my money back for them at their barracks. So that's what I did. I played innocent, got my money back. And then I went and bought some more batteries. I also bought enough bread to fill the basket, and I hid the batteries in the bread. I figured it was safer that way.

However, I immediately got stopped again by another bunch of soldiers. And this time I was scared because if they found the batteries they'd know I was collaborating. One of the soldiers who stopped me said, "Dump out your basket!" But another soldier, maybe one who had a heart, said, "No, all the bread will be ruined." He asked me where I was coming from and where I was going. I lied about where I was going, but I told him—this part was true—that I was coming from their barracks. "Oh really!" said the one who wanted me to dump out the bread. "I'm going to radio over there and see if you're lying." When he found out what I said was true, he didn't make me dump out the basket full of bread. Thank God! Otherwise they would have arrested me, and who knows what could have happened. Maybe nothing too bad, though. You see, at that time the negotiations were going on between the army and FMLN. People were being arrested but not tortured much anymore. Still, I'm glad I didn't get caught.

A little after that incident, none of us were needed anymore to work for the FMLN. Not me, not Jorge, and not María either. She had been with the guerrillas—what was it, seven or nine years?—and she'd finally got demobilized. She came back to be with the rest of us in Santa Marta. My mother was someplace else. She'd left Honduras about the time we did but was living off with some other people she knew. Like us, she continued to help out the FMLN, but she got demobilized too. She was living then near Suchitoto.

This was in '92. The negotiations had about ended, and around then we in Santa Marta heard about the community of Henríquez. We heard the FMLN was looking for some families to go there. And since we'd never liked Santa Marta in the first place, we decided to check it out.

María went with her grandparents to have a look, and they decided to stay. A few weeks later Jorge went to see Henríquez. He came back and told me, "Look, let's go there. I want to be where my father is." He said, "The place is real pretty. It's a little covered up now with over-growth and trees, but once we clean it up it'll be real pretty. Water's a bit scarce right now, but we can take care of that too. It'll be fine." That's what he told me, and I said, "Okay, then let's go. Let's join María and the others."

It's five years now that we've been here in Henríquez. It's worked out well for us here. As soon as we got here, the FMLN people arranged for us to get some things to get started. Every family got this stuff. You got the materials to put up your house. And you got a table like this one here, four chairs, a fumigating pump to use on your crops, a pickax, crowbar, shovel, hoe, and machete. That's what I remember. And the land too—you got a loan to pay for it. And you also got a loan to do what you wanted—say, buy animals like we did. These loans, the way I heard it, came from some international organizations. They donated the money to the government here, and the government used it to pay off the landowners whose land we got, and also to give us these things. Don't ask me exactly who made these donations. Maybe the gringos, I don't know.

Our family is real lucky. All of us are here, except for one of my older sons, who's over in Chalatenango. The rest of us are in Henríquez. Four of my children have their own houses and are raising their families here. How many are we? Let's see, I'll have to figure it out. María has five kids, Beatriz and Marina have two each, and my daughter-in-law has two also. And my mother is raising five grandchildren—they belong to my sister who's in the United States now. So how many is that? Counting my in-laws and our five kids, we're about thirty-five people. We're the biggest family here, that's for sure. Originally, it was another family that was the biggest—the Henríquez family. They were here before us. That's how come our community got its name. But now, for sure, we're the largest bunch here.

We're all pretty satisfied with the place. All except my mother. She's got her troubles here. My sister and her husband took off for the United States. They're trying to make some money up there. And she agreed to mind their children while they're gone. It's been two years or so now, and she's fed up with it. I tell you, sometimes I think she's going a little crazy with all those kids around her. The oldest isn't more than twelve, and my mother goes wild with them sometimes. She's always whacking them for doing the slightest thing, nothing in fact. Just grabs the nearest stick and goes after them. I remember she was tough with us when I was growing up, but nothing like she is now. She can't manage all those kids—they're driving her nuts.

If you ask me, a lot of her nervousness has nothing to do with them. She's real angry about what happened to her in Henríquez. She's the one person in my family who didn't get a good deal here. All the rest of us got our loans and land. But she, she wound up with nothing. Not a centavo, even though she was with the FMLN in the *monte*. It's not fair, but the thing is, she screwed it up herself. Back in '93 when I brought her over here—it was about a year after we settled here—she had to give them her identity card in order to get her loans and all the rest. So what does she do? She couldn't find her identity card—she'd misplaced it somewhere. Figuring it didn't matter, she gave them the identity card of one of my brothers. Problem was, my brother is a carpenter and he'd already been given a loan for 20,000 colones for his carpentry shop. So the people handing out the loans said he couldn't get still another loan to buy the land. The whole thing got messed up like that, and in the end my mother never got a loan to get her land or a house either. The place she's living in now belongs to someone else. They've just been letting her stay there. But now they want to sell it, and my mother has to come up with the money to buy it. I suppose she'll manage something, though she's all nervous about it. And you've seen the house where she's living, right. It's not much of a place. It's not a solid concrete block place like ours. She's angry about it. She feels she got cheated. She screwed it up herself, but I understand why she's angry.

The rest of us, though, we've made out fine here. Henríquez is a good place. And it's getting better all the time. There's a lot to be done, and I figure if we put some effort into it, we'll improve the place more. That's why I've got involved. Maybe I can contribute something to the community. I hope so. All of us are tired of moving around from here to there like we did during the war. We want to settle in, stay here. Henríquez is a pretty good community. I'm hoping it works out for us, the way it has so far. I'd like to stay here from now on.

Niña Dolores

Of the twenty-one houses in the community of Henríquez, five have yet to be rebuilt and refurbished. In one of these Niña Dolores has been living for four years now, some 75 meters down the dirt lane from María's place. A wire fence separates it from the newly built kindergarten.

Like all the original houses of the community, Niña Dolores's one-room structure is smallish—perhaps 7×3 meters—and is constructed of ill-fitting wood planks, a tin roof, and with plastic tucked here and there to keep out the rain. The floor of the house is simply hardened earth. A hammock and three cord beds are the sole furniture she possesses, apart from a couple of broken chairs and a dilapidated wooden table that sit outside on the hardened earth patio.

For the past two years, Niña Dolores has shared her quarters with five grandchildren, as her daughter and son-in-law have taken off for the United States to earn some dollars. Whenever we visited her, the children were romping about the yard barefoot and bare-bottomed (the younger boys). And romping about with them were two dozen or so roosters and chickens, three dogs, and two piglets, all of them moving here and there through the open house.

Presiding over this chaos would be a tough task for someone half her age, and indeed the strain of it all shows on Niña Dolores's face. At sixty-three years, she has a weary look and her sad brown eyes dominate her well chiseled dark features. On the days she knew we were coming, she wore a starched white or pink dress and slippers, but when we showed up unexpectedly she was most often in a tattered outfit and barefoot like her grandchildren.

On all seven occasions when we visited her, however, she greeted us with a warmth and even a cheerfulness: our visits seemed to give her a sense of relief from her daily routine of cooking and washing clothes for her grandchildren. Beyond this, she appeared to enjoy the opportunity to talk at length about her life and was gratified—though somewhat surprised—that anyone else, and especially people in the United States, might be interested in who she is or the life she has lived.

At the drop of a question she would launch into a detailed account, sometimes rambling and sometimes repetitious, but often with an undeniable narrative flare. Perhaps most impressive was her ability to carry on almost oblivious to the clutter and clatter about her—an ability that struck us again each time we set about transcribing her tape-recorded words, pulling her story from the cacophony of roosters, dogs, and children in the background.

What follows is Niña Dolores's story, minus some of the repetition and rambling and, for better or worse, minus the background accompaniment, which seemed an intrinsic though untranscribable part of the whole.

I was born with nothing, and all I've got now is nothing. That's my life, start to finish. Don't ask me why—that's just the way it's been for me.

I was born sixty-three years ago over in the department of Chalatenango, in a little place called Nombre de Jesús. It's near the Honduras border. That's where my father was from—Honduras. I can't say I knew him too well. He left when I was about five. All I remember is that he had this curly hair and that he treated me nice, he never beat me. But how nice could he have been, I ask you? Because he just left and I grew up without the protection of a father. My mother told me he wanted us to go with him to Honduras, where his mother lived. But my mama said no. She was staying where she was. Who knows how it really was between them? Not me, for sure. I just know that from the time he left I never saw him again.

So I grew up alone with my mother and grandmother. And also two uncles who lived with us until they got married. I was the only child. My mother never had another until way later, after I was married. But all the time I was growing up it was only me.

I remember those years real well. I still have a good memory about that. The house, oh yes, I remember it well. It was the usual kind of place, made of adobe, a single room and a kitchen on the side also made of adobe. The floor was like the one here in this house, pure earth. We'd sit and eat on the floor the way you did then. There was a table in the room, but that was for permanent things. All of us would sit there and eat with our hands, our fingers. We had no forks or spoons, and the plates we ate out of were made of clay. You'd make them yourselves. Simple things. If you dropped them, they'd shatter.

What did we eat? *Bueno*, I'm not going to lie to you and say we had fancy meals. No, it wasn't like that. We were poor, real poor. Sometimes, truth is, when the *maíz* and *maicillo* [millet] and *frijol* ran out, well, we'd go hungry. Mostly though, we had something to eat. Tortillas and *frijol*, that's what we ate—breakfast, lunch, and dinner. My grandma also had a few fruit trees—mango, avocado, and papaya—so sometimes we had a little fruit. And she had a few chickens and pigs. Once in awhile she'd say, "This one here looks fattened up enough. Let's have us a feast!" But that was unusual. Regularly, it was beans and tortillas, that's it. All these packaged things you see kids eating today, the curly salty things that come in plastic bags, I never saw any of that as a kid. Supermarkets! There was nothing like that in my time.

What we had to eat was what we grew ourselves. My grandma had this small *milpa*, and my uncles worked it. The *milpa* was left to her by her father-in-law, my great-grandfather. He felt bad for her because it was one of his grandsons who killed her husband, my grandfather. Shot him in cold blood, the way I heard it. I don't know the details. It happened before I was born. I just know that one day, as my grandfather was defending one of his sons, his nephew took out a pistol and killed him. Left him lying there with his brains blown out. Then that whole bunch, the nephew and his family, they left the area. And my great-grandfather, taking pity on my grandmother, let her have the *milpa*. So that's what we had. We grew our *frijol* and *maíz* and *maicillo* there, and we also raised a plant called *jiquilite* you'd make ink out of. We'd sell that ink—or in fact what it was, was blue lumps that you'd make from the flowers of the plant—and it fetched us a little money to buy things.

When I was a kid, I used to help out with this work—making the ink balls. Or I'd help out with other things too. Bringing food up to the hill where my uncles worked the *milpa*. And all the work around the house, like sweeping up, or hauling water from the spring. Or chopping up firewood, or making the fire in the mornings. It was hard work, harder than today in some ways. Like making a fire—you didn't use matches, oh no! You had this "fire rock," that's how we called it. It's a special kind of rock you'd get up in the hills. If you strike this rock with a machete it sends off sparks. So what you'd do is take a little bit of charred remains from the *comal* [clay dish on which tortillas are made], put them inside a dried corn leaf, and then start scraping the machete against the fire rock—*chas! chas!*—until a spark flew and set off the corn leaf. And then you'd build your fire. Go try doing that in the dark before dawn comes. Not so easy, I'm telling you.

That's how it was in those days. You didn't have matches, or other store-bought things—like soap. You made your own soap. A little animal fat is all you need, with some ash for bleach, and a kind of olive to harden it. You cook up this mixture for a few days, and just at the right moment, you stop cooking and take the hardened mass and make your balls of soap. Truth is, I still make my own soap this way. I prefer it. I show my grandchildren how to do it, and we do the washing these days with the same soap I used when I was growing up.

But my life wasn't the way my grandchildren have it. They've got their school, and they've got time to fool around. Look at them running around here! Me, if I didn't work, I got beaten. My uncles would whack me or my mother would grab me by the hair and drag me off to work. Sometimes I didn't feel like working, and I might go off and take a papaya leaf and put some little flowers on it all in a row, and I'd pretend I was a shepherdess taking my little flowers on a walk. Or once, I can remember—I don't know why I started doing it—I found a few threads on the floor and I began rolling them and making a ball out of them. My grandmother saw me doing it and she just grabbed the ball and threw it into the fire. And that was the end of it. I never played with threads anymore.

I hardly ever played with anything. Or with anyone either. I had a girl cousin who lived nearby, but my grandma and mama never let me go play with her. They wanted me alone in the house. And that's the way it was.

There was no school either. The nearest school was 10 kilometers away. You had no buses, no real road. You had to walk on a rugged path. If you got up at dawn it would take you until mid-morning to get there. What we had was this schoolteacher lady who went around to the villages teaching kids to read. You had to pay her something like 1½ colones a month. That's nothing today, but back then it was a lot of money. I started with her, but she'd only come once a week and I wasn't learning how to read. So my grandma and mama stopped it. They said to me, "This learning to read is nonsense. What are you going to do with it anyway—write letters to boyfriends?" And that was it. Only later, when we were up in the refugee camp in Honduras, and now here in Henríquez, I decided to go to reading classes. But I'm too old for learning now. I just go to get away from the house for awhile. I make little scribbles on the paper, but I can't write more than a letter or two. It's a pity. Everybody ought to know at least a little. Almost all my children, Lupe and them, can read some. Me, I never figured it out. My mama said it would only make me lazy if I went to school. "Better to learn how to do something," she said. "Better to learn to work."

I was a meek person, always have been. If I was told to do something,

I did it. When I was a little kid, not more than five, my mama told me, "You're growing up alone without a father, and you're going to have to work to get by." Tiny kid that I was, I answered her, "Look, Mama, I reckon I can make *petates*." I told her that because I'd seen some women making them. You know, the reed mats you put on the beds. "*Vaya pues.* You reckon you can do it?" she said. "Then I'll bring you the reeds and you set to it." And that's how I started making *petates*. I made my first one when I was five years old. I sold it—my mama did, really—for 60 centavos. And my mama said, "*Bueno*, you've made your first, now go on with it. I'm not going to be able to buy you clothes or shoes or anything. You want these things, you're going to have to pay for them with your *petates*."

Since then, I've been making them. Sometimes it was the 1 or 2 colones I'd get for a *petate* that paid for our food. My mama was proud of me. I helped out that way. And if we had enough food, she'd take the money I made and buy some fabric and sew me up some clothes. Nothing much, really. But it was something to wear. Today, I still make *petates*, when I can get some reeds. Here, I'll show you . . . [*Dolores goes into her house and brings back a handful of thin tan reeds and explains how she weaves them together to form a* petate]. I've got bad eyes now, and my glasses don't work anymore, but never mind. I can still weave a *petate* almost with my eyes closed. My hands are used to it now. I've been doing it all my life. My mama told me, "You've got to earn your living," and so I have. Since I was five.

❧

That's how it was in the *campo* when I was growing up. You didn't fool around, play games, or any of that. It was a different kind of childhood then. Soon as you could work, help out, you did. It wasn't like you had a childhood at all. At least, I didn't.

Then as you got older, maybe fifteen or sixteen if you were a girl, you'd already be getting together with someone. Some *novio* [boyfriend] or other would come along. And that was it. You'd get *ajuntados* —with the parents' permission. That's how it worked. You'd get their permission and you'd go off, and soon enough you were raising your own bunch.

How did it happen for me? Oh, the usual way—more or less. The way things happened in the *campo*. We were living in this village on one side of the Lempa River. On the other side, in the department of Cabañas, there was another village. My husband, Joaquín, lived over on the other side. He had a sister on our side of the river, and he'd visit her. You had to swim across the river, or if you couldn't swim you'd hold onto a plank or tree trunk and make your way across.

Sundays, he'd sometimes visit his sister. Back in that time people had this way of gossiping, they'd say, "So-and-so, this girl, she's living nearby." It didn't matter whether the girl was pretty or not, people would still talk about her. So his sister must have said something about me. He was eighteen then, and I was fifteen. So he came looking around. Not talking, just looking, because in that time you didn't start talking like you do today. You just looked. My grandma saw him coming by and she said, "That boy is looking for something, sure thing. He's hunting about for something." Little by little, he started saying things—to my grandma, my mama, and then to me. And then he stopped visiting his sister first, and he'd just come by my house to talk with us. Never with me alone. No, no! My grandma never left me alone with him. She was aware of what men were looking for. She stayed nearby. And back then you didn't go out places like today, or even out of the house strolling by the river. You stayed in the house visiting.

After awhile he asked me to be his *novia* and I said yes. He was good-looking and he had this nice manner about him, humble and polite. And he spoke nicely to my grandma and mama and me. So I said yes. Was he my first *novio*? Yes. Or actually, there was someone who lived right in our village who wanted me to be his *novia*, but I said no. Since he lived so close, I could see how he was, all coarse and vulgar. With Joaquín, I saw him only on Sundays, and the truth is I didn't know him so well. As they say, only later *te sacan las uñas* [the fingernails come out]. A man doesn't let you know who he is right away. Only later you find out.

Anyway, I became Joaquín's *novia* and soon after that we decided to get married. Joaquín went to my grandma and mama—that's how it was done then—and he asked for me. He didn't come alone. He came with a friend. I knew he was going to do it. I sat there saying nothing as he talked to them. You know, putting his best foot forward, promising he'd make a home for us and our children, treat us well, be loyal to me and all that. He made it sound real nice, and my grandma and mama listened to all this and they said he could have me. And that was it. We were given permission to get together. We didn't just get *ajuntados*, we got married as man and wife.

We did it the way you did the ceremonies back then. One day you have a civil ceremony at the mayor's office. That's so everything is registered officially so that later, say, if there's an inheritance it's all written up in the records that you're married. Then the next day, we had the church ceremony with the priest and a party afterward. It was very simple, not with all the luxuries you see people having some places now. I wore a simple white dress, like you'd use regularly, and a little crown of flowers, and simple white shoes. The priest said his words, and then we put on the rings. His godmother put mine on, and his godfather put his on, and that was it. We were husband and wife.

It was a long walk from the church to his house. When we got there, there was some coffee and tortillas to break the hunger, because we'd come a long way. Then we had this fine food that my aunts had prepared together with his mother and sisters. Delicious things, not like what you ate everyday. I remember there was a chicken stew, some *tamales*, I think, and *marquesotes* [a type of cake]. A little music too, and dancing. Guitars, a violin—a nice party. Then in the afternoon it was over. According to the way things were done, Joaquín and some other people brought me back to my house. Right. Back to my grandma and mama's house. I stayed there for eight days—that's the usual time for the bride to stay— and then I went back across the river to be with my husband. He came to bring me.

When I got to his house, that was the first night I'd ever spent with him. Yes, the first time I'd ever been with any man. I was ignorant. Nobody had told me what to expect. I knew, of course, we'd be having sexual relations. A man didn't marry a woman just to look at her, right?

I knew *that*. What I didn't know was how scared I'd be. If I'd known that, I wouldn't have gotten married at that age, I'd have waited more time. Because that night, all of a sudden, I started trembling. *Ave María Santísima*, I was shaking all over! It's strange to say these things. I've never told anyone about this before. Not Lupe, nobody. I was so scared that night, trembling away in front of him. But really, he was kind to me. He saw how I was and he treated me with kindness. There's some men, they say, that just go ahead and do whatever they want. But Joaquín treated me with consideration, he was soft with me. He did it with kindness, he didn't get carried away like they say others do. Thank God for that! Because, I'm telling you, my knees were knocking together something terrible. That's the truth, though God knows, I've never said this before to anyone.

❧

After we got married, for a few years we lived together fine. We lived in our own house over in Cabañas, and he was working the *milpa* he had. His father had owned some land, 23 manzanas, and it got divided between his seven sons when he died. So we had our small plot for raising *maíz* and *frijol*, and I was making *petates* to bring in some extra money. Our life was fine in those first years.

I got pregnant about a year after we were married. I got real big and people were telling me it was a boy. You see, if you get a nice round stomach, then it's a boy. If it's a girl you're carrying, then your stomach is flattened out more. So I figured it was a boy. And I was right. Except it wasn't just one—it was twins. One came, and then a little after, out came the other. Twin boys.

I had them alone in our house. It was in the morning. I had just finished grinding the *maíz*. I'd made the *masa* [lump of dough], and I went out to milk the cow. It was when I was milking the cow that I had my first pains. Joaquín was there working around the house, so I sent him to bring the midwife. He left, but no sooner had he gone when the first one started coming out. I squatted down and out he came. And the next one after him. I knew it would be awhile before the *partera* arrived. She lived off a ways. So I did what I had to do by myself. My mother-in-law had told me how to cut the umbilical cord, just in case I'd have to do it by myself. I had a scissors nearby and a candle. We called it a candle, but it was made out of goat fat or cow fat. I cut the cord and then with the candle I burned the end, near the belly button. I cleaned them both up and put them both in these little diapers I'd made from rags. By the time the *partera* came, I had the whole thing taken care of. She looked them over, Rosa did—that was her name—Rosa looked them over and said it was fine. But then seven days later they both died. From some fever, it was. There was no place to take them, no hospital around, only one a day's walk from where we were. Nothing could be done. They just went.

That's how it was with my first ones. I lost them. After that, thank God, I never lost another—not a miscarriage, and not right after they were born like that. All the rest lived. Lupe came after the twins, and Oscar and Veronica. Thirteen of them, including the twins who died. Always I gave birth at home. Never in a hospital. Either I was alone or the *partera* came. I reckon about half the time Rosa or someone else was there to help me out. That was better, of course. I preferred having some- one there with me. She'd cut the cord, clean them up, and wrap them. It was easier on me that way. Yes, sure, you paid the *partera*. Some money or a chicken, depending on what you had. In money, the usual price was 25 colones if you had a boy and 15 colones if you had a girl. Don't ask me why there was a difference. I don't know. I know I never paid more than a "fiver" [5 colones], no matter what. And usually I gave them a chicken or rooster, which went for 2 colones in the market. They were satisfied with that. If you couldn't pay the 25 or 15 colones, they settled for that.

Was there a celebration after a birth? No, no party or anything like that. A few neighbors and relatives would stop by maybe. But no party. Not for a boy and not for a girl, and not for twins either. What you had, you had. That was it. I had altogether five boys and eight girls. Eleven with Joaquín, and then two with a couple of men after he died. A boy or a girl, it was all the same to me, just as long as they were healthy and not dying on you like the first ones I had. And I think for Joaquín, he didn't care either. He never said one way or the other. If you ask me, though, I think he didn't care because—at least after I'd had the first three or so—he was so busy running after other women, being a *mujerero* [womanizer]. And that was the only thing he took note of. Not his children, not me. That's the way I see it.

❧

He wasn't a *mujerero* in the beginning. At least I don't think so. But most of the time I was with him, that's how he was. Twenty-two years I was with him. God knows how I survived it, all of what went on, the fights and beatings and all that. God alone knows how I survived it!

I remember one time he had this pal of his visiting him at the house. Some man who lived nearby. The two of them were talking, and I was right there listening to what was said. His pal was telling him, "With a woman you've got to tame her like you do an animal. When you pull the reins they got to move this way, and when you pull the reins the other way then they move the other way." My husband sat there listening and I couldn't open my mouth. I was scared I'd get beaten on the spot. Better to keep my mouth shut, I figured.

It wasn't long after that, though, Joaquín began beating me. Before, it was just him yelling at me. Now he started going after me with his fists, or a whip, or his machete. You see, he'd started spending nights away from the house with other women. I commented on it, told him what I thought. Well, this one day while we were arguing like that in front of the kids—I had two then, Lupe and Oscar—he grabbed hold of me and put his machete to my throat. I thought to myself, "This is it. I'm about to pass over to the other side." But no, I twisted loose and ran off, with him swinging at me with his machete. Somehow I managed to dodge him, and he finally stopped. I didn't dare go back into the house. I figured he'd kill me. I stayed out that night at the edge of our property, but I couldn't sleep out of fear, and with the mosquitoes out there eating me up. Only at dawn I went back to the house and one of the kids opened the door. I set about making a fire and tortillas. He heard me, I guess, and he sent Lupe to see if it was me. He came to have a look, with his face all serious, but he didn't say anything. I just went on making tortillas. That whole night I'd spent out in the yard thinking, "This is it. I've got to leave. But where can I go?" I looked up in the direction of the hills, hills that reached up to the sky almost, and I said to myself, "Where under the rounded sky can I go with the little ones? I know nothing. What can I do?" I knew I should leave him, but when God doesn't let you, He doesn't let you. Or maybe it was that Joaquín had put some kind of spell on me. I don't know. I was never able to leave him. Instead, I stayed on, having one child after the other. And all the time putting up with him and his ways.

And it just kept getting worse. Not even a woman in the best of health could have stood it. He'd beat me for any little thing. If one of the chickens I was raising came into the house at night—he hated the chickens, even though I was raising them for us to have something to eat because, God knows, he wasn't providing us with enough—well, he'd take the poor chicken and fling it hard out of the house and start screaming at me. Right in the middle of the night.

And many were the nights he stayed away altogether, drinking with one or another of his women. Or he'd go away for days with one of them, to the coast on vacation, say. And this one time after he'd been gone for a few days, all of a sudden—it must have been midnight— there he was shouting at the door, "Dolores, open up!" It surprised me, because usually he'd show up in the daytime, never at night. I let him in and he didn't say a thing. He just grabbed a light, a candle, and started looking all about, even under the bed. I had no idea what he was doing. I was tired and went back to sleep and thought no more about it. And the next day he didn't say anything either.

It was only years later he told me what it was all about. The day before he died, he told me. I think he knew Death was coming. He had heard the Spirit speaking to him, and he wanted to set things straight. That's the only way I can figure it. Because right before he died he reminded me of the night he'd come back looking under the bed and all around the house. "I was looking for your lover," he told me. "If there had been another door at the back of the house, or a window, I would have killed you. I would have figured he had escaped through there." And me, I listened to all this and I was, well, I couldn't believe it. I had no lover. It was him doing the running around, not me. But one of his women, the one he was with that night, said to him, "Why doesn't your Dolores say anything to you when you stay with me?" And he told her, "Because I'm the one who gives the orders in the house, I do what I want." And this bitch of his says to him, "No, that's not it. It's because *she* has a lover." So right then he picked up and came running home, drunk and full of courage, looking for my so-called lover. And imagine, if we'd had a back door he would have killed me right then. That's what he said, and I'm sure he would have. The way I figure it, he realized later that I had no lover. It was all her gossip, her filling his imagination with lies. Seeing Death coming his way, he felt the load of what he'd done, or had almost done to me, and he wanted to get it off himself before he died and had to face God. That's the way I figure it.

You see, the next day he was dead. Killed by the Guardia in the river. The Lempa River. Shot by mistake, for nothing he'd done. That's right, he got killed instead of another man who the Guardia was looking for. Carlos Lopez was the one they were looking for. The Guardia had orders to bring him in, and if he took off they were told to shoot him. This Carlos Lopez was up to a lot of bad things. He was a crook. He'd stolen one of the neighbor's oxen and eaten it. And he was running a liquor still, and the authorities were out to stop him. I knew that. We all knew that.

But what I didn't know—I only found out later—was that Carlos Lopez had known the Guardia was coming after him that day. Someone must have told him. So he took off at dawn to hide in the mountains. And that very dawn my husband had it in his mind to go over and visit Carlos. I asked him, "Why do you want to go over *there*?" And he said that he wanted to get some bundles of sugarcane. "You have some right here," I told him. "Why go get more from Carlos?" He wouldn't listen to me. He went to Carlos Lopez's house.

A few minutes later—I was just putting the tortillas on the *comal*—I heard some gunshots ring out. I was scared. I knew the Guardia was looking for Carlos Lopez. All I could think was, "Let it not be Joaquín they got too!" I dropped what I was doing, left the tortillas on the *comal*, and went running down to where I heard the shots. There was a group of the Guardia shooting into the river. You know, when the Guardia goes to get someone they don't fire a shot or two—it's a hail of bullets, right? They were firing at a sombrero floating on the water, but then they stopped, realizing there was nobody under it. And then on the other side of the river a man came out of the water and he was holding onto a rock. It was Joaquín. He came up for air, and kneeling right there at the bank of the river was one of the Guardia. He shot him right there, killed him as he was coming up for air. I stood where I was, not moving and not saying a word. I didn't break down or anything.

I was strong back then. I could look death in the face. I just stood there looking as they dragged Joaquín's body out of the river. Then along came another group of the Guardia, about six of them. "Who's the dead man?" they asked. My husband's brother told them. "And who killed him?" they asked. Joaquín's brother answered, "The Guardia killed him." These six guys from the Guardia looked at him and one said, "Maybe he got killed by a stone that was thrown, or maybe somebody's shotgun." My husband's brother repeated, "No, it was someone from the Guardia." And they said, "Hmmm! If you say the Guardia did it, you could wind up the same tomorrow." And that was it. The Guardia took off and Joaquín was left there dead with his blood all over him.

That's how I came to be left alone, without a husband. Joaquín got shot instead of Carlos Lopez and I was left a widow. I had to provide for the little ones myself after that. My older sons helped me. They took over the land their father'd had, divided it among themselves, and they gave me some of the harvest. It wasn't much, but it was something. And my mama helped me out too. She was living nearby, so she helped me some. What could I do? Even when my husband was alive it had been difficult. Now it was even harder.

I went on making and selling *petates*, and I raised chickens and sold the eggs. Sometimes I'd go without eating so there'd be enough for the kids. That's how I managed it. Day to day, you do what you can to get by. You'd try to have enough tortillas and something to go with them, so nobody would go hungry. I did the best I could, that's all. Living with Joaquín wasn't easy, and without him it wasn't easy either.

I went on as a widow for four years, and then I met someone else and got together with him. For a year or so. To tell you the truth, I'd rather not talk so much about it. Not about him, and not about the one after him either. It was stupid. I never had any luck that way, I always got together with someone who acted one way in the beginning and then another way once you got together with him. It's rare for a man to show you who he is right from the start. I had a child with each of those men. After the second one—he took off to San Salvador with, well, with another woman. . . . After that, I'd had it. Better to be by myself than to put up with a man and his ways, and all that.

It must have been seven or eight years after Joaquín died—let's see, he was shot in '73—and it was about in '80 or '81 that the war came here to Cabañas. Lupe and her family had already gone to San Vicente. They were having their troubles there. She told me about that later, when we met on the way to Honduras, when we went to the refugee camp there. And in Cabañas we had our troubles too, with the guerrillas and the army starting to fight all around us. This was about the time the Monseñor got shot, when the war got going where I was in Cabañas.

I wanted no part of it. I was just trying to get by with my children, day by day. But the way things happened you couldn't stay out of it. A person had nowhere to be except with one side or the other. The guerrillas had a bunch of groups. I don't remember all their names, but they joined together and made one big group—the FMLN. If you refused to help out the guerrillas, they accused you of being a *contra*. That's how you were called. A brother-in-law of mine got killed by them this way. He went to a couple of their meetings, then said he didn't want to fight with them. So they dragged him off to the mountains and killed him. You had this pressure on you from the guerrillas, you see. In the beginning they needed food, and they'd come ask you for what you had—some *maíz* or some animals. And God help you if you refused! At the same time you had the Fuerza Armada coming by, hunting for the guerrillas or for people who were helping them. "Collaborators," that's what the army called them. And if the army got this idea, let's say somebody told them—true or not—you'd been helping the guerrillas, then you'd get killed too. So you tell me, what was a person to do? The way I saw it, you had to go with one side or the other or you were dead.

Some people I knew went off with the army. Their sons fought with them and the families left their homes and went to places where the Fuerza Armada was in control. Me, I decided to be with the guerrillas. Four of my older boys had gone off with them and I was alone with two younger ones. The guerrillas came by one day and told me they needed me to help them, to work as a *molendera*. "The army is coming this way and they are going to kill you," they told me. So what could I do? I left my younger ones with my grandma, and I took off with the FMLN. I was forty-six or forty-seven then, but they wanted me. The way I saw it, I had no choice.

I was with them then a year or so, going around the mountains in Cabañas and Chalatenango. One place to the other. I didn't go with arms, I just cooked. I made tortillas for them. Or if there was more time I'd make a meal. Or if we were moving about, I'd carry the pots and cooking utensils. Some young girls and I worked together. I can't remember all the places we were that year, but it was a lot of running around, trying not to get killed by the army that was chasing us from here to there.

After a year or so, I'd had enough. I left for Honduras, where there was a huge refugee camp built by some gringos or other international people. I'd met Lupe and her family as they were fleeing this way from San Vicente, and we all went up there to Honduras, to Mesa Grande. It was a huge place, like a city of refugees. Maybe 7,000 people, all up in this one place. You had your food there and a place to sleep, but it wasn't too good being there. Too hot in those little plastic houses they gave you. I didn't like it up there.

And I had no idea where my sons were, the ones in the guerrillas. I kept praying to God that nothing would happen to them. One of my boys, he was just twelve when he'd gone off with a backpack. The FMLN took him off, and I had no idea whether he was dead or alive.

And then when we were up in Mesa Grande, the FMLN kept sending people to recruit more of us from up there. Some of Lupe's children went off. María, she was the first. I don't know exactly how it was for her, I've never discussed it with her. I don't know if she volunteered, or what. She was a *radista* with them for many years. More than that I couldn't tell you. She never told me about it.

I only know that after I'd been up there awhile, the FMLN came to recruit me. Yes, *me*! They told me I didn't have to join, but they said they needed a woman to take charge of the cooking. All they had in their unit were young girls, and they couldn't rely on them. The young girls would go running off quickly if they heard a plane or helicopter overhead, looking for some pit to jump into and hide. And this wasn't so wise because the people in the planes would see you running, and you'd be in even more danger. Besides this, the girls wouldn't do the cooking in the right way. For example, you need *cal* [lime] to make the tortillas right, to prepare the *maíz* the right way. The girls wouldn't make sure to find any *cal*, and they'd just parboil the *maíz*, and people would have to eat it like that. Not very tasty, really. So for all these things, they told me I was needed. And they talked nicely to me. I figured, "Alright, I'll go back with them."

I wasn't very scared, no, I wasn't. I was pretty brave, and the reason was that I never believed I was going to get hit by a bullet. Some people who knew I was joining them again told me I would get killed. But I reckoned my time wasn't up yet. God wasn't going to call me over to the other side yet, I figured. Even though the army had all their planes and trucks and so many arms, I figured I'd survive it. And I did, as you can see, with no parts missing. Though I'll tell you this, it's only by some miracle that I did survive it and that I'm here telling you about this. Because we had some bad times when I went back.

This one time, the worst time I can remember, was when we got caught in an ambush by the Fuerza Armada. We were about four hundred people then, not only our soldiers but their families and a lot of other people. We were going from one area to another, moving at night so the army wouldn't see us. But they must have known we were coming. We arrived at this place where there was a building, a school I think it must have been. The army was spread all around there and up on a hill above. It was pitch-dark. Then suddenly there was a hail of bullets—in the night you can *see* it. In the daytime you don't see the light of the gunfire, but in the pitch-dark you do. Our people were running and screaming all over. Many got hit, and there they were on the ground in their last agonies. Me, I moved slowly past a wall, then past a tree here and there. A soldier—I don't know if he was one of ours or theirs—told me, "Woman, get out of here quickly if you don't want to wind up eaten by the dogs!"

I kept sneaking along slowly, smelling the stench of dead bodies all around me. I passed by a place where suddenly you heard one of the enemy shout, "Hey! There goes the family of so-and-so," and there comes a hail of bullets and these people were killed. And then in all the smoke—I tell you, you could hardly see where to go—an old man went by carrying his sick granddaughter in a hammock, and some of the army leaped on him and cut him to pieces with their machetes. And his granddaughter too. I tell you, it was pure hell.

Only by the grace of God am I here telling you this. At the time, I wasn't thinking I'd survive it. But I did. I found some underbrush, hid there like an armadillo for a day. And the following night I took off with some others. For days we kept going, with nothing to eat except for three little tomatoes I found and kept sucking on. Nothing to drink either, except that it rained some nights and you could suck the water out of your clothes or look for little puddles on the ground. We kept going on like that until we found a place to be. We must have been walking for two weeks. Pure hell, I tell you.

It wasn't too long after that time that I got out of the guerrillas. Actually, I didn't quit. *They* released me. I was getting too old to keep up with them. I was maybe fifty-five by then. I couldn't keep up with them, marching day and night through the mountains. I was getting ill from it, my face was all swollen, and I was having trouble seeing at night. So they said to me, "Alright, you've had enough. Better if you go back to your house. You can't help us anymore." And that was it for me. I'd been with them altogether maybe five years, and they were right. I'd had enough. It was time to leave.

❧

The thing was, I had no home to go back to then. The Fuerza Armada had destroyed it. I went back looking for it, but it was gone. Scorched to the ground. My mama was living in a place then where the Fuerza Armada was. If I'd gone there, they'd have cut off my head first thing I got there. So I went to this village near Ilobasco where some of my mother's family were living—people who hadn't been involved with the guerrillas. But it was safe there. They had a place and they let me stay with them for awhile. Finally I found out about the rest of my family. It took awhile, but I found out that all of them, all six of my children who'd been with the guerrillas, had survived. Thank God for that! So many others had died, and somehow my family survived.

I stayed over there by Ilobasco a couple of years and then moved to a place near Suchitoto. Lupe found out I was there and she came to see me. She and her family had just moved to Henríquez, and she told me I should come quickly and get a place while I could. I wasn't too enthusiastic about that, but I decided to take her advice and come, to see if maybe I could settle in here.

Everyone here in this community was with the FMLN, one way or another. When the war was starting up the FMLN told us, "*Compañeros*, we're fighting to improve the lives of you who don't have anything. We're fighting so everyone will have things equally. When the war is over you'll get your due." That's what they told us, but it was just a dream. It'll never be like that. The bosses in the guerrillas got their big houses and savings accounts in banks. And others who fought for the FMLN got something, but not all of us. Not me. I didn't get one centavo! There're people in this community who got more than others. Some of them, if you ask me, just joined up in the last days of the war. They grabbed some young person's rifle or did a little work for the FMLN just before the war was over. And they got their houses here, their 3½ manzanas, their bank loans, and all the rest—tables, chairs, beds, gas stoves, tools. You name it, they got it. Some people here, like María and Lupe, they deserved to get things. But not all the people here deserved what they got. And me, not one centavo! For five years I ran around the *monte* busting my ass for the FMLN, until *they* told me to leave. And I've got nothing to show for it.

Yes, I know what Lupe says about why I didn't get my land and house. I've heard her. But it doesn't make sense to me. So what if I gave my son's identity card and he already had a loan! I tell you, there're other people here who had loans for all kinds of things, and still they got their land and house here. The woman who owns this house and land I'm living on now—she's got another place in Chalatenango. She's let me stay here, thank goodness for that. But lately she's been coming by and saying, "Dolores, I want to sell this place. I need the money." She didn't pay a thing for it, but now she wants to sell it to me. For 4,000 colones! That's what she wants.

And you tell me, what choice do I have? I've got to come up with the money somehow. I don't want to be lugging my things here, there. I've had enough of that. And what am I to do with all these kids? My daughter is off in the United States trying to make some money. This daughter of mine, Beatriz, was with the guerrillas. In the hills right above Henríquez. Yes, up there in Mount Guazapa. But she sees how we're all living and she says, "I want a better life than my brothers and sisters have. I'm going to get some money in the United States." She sends me a little to help out, but it doesn't cover things. It's been a few years since she's been gone with her husband, and all these little ones are dependent on me. I'm the one who's got to watch over them.

Lupe and her family are the only other ones I've got here in Henríquez. The rest of my children are scattered about. A couple of my sons are also in the United States working now and sending money to their families here. Others are in different parts of the country, and two of my daughters I've lost track of altogether. These two went to San Salvador, one to work as a *muchacha* and the other doing God knows what. I haven't seen them in years. I guess they figure their old mama is gone by now, killed in the war or just dead. Who knows? So Lupe is the only one I've got here. At least I have her. And at least I can say this—thank

God for this—none of my children got killed in the war. They all survived. Even if I wound up getting nothing, at least my children made it through the war. I thank God for that.

Yes, oh yes, I'm a believer. A believing Catholic, oh yes. Once in awhile a priest comes out here to Henríquez and we have mass in the open air. All of us go. Me, Lupe, María—all of us. But that doesn't happen too often. If you want to go more regularly, you've got to go into town, say, to Suchitoto. Sometimes I do go on Sundays, when I can get away. It relaxes me. I pray to God and to the Holy Mother. I pray for myself, for my grandchildren and family, and for all those who don't pray. They say you don't have to pray to the Holy Mother in your prayers, but I mention her too. She's the mother of Our Lord, and she's generous to all her children, and so I pray to her too. It's good to recognize her, I believe.

Praying at church or just praying at home calms me and makes me feel better. Still, there're days that I get these terrible feelings and bad pains. My legs, my arms, my head hurts. I go gather some plants and roots in the hills—my grandma taught me all about this—and I make a compress and massage my pains, and it helps. I prefer it to the pills they give you in the clinic. It works better for me, and the pains go away after awhile.

The thing that doesn't go away—I don't know how to say this, and maybe I shouldn't be saying it—but it's something I have now, and in fact I've always had it. A sadness comes over me sometimes and grabs me. Some mornings, I tell you, I wake up and I can't stop crying. I try not to let the little ones see me. It just comes over me, this sadness. And I can't get moving or do anything. Then somehow it goes away. I get myself up, make some tortillas, or do a wash, or go up to the *milpa* and see how the *maíz* and *frijol* are doing. And then somehow, it's gone. I'm feeling alright again. People here say soon we're going to be having electricity and the people will be having televisions. And then you've got something to watch—you can get your mind off things. I don't know. I don't expect it will change things for me. I've had this sadness with me all my life, I'm not expecting anything to change that. It's the way I am, and I guess it's the way I'll be till God comes along and takes me over to the other side. That's the way I figure it.

La Familia Rivas

Dulce

We begin the middle-class family's stories with Dulce Rivas de Gutierrez, in part as a narrative shift from the other families, but above all because her life and struggles have been pivotal in lifting her mother, herself, and her children from the poverty of the lower class to the greater stability of middle-class Salvadoran society. And while her story has its own singular style, the struggle links her to other Salvadorans who have managed, or are managing, to break the cycle of poverty for themselves and their families.

Today, at forty-nine years, Dulce is a primary school teacher and has taught for twenty-five years in private and public schools in El Salvador. Now she teaches first grade in the port city of La Libertad, some 30 kilometers from her house in the capital. "We don't have a car, so I go by bus," she says. "A nice ride, but a bit crowded. If you want to know El Salvador, you travel by bus. That's where you can meet everyone."

For the past twelve years Dulce and her husband and their three children have been living in a middle-class neighborhood southwest of San

Salvador. There they rent a small three-bedroom house that borders on a busy thoroughfare. Along this street are similar small attached houses, as well as grocery stores, beauty salons, and a number of *pupuserías* [restaurants specializing in *pupusas*, the tortilla-stuffed national dish]. Day and night, there is a constant flow of traffic and passersby, but for Dulce all this hubbub is familiar and, up to a point, even enjoyable.

An outgoing and friendly woman with an easy manner, Dulce is, as her (chosen) name indicates, a "sweet" person—someone who makes almost anyone who crosses her path feel welcome, students or neighbors or, for that matter, curious interviewers. Her round attractive face is dominated by huge brown eyes that quickly fill with the joy or sadness of whatever tale she is telling or hearing. She speaks slowly, reflectively, and openly; yet occasionally, as she says, "memory fails me when I try to recall some of the hard times."

We met with Dulce over a span of nine months. Apart from several social visits—for example, eating out at a *pupusería* on her street, or visiting in her classroom in La Libertad—we formally interviewed her eight times. The sessions all took place in the tiny and sparsely furnished living room of her house. They were leisurely and long, punctuated by interruptions from neighbors, children, or other relatives. Though her husband was aware of, and had no objection to, our interviewing his wife and daughter, he was never present.

In her typical manner, Dulce regarded these interviews as "conversations with friends," and from the outset she seemed to welcome our visits. Indeed, as the last one ended she told us, "For me it's been a chance to remember and piece together my life. Strange to say, maybe, but I feel *I* learned a lot from it. Really, in a way I'm sorry it has to stop."

So were we.

Where do I start? From the first thing I remember? I tell you, those years—my first ten years, say—were such a jumble I'm not sure what I remember. Before my father died, which was when I was ten, it seems confused to me. I once asked a doctor if maybe the hard time my mother, sister, and I went through might have done something to my memory. "No," he said. "Nothing's wrong with your memory." I guess he was right because now and then someone from those early years shows up, a face from the past, and then suddenly the events and feelings come flooding back.

About my ancestry, I can't really tell you much. My father's family name, R——, is one that comes from Spain. A number of famous Spaniards have that name, so I guess his people came from there some time ago. But I never discussed it with him, so I don't know. My mother may also have had some Spanish ancestors on her father's side. She has talked about this from time to time, but again I don't know. Truth is, I paid no attention. Maybe psychologists can understand this more than I do. I just know that my genealogy never was of any interest to me. Still not. *unlike upper class*

I know somewhat more about my parents' lives. More about my mother's life than my father's. I never had a chance to discuss much with him before he died. As for my mother, most of what I know is what she's told me since I grew up. When I was a kid, I knew almost nothing. My mother, *she* has a good memory. She likes reflecting back on her childhood. About growing up in the *campo* and all the fun she had there. She loves recalling these things. And I tell you, I admire her. Not just because she remembers so much in detail at her age—she's in her late seventies now—but because she has this way about her, her character I mean, that is strong and sure. She thinks of the good things and dismisses all the rest. And really, she *did* have a hard time. Very hard. She just managed not to let it get the best of her.

You see, she was more or less abandoned by her parents. Her mother was some kind of simple person living over in San Ildefonso. Her father had some land there, he wasn't poor like her mother. He took her as his woman for a number of years. They had five children together, and my mother was the oldest of them. Her parents never lived together, and the children were scattered about among the relatives. My mama was raised by her grandma, her father's mother, and she lived there all her childhood. I don't know all the details, but I gather that her grandma was good to her. Her father surely was *not*. He ignored her, and later when he got legally married to some woman, he had another bunch of children—his so-called legitimate children. They are the ones he looked after and the ones who received his inheritance. My mama got nothing. If you ask me, I think it hurt her deeply. But that's not what she says. She only talks of her grandma, and how good "Granny Mari" was to her. You know, she looks at the half-full glass and sees the part that has the water in it. That's her character, and I admire her for it.

Me, my way seems to be that I forget things—especially some of the bad things in the past. I can't tell you much about my mama's life after she left her grandma's place in San Ildefonso, and before she met my father. She told me that she had been involved with some other men—no, she never married any of them—and she had some children with them. But better to ask her about this. What I know is that she must have been in her late twenties when she met my father. And he, well, he was already an *anciano* [old man], maybe fifty or fifty-five. She doesn't like me talking about him this way, calling him an *anciano*. Yet the fact is, from the time I opened my eyes my father was a white-bearded man, who walked with a cane and had trouble seeing. A good man, yes, and I loved him. Still, he was always an old person in my eyes.

The way they met, as I understand it, is that she was his *empleada domestica* [domestic employee]. She'd been working like that ever since she left her grandma's house, supporting herself as a maid in people's houses. My father was a widower, he already had his children and they were all grown up and out of the house. He was in the army, an engineer in the army. Anyway, he needed someone to do the cleaning and cooking in his house, and my mother began working for him. The children she'd had with other men were living with relatives, so she was alone. And then, I guess in the way these things happen, she and he took a liking to each other. And then the next thing she was pregnant—with me. And after me, about two years later, with my younger sister, Doris. That's all she had with him, just us. But unlike with the children she had before us, she made sure we stayed with her. We grew up at her side.

Now, a part that is fuzzy to me—still to this day—is exactly *who* I lived with and *when*. What I mean is this. My parents didn't live together in the same house. We all were living over in Soyapango, about

10 kilometers from the capital. He had this house where some of his other children would come and visit. And nearby, she had her apartment. They hardly ever, maybe never, lived together. She went to do the cleaning at his house and he supported her with some money and paid for her little apartment. I think I used to live some of the time with him and some of the time with my mama and Doris. I'm not sure.

I do know that one time, when I was about six, he took us all to court. There must have been some difficulties going on between them then. I'm not sure how it really was. I do know—this my mama explained to me later—that earlier he had bought her a sewing machine. All her life she had wanted one. She had learned to sew when she was young, and she always said, "The sewing machine is *my* machete." *Bueno,* at one point my father was selling some land, and my mama—she was shrewd about these things—she said to him, "Antonio, I reckon the land you're selling is larger in size than what's in the records. Check it out before you sell." And my father told her, "Alright, I'll have it remeasured. If you're right, the extra money goes to you." And my mama *was* right. So as he had promised, my father gave her the 400 colones—a lot of money in those days. And with it she bought the sewing machine.

Later when there were arguments between them, I guess he had second thoughts, and he dragged us all to court and had my mama sign a legal document stating that the sewing machine belonged to me and my sister. That way, say she got *ajuntada* with someone else, we would be entitled to the sewing machine. None of this ever happened. She never got *ajuntada* with anyone again. But what I remember is that day when we went to court. As we were all walking back—I can see it before me now—there was a fork in the road. My mama and Doris went in one direction and I, for some reason, continued on with him. I went back to his house. And from then on, it seems to me I stayed more with him than with my mama and sister. Why? I don't know exactly, except maybe a certain affection a girl has for her father. I can't really say. And if you ask my mama, she'll tell you I lived *always* with her. So who knows? To me it's fuzzy.

I remember that wherever I was living or sleeping, I spent a lot of time with my sister. We played with the same friends, some children who lived up on this hill. Their father was a wealthy man, a famous painter. We'd go up to their house, it was like a castle, and we'd play games in their big yard. Games girls like, sitting in a circle and singing and telling riddles to each other. Or we'd put on their radio. Every afternoon at four o'clock there was this program with rock-and-roll songs, Elvis Presley and Little Richard and all them. We'd dance together and have a fine time. As long as we were up there in this castle, my mama never worried about us. She knew we were being looked after.

School? Oh yes, I went and so did my sister. My mama insisted on it. She herself hadn't got past second grade, and she was determined that both of us were going to do better than that. She had the idea way back then—and I bless her again and again for it—that going to school, learning some kind of trade, would help us in our lives. She'd tell us, "I don't want what happened to me to happen to you. I want you to have a chance for a different life." It was a sacrifice paying for the school supplies, making sure we got there. But she made sure.

Me, I didn't do so well in the beginning. I got left back in first grade. Maybe that has helped me in my work with some of my first graders these days. I know what it is to fail. After repeating first grade, I seemed to get the knack of it. I liked going to school, and I had the good fortune to have teachers who took a liking to me. Some of them even invited me over to their houses, to visit or eat lunch. Once, I remember, this teacher invited me to her house to eat what I guess was a special meal. Snails! My God, I'd never seen such things in my life, and I couldn't figure how to eat them. I was used to tortillas, beans, cheese, coffee. But snails? When I look back on it, I think it was a fine gesture on her part. She wanted to encourage me as a student, so she invited me over. I think that's the way a teacher should be. I learned from that. Though to this day, I can't remember the teacher's name, or even how she looked. I only remember the snails, *jutes* you call them—little, spiral, ugly things. When I invite students over these days, I've made a point of never serving *jutes*, that I can assure you!

❧

Anyway, the part of my life that is much clearer to me is after I was ten. After my father died. From then on, there're not so many blanks.

I remember my father dying. As I told you, he was always an old person. Even so, he wasn't sickly. We didn't think he was so old that any day he might die. No, he was just an *anciano*. Then suddenly he took sick. Some kind of kidney problem, I think. He went to the military hospital, and we heard he was getting better and soon would be coming home. But then we got a telegram—the very day he was to come home—and the telegram said he had died. For me, for all of us, it was a shock. I couldn't imagine that he was gone.

I remember they had the wake and funeral over in Santa Tecla, where most of his sisters and older children lived. My mama wasn't consulted about this. They told her to come if she wanted, but she had nothing to say about the preparations. She told me this later. We were over there for a few days during the period of mourning, and I remember—this I'll never forget—that some of my father's family asked who we were. We were dressed very simply, not in black. And one of his sisters pointed to us and said, "Oh, they're Antonio's bastards." That's right, "bastards" is what she called us. I was old enough to know what it meant, and of course it was deeply insulting. You see, my father's family never accepted my mother because they considered her socially inferior—Antonio's maid, that's how they saw her. And they saw us as his illegitimate children.

Years later, when Doris and I got our education and married, then their attitude changed. Today, I have good relations with some of them. With most of them really. They're good people. They just had this way back then of seeing my mother as not worthy, not on their level. Though when I think about it, my mama is the one who truly was more worthy as a person—more worthy than they were, more worthy than my father. You know, just before my father died, when he was sick, some of his older children suggested to my mama that she ought to sign some legal papers establishing her as his legal wife. And that way, when he died she would be entitled to his army pension and she'd have some money. I guess it was a kind gesture on their part, the ones who suggested this. But my mama told them, "No, I'm not with Antonio for any gain like that, not for any money." She flatly refused. And later, after he died, she told me, "Your father didn't leave me or you anything more than the street. But he did give me two treasures—you and your sister—and in that way he left me richer than any millionaire." When I heard this I felt her love for my father, and also her own pride and sense of her own worth—and of our worth too. All I can say is thank God for my mama, because even without my father, and without any money, she figured a way to raise us.

❧

The problem after my father died was that we no longer had a place to live. My mama had no money to support us then, and we no longer had any apartment or house to live in. What happened, I guess, is that my father's family must have discussed among themselves what to do with us. I suppose they could have abandoned us altogether, but they didn't. As I say, despite certain attitudes they had, some of them were good people. So one niece of my father's, Carmen, told my mother she could come stay at her house. She had a big place, with servants, and she offered to have my mother come there—though more or less as a person who would work there too, along with the other *empleadas domesticas*. As for me, one of my father's sisters—Amparo was her name—she was the headmistress of a school in Nuevo Cuscatlán. She offered to take me with her, to live with her and be a student in the school. My mother saw it as a good opportunity for me, and I think I did too. But I was a bit scared. I didn't know this aunt at all, and I was scared to be separated from my mama and sister. Especially right then, when my papa was no longer with me. They left it up to me to decide, and after much hesitation I agreed to go.

Now I look back on it, I feel I made the right decision. It was hard, very hard, but it seems like that year made a big change in me. I was a child when I started the year, and a young woman when the year ended. Even physically, I changed from a girl to a woman that year. And I think it was my experience there that helped set the direction for me to follow—to become a teacher myself.

The school in Nuevo Cuscatlán was a fine place. It was located on the main plaza of the town. You know how those plazas look, right? A huge, ancient tree in the center of the plaza, the mayor's office on one side, the church on another side, and then our school on a third side. My Aunt Amparo was a single woman, and as headmistress she called the shots. She put me in with a good teacher—no, a *great* teacher. When this woman taught she made everything come alive. I was in fifth grade then, and here in El Salvador—still today—in fifth grade you study the geography of North and South America. I used to go back to the house after classes and lie there daydreaming about the places she described. It seemed like a whole world I'd never known was opened up to me. I'll always be grateful to that teacher, and my aunt too, for exposing me to these things. To this day, when I have a chance to visit Nuevo Cuscatlán—my aunt is no longer there, she's dead now—I see the old plaza, the same tree and church, and my heart fills with warmth.

The thing is, I got a lot out of that year but at the same time it was very hard for me. I seldom got to visit my mother and sister, and my mama couldn't get away to visit me. My aunt was strict, very tough in a way. Maybe her living alone made her like that. She helped me get a good education, but in her own way she sort of used me—even exploited me, you could say. Part of her idea in bringing me there, you see, was to help take care of her house. She had me do the cleaning and washing up. And often when the teachers would come to her house for lunch, I was the one who had to serve them. Besides this, my Aunt Amparo had a certain head for business. Most evenings, she'd put me to work making these banana slices dipped in chocolate, and the next day I'd sell them to the students. My aunt, of course, kept the money—not me. And then on Saturdays, what she'd do is make money by selling tickets to people who wanted to come watch her television set. I'd make up the tickets and then sell them to *campesinos* who were in the plaza. They were men who worked on fincas in the area, and with the workweek over they'd come to the plaza. On Saturday afternoons there was wrestling on TV, and the men would pay to come watch. My aunt had me running this little business for her. When the men were in the house she made sure I was out of the way, nowhere nearby. Then when they left, I'd be called in to clean up the mess. I can't say I liked this at all, but I guess she saw it as a way of my paying for what she was providing me. And look, she *did* provide me with a lot. More than I may have even realized at the time. Because when the year was over I had become a real student and I was a young woman who had some direction.

At the end of my year with Aunt Amparo, I went back to live with my mama and sister. That was a great relief for me. I had missed them, and it was a joy to be together with them again. They were still with my Aunt Carmen. I call her "aunt," though actually she wasn't my father's sister, she was his niece. She was about my mother's age. I lived with her and her husband, Uncle Alberto, for the next nine years. Me, my mama, and my sister. We had a kind of stability there, and my sister and I were able to go to school there and get our education. The reason we succeeded in this was not because of my Aunt Carmen and Uncle Alberto, but because my mother encouraged us and guided us this way. As we became teenagers, the others told my mama, "Why not send them to work? So-and-so is looking for a maid and nanny." But my mama said, "Look, as long as they're not a thorn in your side, why hurt them by taking them out of school?" And that's the way it was. We didn't drop out of school.

All nine years there at Aunt Carmen's big house we were treated more like servants than family. We didn't live in the main house, but rather in the servants' area. When members of my father's family would come visit—my stepsisters and stepbrothers—they'd go in the main door of the house and be treated the way you treat family. If they happened to see us, they'd say, "Hello, how are you?" But, you know, without any interest. To them we were "Julia's daughters," the daughters of my mama—not like real family.

When it came to eating meals, we ate with the other servants, not with my aunt and uncle. You know how it is in houses like that, right? The cook serves the family and then the servants get to eat what is left over from the table. You'd get the leftovers and also—it was rationed out exactly—two spoonfuls of rice, two spoonfuls of beans, a little piece of meat sometimes, and some coffee. The cook was not too nice about it either because she resented the fact that we could call the owners "aunt" and "uncle," even though our living conditions were the same as other servants'. So there were quarrels now and then. But my mama, she knew how to handle these things with dignity. She taught us not to make too much of the other servants' attitudes, not to be petty like them. Instead, what she did is take her own money and buy us extra food in the market. She was being paid 20 colones a month, and when she had time she'd sew things and sell them. She put up a nice table in our room and we ate there in a kind of dignified way.

Maybe because I was younger, I resented all this and felt the unfairness of it. All nine years we lived in that house, I didn't like the atmosphere there. As I got older I used to look for ways of being away from there. Some of my classmates at school came from families who were well-off, and they had nice houses. Their parents liked me. They saw me as a mature person, I think. I'd be invited to sleep over, to spend vacations in their houses. My mama had no objection to this. It was fine with her.

In my heart of hearts, all those years I was waiting and planning for the time I could move from my Aunt Carmen's house. Not just me. I wanted to get my mama and Doris out of there too. As a teenager, I saved some money by working as a cashier in a department store. And always, always, I kept up my grades. I did well up through ninth grade, what's called *educación basica*. And then I got accepted to La Escuela Normal España, a three-year teachers' college for women. I managed to succeed there too. Today, the training to be a teacher is more lengthy— twelve years and then teachers' college. But in my time, twelve years altogether is what it took. I graduated at the age of nineteen and soon after found my first job in a private Catholic school. I felt I'd entered heaven! I was suddenly being paid 185 colones a month, and I loved teaching the kids.

And you know the first thing I did when I got my paycheck? I went to my mama and said to her, "Mama, that's it! Enough staying here with Aunt Carmen. We're getting a place of our own!" And that's what we did. My mama and sister and I found a small apartment over in the

Zacamil section of San Salvador, and we rented it. Shortly after that, an apartment in the same building was offered for sale. With my money, and some money my mama earned, we were able to afford the monthly payments. So finally, we had a place of our own. And my mama, who'd spent her entire life in other people's houses, at last she could say, "This house and furniture are *mine*, not things that belong to the señora." For me, this was what I'd been waiting for all those years.

As for my work as a teacher, well, I loved that. Right from the start. I love teaching kids in primary school, first through sixth grade. What is it now, twenty-five years or so that I've been doing it, no? About fifteen years in Catholic schools and now almost ten years in La Libertad. And you know, to me it's still as exciting as the day I started. I guess I was born to do this work. It's hard, but never dull. Especially, these last years in La Libertad, in a public school there. It's a great challenge that takes a lot out of you, but it gives you back in the same measure. To teach these kids from poor families is, *bueno*, for me it's a blessing. Look, why don't you come and see for yourselves?

[*The Luz de Soto School sits at the edge of the main road in the sweltering port city of La Libertad. About 50 meters downhill from the school is the sea, and the crashing of the waves competes with the traffic noise from the road. The semicircle of small brick classrooms—covering perhaps a little more than an acre—faces an asphalt basketball court and soccer field. At the mid-morning break (when we happened to arrive), hundreds of blue-and-white uniformed boys and girls came streaming out of their classrooms to join in a pandemonium of separate games.*

Each of the attached classrooms (one for each grade, from first through ninth) has between 40 and 50 students, with about an equal number of boys and girls. All the classrooms have a blackboard in front and well worn wooden desks. In Dulce's first-grade class the walls are covered with the typical decorations of that grade: the alphabet and numbers in primary colors, and a variety of students' drawings. At the end of the mid-morning break, the children returned promptly to class and, after being introduced to the "distinguished visitors,"

put in a solid hour studying the alphabet and numbers, and singing songs. Like
a true classroom maestro, Dulce managed with a gesture here and a firm word
there to maintain order among her 40 students. When the 12:30 bell rang to
end the school day, her first graders lined up next to the door and gave her a
handshake or kiss as they filed out. Four volunteers stayed behind to sweep up
the debris, as Dulce watched over them with a smile of weary benevolence.

Shortly thereafter, the three of us and Dulce went to a nearby fish restaurant.
Along the way, we met at least a half-dozen children as well as some young
adults, all of whom came rushing up to her in undisguised affection. "Former
students," she said proudly. "I try to keep up with them, find out what happens
to them as their lives go on. So many of them are terrific kids, though life has
treated them none too kindly. Believe me, being here in La Libertad has been an
education for me too. I'll tell you . . ."

And so she did. But not that afternoon at the fish restaurant, which was
named La Dolce Vita, a rather incongruous name in the shabby bustling neigh-
borhood. Our meeting two days later was, as usual, in her home and we came
equipped, as always, with our two tape recorders.]

The first fifteen years or so I taught in private schools—wonderful
places that were well equipped, and students whose parents could afford
to send them there. Middle-class or even upper-class kids. I enjoyed the
comforts there, I won't deny it. But then I had to take a break from
teaching in order to help out my husband. He was starting up a store
over in Unicentro [a shopping mall in San Salvador], and he said he
needed my help. So the three kids and I all pitched in to get the store
going—eventually it failed, but never mind that—and that took me
away from teaching. After a year or so, my blood began to call, if you
know what I mean. For me, my blood and soul are in teaching. My old
job was not available then, but I heard about a position in the public
school system in La Libertad. I'd never taught in public schools. Still, I
was eager to get back into teaching. And God knows, we needed my
salary. So I said, "Fine, I'm going to try and get the job." For the last ten
years I've been there.

In La Libertad, you have a very different population of students from
any I'd met before. Almost all these kids come from poor families. I

know, because I've visited so many of them in their homes. It's important for a teacher to do that, I think. That way you get to know the parents, and they are the ones who have the major influence on the kids. But unfortunately, so many of these kids come from homes where there's problems—fathers who were killed in the war or who've taken off, and mothers or grandmothers who are trying to raise the kids by themselves in very tough conditions. You've seen these houses around La Libertad, no? Small places made of adobe and sticks, or real hovels made out of tinplate and cartons. Many of my students live in these places. Their fathers are poor fishermen who spend nights out in their dinghies fishing. That's if they're working at all.

Other kids come from the *campo,* way up in the hills outside the city, sometimes an hour or two away. I know, since I've been out to their houses. They invite me sometimes, say when the first corn is picked, and I swear it's taken me a couple of hours to walk up through the hills just to get there. It amazes me, really it does. These children, six and seven years old, are getting up at dawn and walking all that distance just to get to school. How can you not give kids like that everything you have? And you know, sometimes they arrive and you can see they're not looking too well. I'll ask, "Did you have any breakfast this morning?" And sheepishly, they'll admit they haven't eaten. What I do is keep a small supply of food in my closet—oatmeal, honey, sugar, and a few other things. Otherwise these kids can't focus on anything, they drowse off.

This year I'm teaching first grade. Other years I've taught second, third, and sixth grade. What do I prefer? *Bueno,* each grade has its own challenge. With the first graders, the challenge is to start them off learning in the right way. Make school something they like coming to, I mean. Teaching them to read and write, that's crucial. But just as important, you try to convey to them a way of working together, cooperating and sharing with each other. Some of these kids are pretty wild, and getting them to join in with others is a big part of what I try to do. With the older children, like with the sixth graders I taught last year, they already have a certain capacity and discipline. I teach them according to the government curriculum that's the same throughout the country's public school system—mathematics, language skills, health and natural sciences, geography, and so on. Beyond that, though, I try to open their eyes to all that's in the world around us here. And part of the way I do this is to take them on trips, or invite some of them to visit me in San Salvador.

It may surprise you, but most of these kids—even at ten or twelve years—they've never been up to San Salvador. Not even once in their lives. So some other teachers and I, we'll go on outings to the capital. Take them to the top of Banco Cuscatlán—the tallest building in San Salvador, right?—and you should see their faces light up in amazement as they gaze down at the city below. Or I'll take them to a shopping mall. They've never been in a shopping mall in their lives. I want them to go to these places and to understand *they* have as much right to be there as anyone else. The capital city belongs to them just as much as it belongs to any other Salvadorans. The only thing I tell them, they have to behave themselves and not run around wildly. Like this one time, I took a group to a shopping mall and the kids were fascinated by the escalators. They were scared to go on them. But then Santos, one of the more daring kids, started riding it up and down, whooping with joy. An armed guard came rushing over to him, and Santos, in his usual manner—I mean, in the language he uses naturally in La Libertad—told the guard, "Hey, all I'm doing is riding the escalator. No need to fuck around with me, pal!" Well, it's a good thing I was there, because it could have ended badly. Santos wasn't shaken up by the confrontation, not at all. But *I* was. Since then I've prepared the kids a little better. The last thing you want, right, is for one of your students to get roughed up by a policeman.

More often, though, I like bringing only one student to San Salvador. A student and the parents. I do this quite often, usually with a child who seems to be trying very hard to excel in class. I invite them to stay with me and my family for the weekend. I've been doing this for years now. Originally, I saw it as a way of giving *them* something. And as time passes, I've come to see how much they give *me*. No, not all teachers at the school do this. I may be the only one, I'm not sure. To me, it's a central part of my work there. And the students and their parents react with great warmth to this. Sometimes they'll come up by bus carrying me a three-foot-long fish. I'll cook it up for all of us. But usually what the kids like, and their parents too, is to go over to Burger King and Pizza Hut. That's the novelty for them. And we'll go over to the amusement park, or Unicentro, or the movies. Or just stay in the house. We have cable TV and the kids love flicking back and forth between the 50 channels. To them, it's a world they've never seen before. And for me, it's a joy watching them live it up like this. I'm never so happy as when these kids and their families are visiting us.

How does my family like it? Put it this way, the children are used to it by now. They even like it. When my own kids were younger, one of them might say, "What, you didn't bring candies for *us*—only for your students?" And when the families visit, one of them—my son, generally—had to give up his room for the weekend. By now they're used to it, and the older they are the more they appreciate what I'm trying to do. They know that some of my students are kids who've been delinquents. Kids who've been into petty stealing, glue sniffing, and that kind of thing. Recently, I had one boy here—a former student—who was with us about a month. Miguel. He's a kid who had lived in the streets for five years before rejoining his family and then coming to school. He's a wonderful kid. I've had a special relationship with him, and I've tried to help him along. And you know, he has returned this affection by speaking out against drugs—even giving talks to other kids in the school about his bad experiences. It's a beautiful thing to see, and I tell you, the only way you can get things like that to happen is to invest something in the child. Call it a kind of missionary work, maybe. But that is what is needed.

And my husband? Well, Arturo has been my main supporter in all this. He joins in wholeheartedly. He has the same social ideas I do. Politically, he's a little more, well, more to the left than I am, I'd say. So right from the beginning he's been with me in doing these things. He helps me take the kids and their families around, he joins in with everything. He enjoys seeing the feeling, the love, I have for the students, and also the way they return this love to me. No, without Arturo I'd never be able to do what I want in this way. He's with me 100 percent.

❧

Y ou want to know about Arturo? How I met him and all that? Very
well. It goes back to the time I was studying to get my teacher's
degree. I was living over in Zacamil, as I told you, and then Arturo and
his brother moved into an apartment right across from ours. We became
neighbors. Arturo had come to San Salvador a few years before, when
he was fifteen. He's originally from the town of San Juan Opico. He's
got a big family there, and he's the oldest son. His parents are people of
modest means. His mother ran a small store there, and his father was a
tailor. When he was fifteen, Arturo's parents told him, "We can't afford
any more schooling for you. If you want to continue, you're on your
own." So Arturo came to San Salvador and continued his studies in night
school—to become an accountant. In the day he worked to support himself. As fate would have it, he came to live in the same apartment building where we were.

Later on when we became *novios*, he told me that right from the beginning he'd had his eye on me. He was sort of observing me. For *four*
years! I had no idea. To me, he was a neighbor, that's all. A good neighbor, quiet and respectful and serious. He would bring us fruit and other
things from his mother's store when he'd return from visiting his family.
We were friendly, but for me that's all there was to it. Besides, there
were other reasons why I was paying no attention to Arturo. Wait—I'm
not sure I want you to record this. . . . *Bueno*, it'll be coming out in English, right? And anyway, it was long ago.

You see, the thing is, during those four years I had other *novios*. Two
serious ones, really. One who I was with when I was in teachers' training
school, a fellow student. He was the most brilliant student there, and I
was crazy about him. But I caught him once with another girl, and that
was it for me. And you know what happened? The very day I was getting married to Arturo, he showed up at my house. No, I didn't say hello
to him. My mama greeted him and then sort of sent him on his way. I
haven't heard from him since then.

And then after him, there was one more—Rafael. I met him while
working in the department store. He came to buy a suit one day, and
then a few days later he showed up with his mother. He lived alone with
her. I found that out later. Apparently, he'd gone home and told her
about "a girl with unusual eyes," and they'd both come back to look me

over. Next thing I knew, he was pursuing me, waiting for me at the bus stop outside the department store, and chatting with me. He was very nice, an appealing person. And after awhile we began to go out together, to be *novios*. It lasted for several months, and then suddenly I didn't hear from him for a couple of weeks or so. I didn't make too much of this until one night I had this dream.

In the dream, I was visiting his house and then a girl there came at me with a knife, trying to kill me. His mother struggled with her and took the knife away in order to protect me. I tell you, for days I couldn't get this dream out of my mind. Finally I went to his house and told his mother about it. I could see she was struck. She told me, "I'm about to go away for several days, and I have to tell you I've been very worried. There is this girl coming from the United States. She considers herself Rafael's *novia*. He loves *you*, not her. But I'm very afraid she'll go wild if she finds out about you, and she'll cause you some harm. I've been meaning to tell you to be careful, to stay away these next weeks."

Well, you can imagine my shock on hearing this. I felt grateful to his mother, but angry at him for stringing along two of us at the same time. I decided, "That's it! Enough of him. It's finished!" And it *was* finished. I refused to see him again. But for months after, I was feeling very down. I went to the medical clinic, and the physician there sent me to a psychiatrist. It's the only time I ever went in my life, though God knows, I thought of going later too—during the war. But that's another story. Anyway, I went to the psychiatrist and we talked and talked. It turned out that my deepest sadness was not over losing Rafael. It was the loss of his *mother*. I'd come to admire and love her, and that loss was what I couldn't bear. Somehow, figuring that out helped me. I never did see him again, though I heard from her. The two of them went to the United States, and maybe he married that girl. I don't know. I lost contact with the mother. I don't know what happened to her or her son.

Now, while all this was going on Arturo was keeping an eye on me. I don't know what he ever knew about it. He never said a thing. The one who did say things to me now and then was my mama. I don't know what you've discussed with her, but perhaps you've realized that she has a pretty low opinion of men. She used to warn my sister and me,

"You two be careful, because men only want to play with you. And if you wind up with bellies, you're not going to be able to study, and then who'll want you?" That's her view, and she'd always warn us. I didn't say anything back to her. But it wasn't my experience. The *novios* I had before I met Arturo, and Arturo too, weren't the kind to take advantage of a girl. I mean, yes, they had other girlfriends. Still, with me, Rafael and the guy before him were very respectful. And, if I'm most honest about it, maybe they could have taken advantage if they'd set out to do that. You know, sweet words here, and a kiss and hug there, and who knows what could have happened? I was lucky in that way. They didn't take advantage of me, and I bless them for that. And Arturo, from the beginning he was always respectful toward me.

In fact, the night he declared to me he wanted to be my *novio*, I was truly surprised. We had gone to see some folkloric dance performance, and on the way back he blurted out what he'd been feeling all those years—how he'd been watching me and waiting for the time to ask me to be his *novia*. I was amazed at all this feeling he had for me. I wasn't aware of it. It had even crossed my mind that he liked my sister, but she was not available. She had a *novio*, the man she later married. So I guess he turned his interest toward me. I don't know. I was just very surprised. I mentioned it to my mother, that Arturo was interested in being my *novio*, and she had nothing against it. She seemed to like him, and by then I was getting on in years. I was twenty-four. So maybe she wasn't worrying about me in the same way as before. Anyway, I thought about it and then I told Arturo, "Yes, I'll be your *novia*."

After that, things went very fast. Within a few months of becoming *novios*, we were already making plans to get married. I came to see that Arturo was right for me—a very good man who loved me a lot and was serious and true. And I felt good about him too, I wanted to be his wife. The problem we had, though, was that his family didn't want him marrying me. Not because of me, personally. They didn't want Arturo marrying *anyone* then. His mother and one of his sisters would have opposed any girl he chose, even if she were someone from the "fourteen families." They were just plain jealous. And all of them, his father too, wanted Arturo to hold off any marriage plans because, frankly, they wanted him to go on supporting them and helping them put up their new house. Arturo, though, was determined. He told them his time had come to marry and he had the woman he wanted to marry. And that was it. Like it or not, they had to accept it.

Because of all this, unfortunately, the atmosphere at the wedding was not good. Actually, it was very unpleasant. The civil ceremony was no problem. We had that on February 28, 1973, and only a few people came. There was no party, and no problems. It was the church ceremony we had five weeks later, on April 7th, that was unpleasant. If I had it to do over, I'd never do it the way we did—there in San Juan Opico. His family insisted we do it there in a church where everyone in his family had always got married, and with a priest I didn't know at all. And even though my mama and sister and I put up the money for the food, it was his family that insisted on preparing it their way. Everything had to be *their* way.

Everything except one thing—my wedding dress. That I insisted on being *my* way! His family thought I should wear an all-white dress, the way—how should I say this?—the way proper girls do. Yes, right. The way virgins do. I wasn't going along with that. I had seen a wedding dress in a catalogue that was white, yes, but with purple ribbonwork on the neck, cuffs, and hem. I fell in love with that dress. The color purple has always held a special significance for me—the transmutation, you can say, from all that is bad to all that is good. I wanted my wedding dress to have that purple ribbonwork, and my sister, who's a great seamstress, made me that very dress. I insisted on wearing it, even though his mother and sister kind of raised their eyebrows and let it be known that they opposed me. Arturo said nothing. What I wanted to wear was my business, that was his attitude.

So, the truth be said, I didn't really feel very good at the church ceremony or at the party afterward. The atmosphere was filled with these small resentments and unpleasant innuendoes. It was only when we got away from his family and went off on our honeymoon that I finally felt good. Good to be away from all that pettiness, and good to be with Arturo. And truly, we had a wonderful honeymoon. Eight days. First here, at Lake Coatepeque, and then in Guatemala. To be together, just the two of us, was wonderful.

Was this the first time I was alone with Arturo? Yes, it was. No, I didn't know exactly what to expect. I was a little nervous, for sure. But he was very good to me. I was a little embarrassed, and I decided to talk to him, ask him questions—yes, right then on the wedding night—I told him how I was feeling. That's the way I am. Always have been. I go forward even if I'm a little scared. Arturo gently explained things to me and made me feel comfortable. I mean, yes, there's the embarrassment and some pain too, right? But it goes away with the feeling of being together, the sense of handing yourself over to another. Later, the pain and embarrassment come back, right? Yet in time all that is gone, and what you have is the feeling of oneness, the sense at last that you and the other have joined together.

Today, twenty-five years later, I feel this more than ever. And with each year that we've been married, the sense of our togetherness gets stronger and stronger. Each year there is more understanding and friendship and love. For me, the encounter with your partner is a religious experience, an encounter with God. There is the affection and physical part, yes, but above all I have this sense of a transcendence—that the physical part of love has a spiritual dimension, and that my husband is for me a gift, a gift from God. That's how I view our marriage. It's been like what you say at the altar when you exchange vows. We've been together for better for worse, for richer for poorer, in sickness and in health. I'm very lucky in this way. I really think so.

I don't mean it's always been easy. As I said, we've been together for better *and* for worse. We've had our hard times, our differences—especially, I'd say, in the beginning of our marriage. You see, right away we had our children. Three in three years. I was already working as a teacher, and I loved my job. Raising three small kids and keeping my job was very hard on me. Arturo thought I should take time off and stay at home. He put a lot of pressure on me, and finally I went along. I took a year off. But as I say, my blood is in teaching, and I felt I had to go back—even against Arturo's judgment.

I worked it out that my two oldest were in nursery school where I was teaching. And my youngest, Sara, was taken care of by some relatives and also by my mama. My mama was living nearby with my sister and her husband, and she helped me in the daytime with all my kids. They're still close to her because of that, especially Sara. My mama was like another mother to them. And really, she's the one who helped me get through those early years when I was determined to stay at my job.

Besides my mama, I also had some help in the house from *empleadas domesticas*. I was working the usual double shift, mornings and afternoons—that's the way you had to teach back then—and I needed someone to help with the housework. I didn't want my mama doing it, oh no! So I took on a maid. You can imagine, I guess, that this was a complicated thing for me. Given my background, it was hard to bring in a person and treat her like a servant.

I used to have arguments with Arturo over this. Because what happened is that every maid we had—we had four, I think, over the years— they would sooner or later take advantage of me. I couldn't accept the idea that the maid serves us dinner and then eats the leftovers. I had her eat together with us, as part of the family. And if she had a child, he'd eat with us too. So in time, the maid—look, they were all good people, not malicious—but naturally she'd do things she might not have done if I were tough and harsh. Like, she'd let her child crawl all over our furniture and mess it up. Or she'd run up telephone bills, or in one case, bring in lovers when we weren't there. And me, I could never get myself to fire any of them. I understand these people, how hard life has been for them, and I couldn't throw them out. Arturo would get angry with me. He'd say, "If you treat every person in the appropriate way, in their place, then we won't have these problems with the maids." I don't know, maybe he was right. I just couldn't get myself to be tough with them.

The only way the situation finally resolved itself was when my kids got a little older, and then they were able to help out in the house. That's the way we've done it for years now. No more maids. Now we all pitch in. Everyone does some of the cleaning up, the laundry, the cooking. Oh yes, Arturo too. He buys groceries, cleans dishes, mops up—whatever is needed. He's working hard as an accountant, but when he comes home he doesn't expect to be served. He's very egalitarian in that way. My problem with him was only when I had the maids in the house, and he felt I didn't handle things in the right way. That's when we had our arguments.

The other area of disagreement between Arturo and me—not a real clash, but still there were some differences—was during the war. We didn't see things or feel things in quite the same way. I tell you, just remembering those years makes me cringe. That whole period, all twelve years, I lived in constant panic. Maybe I had something like a war psychosis. I don't know what to call it. I only know that through that whole period I was terrified a lot of the time that something would happen to us, to our family. Me, I wanted to get away. Many friends of ours did go off, to the United States and Canada. If it had been me alone deciding, I would have gone too. But Arturo wouldn't hear of it. "We mustn't run away," he said. "Now is the time that the country needs us. We have to stick it out."

Arturo's point of view about the war was different from mine. He sided with the FMLN. I don't mean he was going around planting bombs and burning gas stations. Of course not. Yet his view was that the only way to achieve certain goals, to have a more egalitarian society, was to use a kind of pressure and force. He felt the war was necessary. I did not. I couldn't agree with him. I knew about the injustices in this society—who didn't know? My point of view was that just because some people have lots of money and land, that's not a reason to go to war. Some of those wealthy people worked hard to attain their money, and if they earned it honestly, without exploitation, then they were entitled to it. Sure, some of the upper class were dishonest and arrogant. But let's be frank about all this. It's not only the upper class here that is dishonest and arrogant. Middle-class and lower-class people, too, are arrogant and dishonest in many cases. It's *people*, it's human nature to act that way. You see it all down the line. Anyone who thinks he has a little more feels he's better than the other, and he tries to make the other feel this. You see it among the poor too. Anyone who can take advantage of another usually tries to do it. So to me, the fact that there were, and still are, inequalities and injustices was no reason to go to war. There was no justification for the kind of violence we had here.

Both sides, the FMLN and the Fuerza Armada, had the view that the end justifies the means. I absolutely reject that. Look at the number of people, families, who perished in this war. In the school where I was teaching, two of my colleagues were shot down as they were walking out of the school. And friends of Sara's, their father was machine-gunned to death as he dropped his children off at school. I lived through those days in constant fear, wondering when our turn would come.

I was teaching in a Jesuit-run school, and the Fuerza Armada was suspicious of the Jesuits. They said the school was preparing students to be on the side of the guerrillas. "You are like watermelons," they said about us. "Green on the outside and red on the inside." It's true that some of the teachers in my school sided with the FMLN, but exactly who I didn't know. Nobody talked openly. I myself was sympathetic to Monseñor Romero. I didn't go to his church, but I appreciated his openness in denouncing injustices and speaking up for the rights of the poor. I just didn't go along with the idea of fighting, making war to change things. Dialogue—that's what I supported. Speak out and speak up, but *nonviolently*. War was not the way. I felt that then, and I continue to feel it today.

Look at the results of the war—*all* the results. True, there have been some changes that are positive. New laws that protect women—or really, old laws against the maltreatment of women that are finally being enforced. And some better social legislation for the poor, and some more land reform for *campesinos*. Alright, that's good. But overall, there's not been any change in the number of poor people we have in El Salvador. If you ask me, we have at least as much poverty today as we had before the war.

So many fathers and sons were killed that you have all these families without a breadwinner. And all the delinquency today—you could see it coming. I'm not an expert on this, I only know what I see in La Libertad and where I work. To me, the situation in El Salvador today is not better than before the war. The war solved nothing and never will solve anything.

The only solution is that people themselves have to turn within, change from within. My deep personal feeling is that for us to have real peace here, it's more a question of each person finding internal peace—peace through God. When each of us finds that kind of internal peace, then the situation in our country will change. Less injustice, less delinquency. And every person, no matter what their station in life, must take a personal responsibility for bettering themselves. That's how I see it. Call it a religious approach to life, a solution through God. To me, this is the way. Not war, and not politics.

My religion? Well, the fact is I don't consider myself as a member of any particular religion. Not Catholic, not Evangelical.* I don't wave the banner of any one church. Yes, I was raised a Catholic and I've taught in Catholic schools. And I have opened the doors of my heart to Christ, that Christ be within me. But I don't want to belong to any one group because I don't want to separate myself off from any other group.

My husband considers himself a Catholic. He goes to mass now and then—not every Sunday. Sometimes I join him, depending on how I feel. And sometimes my daughters go too. But the one who's the devout Catholic is my mother. It's hard for her to get to mass, so she's become one of these "radio Catholics." You know, every morning she listens to mass on the radio. She doesn't go out of her room until she's heard it. She doesn't go to church, but she knows what's going on all over the country in this church or that church, because she hears it over the radio. I respect her way. She's deeply religious and I respect that.

Now my sister and her children, they've joined up with the Evangelicals. My son, too. I understand them. I can see what they like in the Evangelical churches. You see, the Evangelicals have these small churches usually, and they're more involved in the communities and with individual families. Their church services are more animated, with music and singing. As I remember, it was soon after the war started that

*Over the last fifteen years a Protestant sect, the Evangelicals, has come to include about 18 percent of the Salvadoran people ("La religión de los salvadoreños en 1995," *Estudios Centroamericanos* [September 1995]: 851).

the Evangelicals started to have a growing influence here. A good influence, I think. My son, Gerardo, he's taken up with them recently. He was studying to be an industrial engineer, and then a couple of years back he said he had this call in his heart to do something more for humanity. Now he's studying to be a missionary. That's his way, and it's fine with us, though being an engineer would have been fine too.

And Sara, she's got some of that—how should I call it?—some of that "missionary spirit" in her too. With her, it doesn't have so much to do with serving any church. It's more a kind of social activism, I'd say. Two years ago she went up to Chalatenango, to one of the communities that had formed there after the war. She went up there as a volunteer teacher for a year. Truth is, Arturo and I didn't want her to go. There had been a lot of fighting in Chalatenango during the war and we were worried about her. But the Jesuit group at her school was sponsoring the project, and so we said, "Alright, go ahead." Since then she's kept up her ties with the community, and I know she wants to go work there more. "Fine," I tell her. "But finish your studies first. Get that behind you." I respect her convictions, her determination to help the people up there, but frankly—I guess I'm speaking like a mother now—I'd feel less worried if she stayed around here and spent her vacations with us, with *her* family, instead of running up to Chalatenango to be with other families every chance she gets.

The main thing, though—and my husband and I are together on this—is that all our children need to get their education. Let them study what they want, but they have to have a way of earning a living. We know how easy it is to wind up in rough straits if you don't have a good education. I see this in my work with the students down in La Libertad. Some of those kids are very bright and could do well in university. But very few make it there. Their parents don't send them. They can't afford the expenses. So what happens to those kids? They finish ninth grade, at most, and then the next thing they get *ajuntados*. The girls are raising kids and the boys are out on fishing boats or in the *campo* trying to make a living. It's a pity. They can't break out of the cycle of poverty, even though they have the native ability, the intelligence, to do so.

With our children, thank God, they already have got the push they needed. We sent them all to private schools, and now to university. For Arturo and me, frankly, this has been difficult. His salary and mine can hardly cover all the expenses. But we manage it somehow, because we know what it means. What our children do in their lives is up to them. I'm not looking to see them move into the upper class, or anything like that. For that you need family and social connections, or some kind of lucky break, or some great determination and skill at making money. My kids are not like that. They're fine children, with social consciences and dreams of making some kind of contribution to others. I'm proud of all three of them. I don't know exactly how it'll turn out for any of them, but I feel things are going in the right way. Arturo feels the same.

When they're finally off on their own, well, then Arturo and I will have more time to do some things together. Maybe even go to the United States—for a visit, *not* to live there. Now *that* would be nice. I've always wanted to see a little more of the world, ever since that geography class I had back in fifth grade. South America, North America, Europe. Who knows? Maybe it'll happen. I certainly hope so. But right now things are good enough as they are. Things have worked out more or less the way I hoped. I thank God for that. I feel my life, our lives, have been blessed.

Niña Julia

Just a fifteen-minute drive to the west of Dulce's house is the suburb of Merliot—one of many districts that have sprouted in and around the capital in recent years, principally to house the city's growing middle class. As in other such districts, the conveniences and trappings of this new wave of life are in evidence: supermarkets, fast-food restaurants, and that hallmark of suburbia, the shopping mall. Small, boxlike cement houses are the preferred (or at least, the affordable) architectural form here, each one with a car parked out in front.

Niña Julia Rivas has lived in Merliot for three years together with her daughter Doris and her family. Their cement-block house sits on a hillock overlooking the shopping mall. The house itself is small, but Niña Julia has now what she never had before: "my own bedroom with its own bathroom—a real luxury for me!" And indeed, after a lifelong odyssey of dwelling all over the country, Niña Julia appears to have settled in here, in a room of her own.

At seventy-nine years and with aching legs, Niña Julia spends most of her time at home these days watching TV, crocheting, or helping Doris with some of the cooking and housework. She walks and talks slowly, but her dark-brown eyes exude an alertness and a ready sense of humor. Eschewing jewelry and makeup ("Those are luxuries I do *not* need," she says), she also dresses simply, most often in house slippers and in patterned cotton dresses.

When Dulce first introduced us to her mother, Niña Julia greeted us with a certain reserve. She was friendly and gracious in her quietly dignified way, but she was also guarded about what she would say. In short, she let us know that she was not one who opened up easily, certainly not to strangers. And, in fact, even though she agreed that day to be interviewed for the book, she kept a cautiousness over the first three months—that is, three interviews—we had with her.

Eventually, Niña Julia began to let down her guard. Interestingly, what seemed to help in putting her at ease was a decision we made at the end of the third interview: to have only Gloria Leal and Marta Pineda carry out the balance of the interviews. As Niña Julia's narrative would make clear, she had a history of reasons to confirm her suspicions of a man's motives and behavior. Thus, her last five interviews were with Gloria and Marta, or sometimes just with Marta, who came to develop a daughterly rapport with Niña Julia.

Asked what name she wanted to adopt for the book, Niña Julia hesitated and then said, "*Bueno*, if it can't be my own name, go ahead and call me 'Julia.' That's my mother's name, God bless her memory. I think that would be a good name for me, don't you?"

Accordingly, what follows is the story of Niña Julia: daughter of Julia and mother of Dulce and Doris and, as she explained, a few others as well.

I was born on February 15, 1919. But that's not what's written on the records or on my identification card. My birth date there is February 19th. What I was told is that my parents forgot to report my birth on time. You had eight days to report a birth. If you were late you got a fine of 5 colones. To avoid paying the fine, they said I was born a few days later. After all, who was going to know anyway?

I wasn't raised by my mother and father. It was my Granny Mari and

Grandpa Mauricio, my father's parents, who brought me up. They're the ones who were like parents to me, and I lived with them all my childhood—until I left home at seventeen.

Why was that? Well, my mama was a poor woman. Real poor. Her mother had died when she was young, and my mama had only one brother. This brother and my mama, the way I heard it, were working on my grandparents' farm. Yes, Granny Mari's farm. My grandparents had a pretty good-sized place. They were raising cattle. Over in San Ildefonso, in the department of San Vicente—that's where I'm from. And the way it must have happened is that their son, my father, met my mother that way. I don't know how it happened really. Nobody ever informed me of any of that. I just know they got together, but I think he lived in one house and she lived off alone or with some relative. They had five kids. I'm the oldest. I've got a twin brother, a few minutes younger than me, and there were three more. I don't know them too well, since we were all living apart, with one or another of my father's family. My father never took my mother as his legitimate wife, you see. It was only after he got tired of her—God alone knows how it was—he then found himself a woman to marry, and he had a heap of kids by her. Those kids were the ones he left his money to when he died. Me, I never saw a centavo of it. And my mama, he didn't take care of her either. She died a poor woman, a couple of years after my father left her, with no children and no money. God bless her memory, my mama Julia.

But God watched over me, yes He did. Just like it says in that psalm: "Though your mother and father abandon you, God will never abandon you." God made sure I had someone to take care of me—my Granny Mari and Grandpa Mauricio. All ten of their children had grown up and were living out of the house when I was born. So Granny Mari said, "Alright, bring her to me. I want to raise her." And that's the way it was. She took me and my twin brother, Mingo. Though later on, when he was five years old, my father took Mingo to go be with him and work on the ranch. Because I was alone then, Granny Mari treated me like a princess. My Grandpa Mauricio, too. I had it real good with them. A good life is what they gave me.

We lived in the town of San Ildefonso. Back then it was a small place, no more than a thousand people or so. About a league's distance out of town—a league was like 4 kilometers—on the road to the town of San Vicente, that's where my grandpa had his ranch. He was a hard-working man, Grandpa Mauricio. He had started out growing indigo and made good money there, and then he invested it in land and cattle. By the time I was born, he must have had 150 or 200 head of cattle out there at his ranch, and maybe 50 manzanas of land. No, I wouldn't say he was rich. He didn't see himself that way. He saddled his horses with those simple saddles, not the fancy kind so people call you "*Don* So-and-so." No, he was just Mauricio—a simple person like the people who worked for him. He had been born a simple person, and even with his 50 manzanas and cattle he stayed that way.

When I was young I hardly ever went out to the ranch. I stayed at home with Granny Mari. As soon as I was old enough, I helped her around the house. Sweeping up or making tortillas or whatever. She was a good cook and I learned what I know from her—making stuffed chicken, *marquesotes, atoles* [drinks made from cornmeal gruel]. These days the art of cooking is gone, isn't it? People eat whatever you get from the supermarket or the Pizza Hut. Back then we ate differently. All the fresh butter and cheese and meat, and all the vegetables and fruits my grandpa grew out at his farm. Oh yes, we ate well.

And the house we lived in, I liked that too. It was the same size as this one here, but made of red adobe bricks. My father built it. And he made some of our furniture too, closets and beds. He was good at that kind of thing. The way the house was, we had this one big bedroom. My grandma and grandpa and I, we each had our own canopy-covered bed, with the beds separated from each other by white curtains that you drew closed. Back in those days a couple slept in separate beds, not like today where they have one bed for both of them. And I had my bed, like I say, and just on the wall above was a picture of John the Baptist. From the time I was young I learned to say my prayers before going to sleep. To this day I do it, and I cross myself, otherwise I can't fall asleep. But even crossing myself and all, sometimes I used to get these nightmares. I still do. I'd get this nightmare where people are lifting me up, taking me away, and it seems like they're about to break me, but I manage to shout, *Ave María Purísima! Dios Santísimo!* And then they lower me gently down and I'm alright. I've had this nightmare since I was small. I don't know why. Some people used to say you get nightmares when you sleep on your back with your arms crossed over your chest and your mouth facing upward. My daughter Doris says it's because of some medicine I'm taking for my diabetes these days. I don't know. I just know I've always suffered from nightmares, but with the protection of God and the Holy Mother, I always manage to find my way to safety.

What else can I tell you about my childhood? School? Oh yes, I went. Granny Mari saw to that. She wanted me to learn. When I was five or six, there was a lady who came to our house and I learned my letters from her. After that, maybe when I was nine, I went to school in town. These days, out there in San Ildefonso, I think they have a school that goes up to twelve years, but back then they had a school that only went to second grade. It wasn't a school building. Just an adobe house and a courtyard, and one lady who taught both first grade and second grade. First grade in the morning and second grade in the afternoon. Bless that woman, she was a fine teacher and like a mother to us all. We had good equipment too. Blackboards and desks, books and pencils. We had these things thanks to General Martínez, the one who put down the Communists. You can look it up—I think it was in the early '30s. A great leader, I admire him. Because of him we had our things at school. He was the one who arranged it.

Anyway, I went to that wonderful little school for three years. After second grade, I repeated it because that was all you had there. So I stayed on to learn more. I learned how to read and write in those three years. I can read a newspaper or book, though writing is a little hard for me. I confuse some of the letters, like "b" and "v," which sound almost the same. But I can write a note or letter if I have to. And I can read the Bible too—that's something one ought to know how to do, right?

My grandma wanted me to learn more. She told me, "It's the only wealth I'll be able to pass on to you, so you should continue." Problem was, the nearest school that went past second grade was down in Berlin, which was quite a ways off. One of her daughters lived down there and I could have stayed with her. Yet I kept thinking, "What if Granny Mari dies while I'm down there? Then I won't be able to come back." So I refused. She encouraged me, I'll say that, but I plain refused to go. And in that way, I wound up getting no more education.

I preferred to stay at home with my grandparents. I felt best that way. My own mama, Mama Julia, was still alive then and living in San Ildefonso. She died a little later, when I was about thirteen. Granny Mari, bless her, encouraged me to visit her now and then. But I didn't spend so much time with her. I mean, I loved her—because of her I am here, right? I always paid my respects to her. If I saw her walking in the street, I'd always say, *Buenos días, mamá*. And I'd press my hands together like this [*Niña Julia presses her hands together as if in prayer and slightly bows her head*]. I respected her and loved her. When she died it was hard for me. I missed her. I had a connection with her always, even if I wasn't raised by her, and even though Granny Mari was the one who was more like a mama to me, the one who provided for me and protected me.

Granny Mari liked to have me around her, so I guess when I refused to go to school in Berlin it was alright with her. She would have been alone in the house if I'd gone, and this way we stayed together. That's how it was, the two of us most of the time doing things together. I had a few friends who lived in houses nearby, and we'd play some. You know, the way kids do. Tag or dueling with sticks—I was pretty good at that—or other games. Or once in awhile I'd get together with my friends and we'd make a small bonfire somewhere outside. Granny Mari had this store where she had all kinds of things, like sugar and coffee and *plátanos* [plantains]. She used to get loads of stuff brought to the store, brought on mules or horses. I'd go grab some things, and my friends and I would make a meal around the fire. Drinking coffee and eating fried *plátanos*, like adults and all.

That's the kind of thing I'd do to amuse myself when I was a kid. And when I was alone with Granny Mari it was also fun a lot of the time. She had this thing she used to do, kind of a hobby but she made some money out of it. Making paper flowers. I used to love doing it with her. The way you'd do it is that you'd make them from wire and paper. Little bunches of flowers. You'd attach a yellow paper to the rolled wire stem, and this yellow paper was the base of the flower. And then you'd attach little paper cutouts of petals. You'd glue them on. The glue came from the spine of a certain tree that grew out there in the *campo*. We'd buy this glue for 50 centavos a pound. You can still buy it today, but it goes for about 10 or 15 colones a pound. We called it "spine glue," and you'd put the petals of the flowers together with it. Or you could use another paste to put them together, something called "starch paste," which you make by putting starch in boiling water with a little lemon juice. It holds the petals together well too. I really liked doing this work. It was my way of entertaining myself on those days when there wasn't something else to do.

You see, in those days—back as a kid, I mean—work was like fun. A lot of it was, anyway. Like washing clothes, that was fun in the winter. In the winter, you see, we didn't have water in our wells for washing clothes, so you'd go all the way to the river. The river was out where my grandpa had his ranch and farm. We called the river Rio San Antonio, because some people had found a slab with San Antonio on it at the bottom of the river, so they named the river after him. It was a beautiful spot right at the base of a mountain. Granny Mari and I would go wash the clothes out there in the winter. We'd ride out on horses. Oh yes, I could ride. I taught myself. What, you think people were going around giving riding lessons in the *campo*? No, you'd learn by yourself or you didn't learn at all. I could ride bareback or with a saddle like the kind men used. I'd carry the wash down to the river and later bring back water in containers, one on each side of the horse.

When we were down by Rio San Antonio, you had to go with others. With men carrying rifles. Since the river was at the base of the mountain, coyotes and ocelots would come down there drinking. And one time they found an alligator in the river—in the pool they'd formed down there for bathing. In the men's pool, it was. They had their pool, and the women had their own place to bathe—a smaller pool. I liked sitting by the pool and playing with the water. I couldn't go in swimming because

I never figured out how to do that. And, of course, nobody taught you. Still, I loved being down there at the side of the pool and the river, slapping at the water and cooling myself off.

I especially loved being out there at Grandpa Mauricio's ranch when the cows were calving and they'd be with their calves mooing softly, peacefully. There were goats out there with their kids—baa! baa! baa! That's how they'd go. And the young horses whinnying. How wonderful that all was! My grandpa had these fruit trees down there, mangoes and oranges and lemons, and he also grew a kind of pineapple that was delicious. My Lord, he had everything growing out there, *maíz* and *frijol* and sesame, and all kinds of vegetables. Every way you turned, he had something growing there. I swear, it was a paradise.

Some evenings we'd all go down to the river and spend the whole night there. *Lunadas* [full moon parties] is what we called them. I was about fourteen when I started going. Maybe five or six families, adults and children, would all go down to the river in oxcarts. You'd arrange with the fishermen down there to catch you some fish and river shrimp, and you'd bring along big pots and frying pans to cook them up, fried or in a soup. Some young men from the families would bring along their guitars and we'd spend the night singing. It was beautiful, I tell you. My aunt—one of my father's sisters—was the one who organized it all. It was her idea. She watched over the whole party and she made sure there was no liquor there. Because you know how it is with men when they get some liquor in them. They start grabbing some girl, going around kissing and embracing this one or that one, and then going on to other things too. My aunt didn't want any of that, and since people respected her, they didn't bring along any *chicha* or anything. So nothing bad ever happened. It was always a good time with no dangers of that sort.

When I got to be sixteen, around that age, my father had this idea to marry me off to someone. I didn't know the man at all, but my father said he'd be good for me. My father wasn't insisting or pushing hard. He was just telling me that's what I could do, and he'd arrange it.

But one of his sisters, my Aunt Isabel, told me not to follow his suggestion. Aunt Isabel was an aunt I relied on for advice. She loved me like I
was her own daughter. And she said, "Yes, that guy has his lands just
like your father says. But all he does is hang around street corners, and
he likes his liquor. That kind of man isn't for you. Tell your father you're
not interested." I trusted my aunt far more than my father, so I told him,
"No, I don't want so-and-so." And my father accepted it, he made no
big deal out of it.

   Truth is, my father wasn't very interested in me one way or the other.
Never was. From the time I was small, I knew that. I'd see him now and
then, especially down at the ranch, but all I'd say is, *Buenos días, papá*,
and that was it. My father was a strict man, at least with his children.
With his friends he used to laugh it up and have a good time. With me,
I never saw him laugh or smile. I can remember this one time—I swear,
I'll never forget it—I wanted this pair of new shoes. An aunt of mine
had this store where she sold clothes and shoes. I think you call them
"tennis" shoes. They were a new type of shoe and she'd just got them.
Bueno, as she was showing them to me, my father came in and my aunt
said to him, "Look how good these shoes look on Julia. You ought to
buy them for her, they're only 6 colones." And you know what he answered? He said, *El que quiere celeste, que le cueste* [The one who wants a
lot, let him put out for it]. I must have been seven years old at the time.
My father wasn't a poor man, he had his cattle and all. Well, I went
home crying to my grandma. When I told her what had happened she
said to me, "Never, never go asking anyone for anything. Not your father, not anyone. Remember well what I'm telling you!" And I never
forgot. I've always tried to keep that in mind. I never again in my life
went to my father and asked for a thing. When he died and left all his
land and money to his other children, I never uttered a word. One of his
children even advised me that I could do something, try to get some
money for myself. But I did nothing. "It was my father's land and
money. He was free to do with it what he wanted," is all I said. I never
expected anything from him and I never got anything from him. When
he died it was like, well, like just any other person in San Ildefonso
had died. I didn't even go back there for the funeral. He was my

father and he was gone, yes, but for me he'd never been a father except in name only.

~❧~

By the age of eighteen, I'd already left San Ildefonso. My grandma hadn't wanted me to go, but I felt I had to leave. I had my reasons—let's say, reasons to make me feel I would be better off leaving and going elsewhere. You know, finding work and making a life of my own somewhere else. My grandparents were getting older then. They died a few years after I left, God bless their memories. Them I loved, and I returned for their funerals. I surely did. I owe them a great deal—everything! I guess if I had stayed with them it would have hit me much harder. But as it was, I'd been apart from them for a few years, living my own life elsewhere.

After I'd left San Ildefonso, I wound up working in a few different places. I didn't have my education, I told you that, so I had to find work as I could. I went to the town of San Vicente, not knowing where I was going to live, except I knew some girls from my town who were living there. I found work in a bakery. Good work. I liked making bread, and the owner let me stay there, live there in a room. That's how I made my way for awhile. After that, let's see—well, eventually I got a job over in Berlin, where my godmother had her house. I worked for her as a domestic. Cleaning up, doing laundry and ironing. I was there a year or so, and then I met this man who offered me work where he was living—in Mercedes Umaña. He said he was a widower with kids to take care of, and that his mother was sick and couldn't do it. All that was true. He offered me a decent wage to work for him, so I decided to take the job. The part that wasn't clear is that he had other ideas in his mind besides my taking care of his kids. That only became clear after I got there and was working awhile. I thought about it then and decided I wouldn't refuse him. If he wanted to get together, alright, I would get together with him. No, we had no marriage ceremony. We just got *ajuntandos*, that's all. We lived together, me and his children and his mother.

Jaime—that was his name—he was a farmer and he had his lands there in Mercedes Umaña. He raised all kinds of vegetables, and he used to sell them in San Vicente. Besides that, he used to build houses, the kind you make out of sticks with mud. You know, you put up the frame of sticks and fill in the mud that hardens and makes solid walls. I used to help him in this work. In this, and in the fields too, plowing and sowing. We worked together, and I worked in the house too. Lots of work, believe me, but I always knew how to work hard.

Jaime and I were together for three years. Then he died. I tell you, I always had bad luck with men. Sooner or later, they died or got killed. With Jaime, the way he died was in a road accident. He was on his oxcart going to San Vicente in order to buy some *dulces* to sell. He was traveling on the main road, the Pan American Highway, and a car came along and somehow he got thrown off the cart. He was all banged up. They brought him to the hospital, and the doctors took one look and said, "This one is a lost case, finished." And that was it, he died there.

For me and Yannett it was a terrible blow. Without Jaime it was hard to support ourselves. Yannett? Oh, she was our daughter. She was two when her father died. I'd had her shortly after I got together with Jaime. A beautiful child, an angel. A real angel! Jaime was just in the process of arranging for me to have some land in my name. He was going to sell some pigs and buy the land. That way I would have had something. But then he got killed and I was left with nothing. His other children and mother got his lands, and since his mother and I never got along, there was no point in staying in Mercedes Umaña. So I took Yannett and went back to my town, San Ildefonso. No, not with my Granny Mari. She was no longer alive. I stayed with another relative in town.

That's where I was for the next two years, me and Yannett, until suddenly—in a few days—Yannett was gone. To this day, it's hard to talk about, really. Oh God, I loved her—my Yannett! Such a wonderful child. Chubby like an angel, and full of fun. Everyone who knew her loved her. She was always singing and dancing. Always. Then, God alone knows why, she took sick. Some kind of fever, and her stomach was bad, and soon she wasn't able to talk. She closed her eyes and was moaning. People told me, "Take some lemon juice and mix it with corn-starch and put it on her head." The idea was to bring down the fever this way. I did that and I thought she might be getting better. She opened her eyes and began to talk. "Bring me an *atole* and some sweets, Mama," she said to me. And then she asked me to lay her down on the table and cover her with a shawl. I thought, "May God be blessed, you're getting better." But no, she wasn't really getting better. I understood later, she sensed she was going to die.

That night, just before she died, she was still lying on the table, and she suddenly said out loud, "There's my papa! The light—Mama, put on some light because Papa's here!" I'd put out the candle so we could sleep, and so I quickly relit it. And Yannett repeated, "There he is, Papa!" I didn't see him like she did, but I tell you, I believe in spirits. I believe Jaime's spirit was there in the room then. I don't believe in all that witch-craft that *curanderos* talk about. Rubbish, in my view. But spirits, oh yes, they exist. So I waited until Yannett fell asleep, and even though I didn't see Jaime's spirit, I began talking to him. Just the way I'm talking to you right now, I said to him, "Look, Jaime, leave the girl alone. She can be disturbed by this. Since you left us alone with nothing, now please leave us alone at this time. Leave me be with her in peace, and go wherever God has you. But stop disturbing me so much with the girl."

A few hours later, around one in the morning, Yannett was gone. She took her final breath as I sat there by her side. To me, it was as if the light in the world had gone out. I couldn't do anything. But you know how it is in those small towns, right? No sooner does someone die than everyone knows about it. Already by two in the morning people were coming over for the wake. They brought big pots of coffee and platters of *tamales*, the way you did it. And some people went and bought a white casket and the sheet and all the rest so we could dress Yannett. I had hardly a colón to my name—I couldn't have done anything without this help. Besides, I was almost too broken to move. We had to bury her the next day, right? Because back then, unlike, nowadays, they didn't have ways of preserving the body. We had to do it quickly. So people helped dress her the way they do—like an angel. Because that's the idea, the little ones are like angels returning to God. We dressed her in white with wings like an angel, and with ribbons on the corner of the white casket. Then in the morning we carried her out to the cemetery and set my angel, Yannett, to rest.

After that, I collapsed. Already, from the time she died, I felt this sickness in my heart, a terrible pain. And for the next few days I kept feeling I was going to faint. People would stop by and mention her name, or something about her, and I would feel such a pain in my heart. I couldn't stand it. I felt I was going to die myself. Believe me, there is nothing harder than losing a child. Not when my mama or grandma or grandpa died, no, I never felt anything like that. It's the hardest thing I ever went through in my life.

A friend of mine in San Ildefonso finally told me the only way I'd get better is to leave the town. I knew she was right. She had a cousin who was a doctor way out east, in San Miguel. She arranged for me to go out there and have him take care of me. And that's what I did. I spent a year out there recuperating in San Miguel. I didn't have anything physically wrong with my heart, I was just overwrought by losing Yannett. It took a year before I felt well enough to leave and try to go on with life again.

For the next couple of years or so I bounced from here to there. I went back to Berlin, where I met someone who put me to work selling eggs in the market there. Later, I got hold of a *canasta* [straw basket] and went around selling oranges myself for awhile, until I met a señora who asked me, "Do you know anyone who might be interested in taking care of two children?" I told her, "Yes, I can do it." So I did that for awhile, until the señora and her family left the area—I still have a photo of the two boys. And, let's see, after that I did housework for a dentist, and I helped a lady who was running a little café. And then I started making money sewing clothes. I had learned when I was young how to sew by hand. I had no sewing machine then. I made an arrangement with a señora who sold clothes in the market—over in Soyapango, this was. I had a small room over there, in a group of rooms where people live and share the bathroom. I was managing this way, you see, making my way alright. And about this time, I met the father of Dulce and Doris.

The way that happened is that a daughter of his was looking for someone to do the housework at her father's house. Jacinto, her father, was a retired engineer, a man who had worked in the army as an engineer. He was some kind of officer. He had his house in Soyapango, but his wife had died and his children were grown up and no longer living with him. This daughter of his asked me if I would go do the washing and some cooking for him. "Alright, I'll take the job," I said, because I needed the money and he was offering 20 colones a month.

But again, the same thing that happened with Yannett's father now happened with Jacinto. Soon after I started working there I could see he'd taken a liking to me. He was an older man and I was about thirty at the time. A decent man, a good man, but I can't say I was looking for that. I wasn't living in his house. I kept my own room and was only going there to work. Yet he kept showing his interest in me, and I was like maybe yes and maybe no. Until finally I figured, "Well, yes, I'll go along with him." And soon after that I got pregnant—with Dulce. I didn't move in with Jacinto. Never. Only at the end, just before he died, I went to his house to take care of him. Before, no, I kept my own room. I didn't want to live with him because I didn't want to be dominated, I wanted no part of that. It wasn't so I could fly around like a butterfly, no. I just didn't want any man telling me what to do, and that's what happens when you live with a man, right?

So I stayed in my own place. With Dulce, and after she was born, with Doris too. I took care of Jacinto's house, and he paid me my 20 colones a month like always. And he helped me out with other things too. I continued to make money sewing clothes. Jacinto had bought me a sewing machine. I also was selling things just outside the place where I lived—oranges, sugarcane, and firewood. I liked having all these ways of working. When you put it all together, it gave me enough to take care of Dulce and Doris and send them both to school.

Then what happened is that Jacinto died. Nobody ever said exactly what it was. He died in the military hospital, but in the weeks before he died I stayed with him and took care of him. I did what I could. If you ask me, the thing that killed him was his bad feeling, a sadness—how do you call it?—yes, a depression. He had lost a lot of money in a real estate deal just before that. And what he did is take to his room, close the door. And he refused to take a bath or even eat. His children brought doctors to see him, but Jacinto wouldn't take the medicines. Naturally, he got weaker and weaker, until finally they took him off to the hospital and he died there.

For Dulce and Doris it was a hard thing. Of course it was. They were suddenly without a father. And we had no place to go. The room we were living in had belonged to him, and I had no more salary from him. And he hadn't left me with a colón. Though he did leave me with two jewels, Dulce and Doris. For that, I'll always be grateful to him, God bless his memory.

Fortunately, some of his family were good people and they stepped in to help us out. A niece of his, Carmen, she had a big house not too far away. She offered me to come live there—not like a guest, no, but as someone who'd work there. She had her domestic help, but she made room for me too. Me and my girls had our room there. Doris and I went right away, and later Dulce—she went to Nuevo Cuscatlán to study for a year—then she came to live with us too. That's how I managed it. Señora Carmen gave us shelter. She paid me a salary, and that way I was able to keep my girls with me and make sure they got their schooling. That was important to me, that they get educated, so they wouldn't have to live a life like mine, working all around.

Did I mind being a domestic at Carmen's? No, why should I have minded? I was grateful to have a place to be, to have the stability. Look, to me the main thing was to work. Housework in someone else's house or in your own house is the same work. Nothing wrong with it. The way I see it, there's no reason to be ashamed of any work you do. Work is a blessing from God. It is an honor to work. That's the thing, you see—to do honest work. Not to be a crook or something like that. Or like what happened to some women I knew, like my friend Juanita. She wound up working in a brothel. I remember seeing her this one time after I found out where she was working. I said to her, "Juanita, dear Juanita," I said to her because I loved her, "Why not go look for some other work, some other way of making a living?" But she just said to me, "This is my life. My husband abandoned me and I don't feel well. This is all I can do." Sad, no? There's other work out there to do, and a person can do it if they set their mind to it. Me, I was born a twin, right? Yet I've been managing independently my whole life. You can do it if you set your mind to it. And I did it, yes I did. There's no shame in what I've done, the way I see it.

And look at Dulce and Doris today! Professionals. One's a teacher and the other is a secretary, though she's not working right now. And look at their children, all of them getting their education. And my other daughters, they've made out fine too. One's over in Santa Ana working as a seamstress in her own house, and another works in San Salvador with the Social Security people. Their kids are doing fine too. They got their schooling too, and one of my grandsons is already a lawyer, the way I heard it. So I'm happy. All my children did alright. They made their way in life and have had it better than I did. Thank the Lord for that. They all have done fine.

Yes, I know, I haven't gone into that much. I haven't told you about my other children. I haven't got around to it. Right, they're all girls—four daughters. I had six children altogether, counting my Yannett who died and a miscarriage I had. I probably could have had ten or more if I had wanted to, because for me giving birth was easy. No complications. In my mama's family many of the women had troubles that way. My mama, too. She died giving birth to my stepsister. No, not my father's child, another man's child. That's how my mama died, the way I understand it. But me, I always had it easy. Not even much pain— whoosh!—out they came.

My first? That's Claudia, the one over in Santa Ana. She's a grandma herself now, Claudia is. Let's see, she's got to be about sixty because I had her when I was eighteen myself. You see, she's the reason I left San Ildefonso and Granny Mari's house. I got pregnant and I had to leave.

You know, I've never gone into this with Claudia. Not with Dulce or Doris either. None of them really know the story. Better not to inform them, I always figured. But look, I'll tell you. These things happen, right? Besides, it wasn't exactly something I did. In a certain way I was the victim, you could say. Someone, Claudia's father, set a trap for me and he caught me.

I was seventeen at the time. This fellow, Alfonso—the one who trapped me—was maybe twenty or twenty-two. He came from a good family, but he himself was no good. I'd see him hanging around the town now and then, and always he was trying to start up with me. I tried to avoid him, to ignore him. Then what happened is that there was a Christmas Eve party at my friend's house, and when I got there I saw he was there too. People were talking and drinking, in this room or that room. It was a big house. Then I made the mistake of wandering off to this room where nobody else was, and in he came all puffed up with courage like some men get when they've had a few. Before I knew it he was all over me, forcing himself on me. I couldn't do anything about it. He was a violent man and I was afraid to yell. I also didn't want to make a scandal, which is what would have happened. So I kept silent and let him do what he did.

After that I felt bad. But I also figured, "Alright, he got me, so I might as well go on with him." Why? Because the way men are, you know, he'd go around saying I was his, and he'd act real sure of himself, and I didn't want people gossiping about me. I decided the best thing was to make light of it. And so when people began saying to me, "I hear you and Alfonso have got together," I'd just say calmly, "Well, what's the big deal? He's a man and I'm a woman, so why shouldn't we spend time together now and then?"

You see, in a small town like San Ildefonso, there were no secrets that stayed secrets. Sooner or later, things were found out. And look, lots of girls were victims, and often there were scandals happening. In my family a cousin of mine married this girl. On the wedding night he discovered that she was, well, that the pitcher had already been broken. Men know these things, right? No, not because there's blood or no blood. Because at twenty a man is already a womanizer, he's had his experiences and he knows the difference between a girl who's a virgin and one who is not. So he beat her. He beat the truth out of her. And the truth was—this was unusual—that the one in town who'd got to her was the priest! Nothing much happened to the priest, except of course he had to get out of town, go someplace else—where, I'm sure, he did the same thing again. The girl, though, was marked from this. Her young man,

my cousin, gave her back to her parents and she had to live with everyone knowing this about her.

That's how it was back then. And these things are still going on.
The girl's the one who gets the bad name. Now, with me, even though
it wasn't my fault, I knew I would have this name. So I decided to
openly let it be known that Alfonso and I were going together. I knew
he would never marry me, that was obvious. He told me himself shortly
after that night. He said, "You think you're the only one? I've got six
women now, three of them pregnant, and another who's about to fall
my way." He was what you call a *picaflor* [hummingbird], going from
flower to flower. I just told him, "Fine, do what you want. This is the
only life you've got, so don't lose time." This would make him angry
because he wanted to make me jealous. But thank God, jealousy is not
something I've ever suffered from. Never. I didn't care who else he
went with.

The thing is, though, I got pregnant from him—with Claudia. *That,*
nobody knew. Not Granny Mari, not my father. Only Alfonso knew. My
grandma was a very understanding person, she wouldn't have forced
me out no matter what. But her sons, my father, they would have forced
me to leave. Maybe they would have beaten me too. Once people would
have started saying, "You've got a pregnant daughter staying in your
family's house, do you?"—well, my father would have come tearing
after me. To avoid that, you see, I decided to leave the town. I wrote
Granny Mari a note saying why I was leaving, and that's when I went
to the bakery in San Vicente.

For me, there was never a question of trying to abort the baby. Oh
no, God save me! I would never do a thing like that. Even though Alfonso had told me, "Whether it's a boy or girl, I'm taking it. *My* family
is going to raise it!" I knew he'd probably do that, but no, I wasn't going
to abort a baby. Never! Instead, when my time came, I went up to Santa
Clara. It's north a ways from San Vicente. I had an aunt there. I call her
"aunt" because she has my same surname, though she was only some
kind of distant relative. This aunt was a *partera*, and I figured she'd help
me with the birth. And she did. She was a good *partera*, and I didn't
have to pay her like you regularly have to do. Yes, I had all my children

with *parteras*—all except my third daughter. I had her in a hospital. Either way is alright, though I think it's safer, surer, in a hospital, no?

Anyway, I had Claudia up in Santa Clara, and since it was my aunt, she let me stay awhile. Actually, I was there almost a year. Not doing much, just taking care of Claudia. I knew I couldn't stay there on and on, I had to go find some work. Then what happened, just like he had said, Alfonso's family came and insisted I turn over Claudia to them. I didn't want to, but what could I do? I knew that if I found work as a domestic, or whatever, I couldn't look after her easily. Alfonso's mother wanted to raise her, and they were people with some means, so I decided to give her over to them. I felt awful, terrible, but I told myself maybe it was better for her. They could provide for her in a way I couldn't. And you know—I wasn't thinking this at the time, only later I thought about it—it may have been the same thing that happened with me and my mama. My mama, God bless her memory, took care of me and Mingo for a year and then passed us over to Granny Mari. The same, no? I never asked anyone how it really was. Yet when I think about it, sometimes I reckon it happened the same to my mama as it happened to me.

The difference is, I always saw my mama when she was alive. With Claudia, I hardly ever saw her. I was living too far off and I seldom saw her. It wasn't until later, when she was eighteen and came to where I was in Soyapango, that I saw her some. I helped set her up to work in a store there. Then she got pregnant and went off on her own. Today, I still don't see her too much. She's way over in Santa Ana in her own house and making her living as a seamstress. She sends me things sometimes—clothes, shoes, and 100 colones once in awhile. I love her and she loves me. I feel blessed by God and the Holy Mother that she turned out—all my children turned out—as they did.

What happened to Alfonso? Years back he died. He got shot. This was about the time that Claudia left San Ildefonso and came my way. I wasn't there, but the way I heard it, he got shot at his daughter's house. By then Alfonso had married and he had a heap of kids. *Bueno*, he was at his daughter's house when some men came by. As I understand it, they were looking for her husband. Something to do with another woman, some skirt-chasing, I think. And since her husband wasn't there, they shot

Alfonso, the father-in-law, instead—to settle the score, I guess. A shame, if you think about it. All those children Alfonso had, and they got left alone. Claudia too. That's how she lost her father.

⚬

I tell you, with me sooner or later the fathers of my daughters got killed or they died off. Sometimes I wonder if it has to do with me. People say there're women who have this thing, a white-colored spleen in them. A woman who has that, they say, shouldn't get together with men. Because if she does, then the men die one way or the other.

With me, they all went. My third daughter, Yannett, her father went too, without her hardly knowing him. She met him once, when she was seven years old, but he died when she was ten. At least she met him. To me, that was important. I wanted my girls to know their fathers, if they were crooks or whatever. They should at least know who their father was. That's how I saw it.

Yannett? Yes, that's her name. Right, the same as my second daughter who died. Well, I wanted to keep her memory alive, so I decided to give my next daughter the same name. She knows, for sure. I told her about her sister who'd died. She knows how she got her name. It's alright with her, sure. Yannett—she's the one who works now with the Social Security. A fine girl, she's done very well. Though I didn't get to raise her either. No, it wasn't someone on her father's side who raised her—oh no! It was my favorite aunt, Isabel, the one who always gave me advice, she's the one who brought up Yannett. Yannett is always asking me about her father—still today she does, but I don't tell her much. Just that he was an army officer, a lieutenant. More than that I don't say.

Because what happened there is the same as happened with my first, with Claudia's father. I got trapped the same way. This was when I was working in Soyapango in the café. I was there one evening when we had this storm, a real tempest. I couldn't go home, so the señora who owned the café told me to stay. A few of us stayed, including some customers. One of these was a lieutenant, a man who used to come by now and then. *Bueno*, I went off and lay down. In the night this lieutenant came over and, well, I couldn't fight him off. But I didn't yell either, because I didn't want anyone wondering what was I doing with this married man. And that was it—from that I got pregnant.

When I realized I was pregnant I went and told him, and you know what he said to me? He says, "Oh yes, I know. I know when I've left a woman pregnant." And then he says to me, "I can't help you right now. I'm flat broke. There's no way I can manage it." That got me real mad. I told him, "Well, thank God, I *can* manage. I'm a free woman, and I'm going to show you how a free woman manages things!"

And I *did* manage! I gave birth to Yannett over in the Maternidad Hospital in Soyapango. They don't charge you anything there. Then I went back to work, selling and sewing. I wasn't making much money, but I managed it. Sure, I did. It was about this time that Jacinto's daughter asked me if I'd work for him. Since I needed the cash I took that on too. Then, like I told you, Jacinto and I got together after a few months, and I got pregnant with Dulce. I was up visiting my Aunt Isabel in San Ildefonso when Dulce was born. That's why Yannett wound up being raised by Aunt Isabel.

You see, Dulce got sick up there right after she was born. Some kind of sickness with sores all over her head. I wasn't thinking it was very serious. But you see how God is, He watches over us. A señora came by and told me the sickness *was* serious, and unless I took her to a hospital immediately she might die. So I asked my aunt to watch over Yannett for awhile, and I took Dulce to a hospital in the Soyapango area. And, thank God, they saved her. When she was well, I sent a telegram to Aunt Isabel—there weren't telephones around where I was—and I told her I was planning to come fetch Yannett. She wrote me back saying, "No, better to leave her with us. Why go around with two little ones? We've got accustomed to her here." I thought about it, and I decided maybe Aunt Isabel was right. When I was up there before, I could see they really did love her. My aunt and two nieces were crazy about Yannett. My aunt had had two sons, but both had died—one of them not too long before, cut to pieces by two drunks with machetes. She'd had a hard time, Aunt Isabel. And I myself knew what a good person she was. I figured, "Alright, I'll leave Yannett with them, and I'll visit when I can." Which is what I did.

Today Yannett is living in San Salvador and she's a widow herself. She's got four grown children, and she's managed fine. We talk a lot on the phone, and once in awhile her son drives her over here to see me. She's always passing me a few colones when she comes. She's a fine person. The only thing that troubles me with her is that she keeps asking about her father, who he was and how we met. I don't want to tell her. What good would it do at this point?

For me, I tell you, I haven't had much luck with the men I was with. Two of them I didn't even choose, they just trapped me. And with the two I chose, they died off. The way I see it, even if you choose carefully or try to do so, getting together with a man is the same as buying a lottery ticket. You never know when you buy one whether you're going to win or lose. Isn't that so?

ॐ

I will say this, my daughter Dulce has had some good luck this way. Her husband is a fine man. A hard worker, a man who knows how to support a household. With me, he's friendly and generous. Christmas comes along, or sometimes even without Christmas, he'll give Dulce some money to bring over to me. He's not a rich man, but he's generous with what he's got. A good man.

Doris's husband? *Bueno*, let me put it this way. I've been with him and Doris all their married lives. I know him up close, you can say. When they got married, they moved into their own place in Zacamil. I went and lived with them. Doris's husband didn't oppose it. Many men don't like having their mothers-in-law around, but he didn't object. Maybe because he saw I was helping them economically. He had just finished his studies to be a doctor, and young doctors don't have much of an income. Doris was working as a seamstress and as some kind of secretary at Hotel Camino Real. And I worked at selling things in order to help out. From the beginning, though, Doris's husband and I didn't have that much to do with each other. He's a man who, well [*Niña Julia tilts her head back and gestures as if drinking from a glass*], one of those. Yes, he likes having a few. Always has. Some bad things were going on there for awhile. So I wanted to stay, be with Doris and be sure everything was alright.

And that's how it's been. I've been with them for twenty-four years, since they got married. Today, things are smoother. He's making more money now, though he doesn't know how to manage it. And Doris's children are doing well. Her son's in the university, and her daughter plans to go soon. Things are alright here. Peaceful, more or less.

I guess the hardest time we had was back in the beginning, because of his problems and also the situation. The war, I mean. Over there in Zacamil was a bad place to be during the war. Dangerous. All of us were living with lots of tension. Dulce's family too—they were over in Zacamil nearby. Bad things were happening regularly then. Lots of shootings and bombs going off. The taxi driver living a few houses away from us got machine-gunned to death. And my granddaughter, one of Yannett's girls, had a bomb fall on her apartment. On the fourth floor, over near us. Thank God, she and her kids were out at the time. When they came back there was a huge hole in the apartment—everything was burned and destroyed, all the appliances. At least, *they* weren't touched. Nobody in my family and no close friends died in the war, thanks to God. But there were many who perished. Over in Zacamil was a bad place to be. That's why we moved out of there. Doris's family and Dulce's family, too. We all moved out of there.

I can't really tell you why the war started. I don't know much about that. I suppose it was the ambition of some people to have a spot for themselves, to get some power. The guerrillas, the FMLN. They figured it was the easiest way to get power. They said they wanted to put in communism, you know, that everyone should have equality, not that one should have three pairs of shoes and the other one pair. I can't say I know much about that. What? Am I going to tell you I've been reading books about communism and I know what it is? No, I don't know what it's all about. And really, it doesn't interest me at all.

I never had any interest in politics. When I was growing up, I was like living in the jungle. I didn't know anything more than that you get up in the morning, eat, work, sleep—that's it. My grandparents and those around me used to say, "What difference will it make if Pedro gets elected or Juan?" I grew up not interested in these things. And I'm still not interested. Some people these days are saying the FMLN is soon going to be in charge here. If it happens, people will have to accept it. You have to accept what comes your way. Me, I doubt I'll be here so long to find out. Maybe I'm fortunate in this. But anyway, Pedro or Juan, it's the same to me. I was born without politics, and I'm going to die without politics.

What matters to me is not politics. Religion, that's what matters to me. I'm always telling people—this is something I'm sure about—I'm saying, "Put yourselves in God's hands. Pray. For God alone will never abandon you." I've learned that about life. I say my prayers to God. And to the Holy Virgin—María Auxiliadora, Señora del Perpetuo Socorro, la Virgen del Carmen. I pray to them all even though I know they're all one. All are the Virgin Mary. I listen to the rosary every morning and I pray every night. I'd like to go to mass, at least on Sundays, but the church is a little distance from here and nobody takes me. Though maybe, Marta, you would like to go with me? [*Niña Julia laughs.*] Sure, if you'd like to take me, I'd be grateful.

My daughters don't have the time or, I guess, the idea of taking me. Their father, three days before he died, told me to be sure Dulce and Doris followed the religious path. I tried to do what their father asked, and I prayed to God to guide me in the right way. What happened, though, is that both have their religious beliefs, which are not the same as mine. Dulce says she doesn't belong to any one religion, and Doris has gone with the Evangelicals. Me, I'm Catholic. That's how I was born and that's how I'm going to die—Catholic. I don't go with Doris and her children to their Evangelical church because they have some ways of thinking I just can't see the same way. They don't believe in the Virgen Santísima, they don't pray to her. Now, tell me, how is anyone not going to pray to their Holy Mother? How do you not honor *Her*? Also, they don't believe in the soul, or in heaven and purgatory and hell. When I pray, I pray for myself and for the eternal rest of my brothers and sisters, my grandparents and Mama. The Evangelicals say, "Why pray for those who are dead?" They say, "Pray for those who are living." I do. I also pray for the souls of those who've gone. So, you see, they have their ways and I have mine. They go their way, and I go mine. I mean, I stay here—in my room. I pray here. And God hears my prayers here, even though it would be good if I could get out to mass once in awhile.

That's my life these days, more or less. I listen to the rosary on the radio, and then I straighten out my room, clean the bathroom— you've got to clean it every day if you don't want *cucarachas* [cock- roaches] running around—and then I'll have my breakfast, some toasted tortillas and coffee. Then I'll clean up the dishes, maybe do a wash, water the garden. Just like this [*she snaps her fingers*], real quick. I always keep a little sack ready, just in case I have the chance to go out. Sometimes Dulce or Doris will take me down to the Merliot shopping mall. I like looking into all those windows, and if I have a few colones I'll buy something. Or we'll go over to the supermarket there. I like that too— all these things you can buy nowadays! But mostly, I don't get the chance to go out. With my legs, well, I don't get around that easily, you see.

I'm just a little short of my eightieth birthday, you know. That's a long time for one person to live. I would like to work, I have ideas, but no strength. Really, I think I've lived long enough. I've enjoyed my life, in spite of everything. That's right, in spite of everything that's happened over the years, the many times I've fallen and risen again, living here and there, the storms that have come, the hurricanes. Everything has gone by and I'm still here. But now, going on eighty, it's enough. I've lived enough. Whatever sufferings I've had, *bueno*, what I want to say is that I've forgiven everyone. Everyone and anyone who did me harm or wanted to, I say, "God forgive them, because they don't know what they do." Isn't that how it is? I leave it to God to judge. In my heart I have peace, in my mind I have tranquillity. God knows what is good or bad. It is for Him to judge. God, my God, I leave it all to Him. I have no fear of death. I am at peace with God and the Holy Mother. I am ready to leave this earth, ready to go—whenever. Not too long from now, I ex- pect.

Sara

Sara Gutierrez Rivas is the youngest of Dulce's three children. At twenty-one years, she is a slim and shapely young woman who moves with the gentle and sure grace of a dancer. Three small silver earrings peek out from under her long brown hair, and a purple heart-shaped amethyst hangs on a gold chain around her neck. Like her mother, she has huge coffee-colored eyes. Yet in Sara there is seldom a sadness, but more often a radiance—the radiance of a young woman in love with life.

Currently, she is in her third year at La Universidad Centroamericana, studying communications ("I chose this field," she says, "because we are not well developed in this area in El Salvador. And, after all, what is more important in society than how we communicate with each other?"). And indeed, in her soft-spoken manner Sara is an excellent communicator. She has developed her own perspective on many matters—one that differs considerably from that of her mother and grandmother. She states her views diplomatically and deferentially, but she also leaves no doubt that she holds these opinions with conviction.

As Sara readily acknowledges, her outlook has been tempered by the war and its uncertain aftermath. In 1995, on graduating high school, she spent a year in Chalatenango working as a teacher in one of the newly repopulated communities. This experience (which she undertook against the wishes of her parents) evidently had a profound influence on her. Though it is not her style to wave ideological banners, Sara now sees herself as a clear supporter of the political left; and her feminist outlook simply goes without saying.

We met her in the fall of 1997 and had seven interviews with her over the following ten months. As with her mother, the venue for these interviews was always the family's small, wooden dining-room table. Family members often came in and out as we talked, though usually they left us to talk alone with Sara. She, in any case, was unperturbed by these comings and goings; and only when talking of her *novio* did she make sure that her words went unheard by others.

What follows are some of Sara's wanderings and ponderings—told with sound but no fury, signifying much about her developing life and, perhaps too, the evolving position of women in El Salvador.

W hen I think back to my earliest years, the person who stands out for me is Mama Ia. That's how my brother and sister and I call my grandma Julia. She's the one who was there taking care of me when I was small. My mother and father worked. Mama Ia lived with us in Zacamil, and everyone tells me I wouldn't go anywhere without her. If our family went for a trip, I'd put up a fuss and wouldn't go unless she joined us. I was very close to her. In a way, I still am.

But for years now she's been living over at my aunt Doris's house. The most we see her now is a week or so. I think she moved in with Doris's family when my cousins were born, and she stayed there because, well, because Doris had some family problems. With her husband, I mean. He drinks. And let's just say, my granny felt she ought to stay over there where she was needed more.

Selfishly, I wish she were living with us now. I even think it would be better for her. We'd pay more attention to her than they do over there. I know *I* would. I enjoy being with her, talking to her and hearing about her life. To me, she's a person I truly admire—what she managed despite everything, no?

You've been talking to her, right? So you know how hard her life was. I imagine you know more than I do even. Having to raise her daughters as a *soltera* [single woman] must have been tremendously hard on her. To put up with being a maid in your own relatives' house—hard, no? It brings tears to my mother's eyes whenever she talks about those years. The humiliation of it all, I mean. But Mama Ia, I don't think she felt humiliated by it. She did what she did in order to help push her daughters forward in life. Others devalued her, but she never lost a sense of her own worth. I can feel this when she talks. She has this composure, this understanding about things. And she *did* accomplish what she intended. My mother is deeply grateful to her for that. Each month when my mama gets her paycheck, she goes over to Mama Ia's and gives her a share of it. I tell you, I admire the way they are with each other.

I would like the chance, really, to know my grandma even more. When you're a child people don't explain much to you. I know, for example, that she had five children, but with whom and when I can't really say. I don't even know much about how she met and fell in love with my grandfather. There must have been someone before him, but I don't know anything about it. I suppose my mother knows, though she hasn't said anything either. And I don't ask. Maybe I ought to. Yet it feels a little disrespectful for me to pry into these things. Mama Ia must have gone through a lot. This is something I realize now, since I've grown up. I can tell. As a child I had no idea. To me, she was Mama Ia, who bought me clothes and dolls whenever she had some money, the person who took care of me. I loved her then and love her now. But when I start talking about it, I realize how little I actually know about her life.

When I think back about my childhood—the years before I went to school—it all seems so fuzzy to me. I once fell on my head when

I was six, and sometimes I think my memory got somewhat jostled by that fall. My sister, Yolanda, and I were over at my cousin's house. The three of us were playing with dolls. *Bueno*, we wanted to go up to the second floor they were constructing, and it meant going up a cement staircase. Yolanda is older than me, but she was scared of falling. So I said, "Give me your dolls, and I'll take them all up." I had my hands full and couldn't hold onto anything. So sure enough, I fell back onto a cabinet with all these porcelain things, and whaaack! my head got cut up badly. They sewed me up at the hospital and I'm fine now, but I've always wondered if that blow to my head made me forget so many things. Because really, those years are hard for me to remember. I don't seem to recall much.

I know I liked it over there in Zacamil. We moved from there when I was four years old—I think because of the war, though I'm not sure about that. I recall that over in Zacamil, which was a poorer area than here, there were lots of kids around all the time. You always had someone to play with, and I can remember vaguely roller skating and riding bikes. Yes, I played with both boys and girls. That was perfectly alright with my parents, they had nothing against that. Remember, I have a brother, Gerardo, so I was used to having him around with his friends.

Gerardo's a fine guy—he's over in Guatemala now studying to be a missionary—but back then he could be rough on me. *Here's* something I *do* remember clearly. I had my favorite doll, Yemi. A big plastic doll I'd received on my first birthday, I think it was. Yemi had these huge eyes that opened and closed. That is, before Gerardo got it into his head one day to jump on Yemi, and when he did, Yemi lost one of his eyes. I was furious with Gerardo, but I didn't say anything to anyone. All I did was console Yemi about the loss of his eye. To me, that was one of the worst things I remember from those years. That, and the fall from the staircase, and, oh yes, another time that I fell from a table [*Sara laughs*]. I was playing Superman with Gerardo. I got up on the table and leaped off, thinking maybe I could fly. And, of course, I wound up banging my head again. I think I was four then. It was before I went to school, to first grade, I'm sure of that. By then you've figured out you can't fly, right?

The place where I went to school from first grade through high school is La Asunción—a girl's school run by nuns. I went there along with Yolanda. She didn't like it much, but I did. My closest friendships today, even though I've been in university for three years, are girls I met at La Asunción. We grew up together and some of us are still really close.

The people who run La Asunción are the nuns there. The director, the coordinators of each grade, all are *hermanas* [sisters, nuns]. The teachers themselves are ordinary people like my mother. Though my mother didn't teach there. She was at another school.

At first I found it a little hard—the discipline is quite strict in religious schools. But later I realized that we had it easier than in other religious schools. Places like Betania, it was even stricter. Over there, the nuns go around in these long robes, and when you pass them in the hall you have to say *Bendito* and bow your head toward them in a reverent way. The nuns there are people you can't talk to. But at La Asunción there was none of that head-bowing—just a normal hello. And some of the nuns at my school were really approachable. You could even talk to them about boys. If you were talking to your friends about boys—like what happens in seventh and eighth grade, right?—and one of the nuns passed by, she might even join in the conversation, in a normal way. In my time at La Asunción it was an all-girls school. Now they're beginning to have boys there too, through sixth grade, I think. Maybe it's better that way. I can't really say. For me, being in an all-girls school was good. It gave me confidence to be just with girls in school. And especially in the upper grades it was easier not to have to deal with boys—to be distracted, no?

The distraction we had at school, if you can call it that, was the political situation in the country. The war. The older I got, the more I became aware of what was going on. The nuns talked about it and we, the students, talked too. In my first years at La Asunción, I knew things were happening, but nobody told us much about it. Not our teachers, and not even my parents. I guess they were trying to protect us, figuring we couldn't handle knowing the country was at war.

Yet even in first grade I knew something was happening. In San Salvador it wasn't like up north, like in Chalatenango, where there was fighting constantly going on between guerrillas and the army. Still, you'd see things on TV, and in the street you'd see burned-out cars and buses. And now and then something would happen in front of your eyes.

I remember one morning—this was when I was in third grade—an incident happened at La Asunción. We had just arrived at school, a little before seven in the morning. I was in my classroom, which faced the street. And just outside, suddenly, there were these gunshots. The teacher yelled at us, "Stay away from the windows! Get back!" There was a lot of shooting going on outside, and in a few minutes the ambulance came whirring into the area. Nobody said anything to us, not our teachers or anyone else. Only later I found out that the father of two girls had been shot down as he was bringing his daughters to school. He must have been someone involved with the FMLN, I later realized—I mean, years later I realized it. He was a well known union organizer, and some government soldiers, or others, killed him that day. At the time, I can remember coming home and telling my parents. They knew about it, but they didn't go into explanations with me. My mama doesn't like discussing politics. And my papa, when bad things like this happened, he'd say something like, "My daughter, the situation in the country isn't good. There're people here who aren't happy with the way things are and so they are doing things."

That was my father's way of talking to me, to us, when we were small. In a vague way, not really saying too much. He must have figured it was better not to involve us. He never told me when I was young that he himself sympathized with the guerrillas. And it wasn't until years later that I realized—my mama told me this—that she and my father had gone to the funeral of Monseñor Romero. Remember that? I was only three at the time, and they'd left me with Mama Ia. They went and they were shot at by government troops, or paramilitary people. A whole lot of folks got killed that day, and apparently it was an awful scene, with the mourners trampling over each other as they fled for safety. My mother was in shock from it. And the way I understand it, she wanted to leave the country after that. It was my father who said, "No, now is when the country needs us. We have to stay." I'm sure they had some arguments between them, but as a kid—you know, six or eight—I wasn't aware of their differences.

On the TV all you'd hear was the government's side of things. The TV commentators would say, "The guerrillas have done this and that." Or they'd say, "The guerrillas have gone into this place." The guerrillas were always the bad guys in the movie, right? But when I got a little older, maybe in seventh or eighth grade, my father would say small things that, well, that didn't directly contradict the government line, but he was suggesting that there was more than one way of looking at things. And at school, too, the nuns also indicated that there was another side to the story. They never took a clear position against the government. They never said, "We support this group, this political party." Oh no! It was prohibited to do that. You weren't allowed to engage in politics in the schools. But what happened is that almost all of my classmates were from families who supported the right wing. They supported the ARENA party. So the girls would go around singing the ARENA hymn, and they would say how much they liked those red-blue-white ARENA colors. For awhile when I was younger, I figured I was with ARENA too.

But as I said, around the time I got to be in eighth grade, or ninth grade for sure, I began to have other thoughts. I'd seek out a few friends here and there, and we'd talk to each other about what we called "the national reality." I wasn't an FMLN supporter then, because in my mind the guerrillas were still people I was afraid of. Yet I'd begun to see that there was a whole other reality that had to be considered. And at home, by then it was clear to me that my papa was seeing things the way I did. My mama not so much. She was against the fighting and refused to take sides. Yet my papa, he wasn't fighting with the guerrillas—no, nothing like that—but he was a sympathizer. That became clear to me.

What really changed me and made me feel things with even more conviction was the experience I had after I graduated high school. The war had ended in '92, and I graduated in '94. The nuns from our school were involved in various projects in some of the repopulated communities where the fighting had taken place. Lots of poor *campesinos*, in the north especially, were trying to rebuild their lives in these new communities. And some of the *hermanas* were up there helping in these projects. They'd been with the people during the war—not fighting with the guerrillas, but helping in humanitarian ways. And after the war, they continued to help out any way they could. I was aware of this when I was in high school. I had talked with some nuns and friends about the work the nuns were doing up north. And, well, I decided I wanted to go there myself, see if I could contribute in some way.

At first when I approached my parents about going, they were like, "Alright, that's fine." My mama told me, "If that's what you want, go forward with it!" I figured I had the green light to go. Then six months later, when I was about to leave, they suddenly changed their tune. On the one hand, since the project was organized by the *hermanas* and I was going to be living with them, well, it appeared safe. But on the other hand, my parents knew—we *all* knew this—that the area I was going to, Chalatenango, was an area where some of the worst fighting had taken place during the war. So now my father started telling me, "Finish your studies at university first, then go do this." And my mama started talking about all the dangers up there. Even Mama Ia, who was always so calm, she too started saying to me, "Sara, just the other day there was an attack on a bus, someone got killed, some girls were taken off to who knows where." And on and on, in that vein. Nobody told me, "No, you *cannot* go!" They simply tried to talk me out of it. Yet by then I was determined to go. I told my father I'd go for six months and then come back and take the examination to enter university. That was my intention when I left, though after I was up there for six months I couldn't leave. I felt I had to stay. I *wanted* to stay the full year. And so I did.

The community I went to was San José las Flores—a large community of maybe two hundred families. I lived there with the *hermanas* in a place that had once been a monastery. It was a good-sized building made of adobe bricks, and three *hermanas* lived there. I had my own room—*bueno*, actually a corner of the library that they curtained off so I could have some privacy. I ate all my meals with the *hermanas*, except when someone in the community invited me for lunch or dinner. It was comfortable enough, and yes, it was very safe. My parents even came up to visit a couple of times, and I think they calmed down some when they saw how it was.

When I first arrived there, it wasn't clear exactly what I would be doing. The way it works is that a volunteer comes to the community, and the directorate of the community decides where the volunteer can be helpful to them. There were lots of volunteers who had been to San José las Flores before me—and still volunteers go there. Most of them were foreigners, people from Spain and the United States. The city of Cambridge in Massachusetts is a "brother community" with San José las Flores, and there had been some volunteers from there before I arrived. The strange thing is, I was the first volunteer from within El Salvador. I think the people appreciated it, that someone from here came to help out.

Anyway, the way they decided to use me was as a teacher. That was fine with me. If they had wanted me to help organize a sewing project or anything else, I would have done that too. I was willing to do whatever they asked. At the time they told me, "We need you as a teacher— that's what we're lacking." You see, during the war all the schools up there had been closed down. The *campesinos* had been moving from place to place, and what they did is form *escuelas populares* [people's schools]. They didn't have real teachers. Those who could read and write a little taught the kids to read and write a little, so they'd have something to help them get ahead in life, not just be illiterate. They didn't have real classrooms either during the war. Wherever they were, in the mountains or even in caves sometimes, they'd do their teaching. Now that they'd resettled in San José las Flores, they wanted to set up real schools. But the teachers they had right then, people from the community, couldn't teach the upper grades. They hadn't got that far themselves. So they turned to me and asked if I'd teach sixth and seventh grade. I'm not a qualified teacher either, of course, but I figured that with some effort I could do it.

I taught two shifts, sixth grade in the morning and seventh in the afternoon. I was teaching everything—everything that the Ministry of

Education demands. Classes in the Spanish language, social sciences, natural sciences, math, even English. The way I knew what to do is that various teachers from the communities in the area would get together every fifteen days, and we'd work out our course plans according to the ministry's guidelines. That's how I got my support. Did I ask my mother for help? *Bueno*, I would have benefited, I'm sure, if I had consulted her. But I only saw her a few times that year, and to be honest, I wanted to do it on my own. That's the way I am. If I possibly can, I like to figure things out for myself. And with the support of friends up there, I was able to manage it. I'm not saying I was a great teacher, but I managed. And I think I did alright with the students.

The ones in my classes were about twelve or thirteen, with a few who were even older. Mostly girls, because boys at that age are already off working with their fathers in the *milpa* or they're working outside the community, say, in road construction. Many of the girls, too, would stop going to school after seventh grade. Either they were needed at home, or just as often they'd get together with some boy or simply get pregnant. There was a lot of that going on in my time there, particularly because there was a big road crew in the area and the girls would go off with this guy or that one and get pregnant. As a matter of fact, in my natural sciences class I decided to discuss the matter of pregnancy and reproduction and contraception with my students. They listened very seriously—I mean, with a few titters here and there—but, oh yes, they listened carefully. The problem is that so many of these kids, these girls, get very little affection or even attention at home. Their parents are too busy. So the first guy who comes along and showers them with attention, they fall in love and go running off with him.

For most kids, though, they managed to avoid this kind of thing. They studied, they wanted to learn. They know it's their only way of going on to something else and improving their situation. I liked teaching these kids. It was hard work for me, I was busy all the time preparing, but I loved it. And don't get me wrong, it wasn't just work. It was fun. Even in class we often had fun. I didn't run my classes in a strict way, the way I was taught in La Asunción. I had a kind of easy relationship with the students. I joked around with them, and they teased me back. Like one day I came in wearing a pair of slacks that was torn a bit. They immediately began saying to me, "Well, we see you've decided to take up the latest style now!" Things like that. Or sometimes during the rainy season we'd go out and play soccer. The soccer field would be full of mud, but we'd play anyway, slipping and sliding and getting covered with mud. And then we'd get into mud-ball fights. Yes, me too. And everyone would go home that day looking like the soccer field itself. No, the parents and *hermanas* said nothing to me about it. It was alright with them, I guess. And for me it was a way of really being with my students, being close to them. It made the work we did in class easier and better, I think.

I came to know many of these students really well. Their families, too. And they'd invite me to visit them, to eat with them. These people didn't have much. They're all *campesinos*, and they're living off the *maíz* and *frijol* they grow, and maybe a cow or two they might have. In some communities the people have more money because they have a relative who's gone to the United States and sends back some dollars. But not in San José las Flores. They don't have much.

Whatever they had, though, they served you when you came over. They'd always say something like, "Please forgive us that we don't have much to give you, that the food isn't this or that." Then they'd try to fill you up, almost as if it were the last meal in your life. They imagine you can eat the way they do, or even more. For me, a tortilla with some beans or cheese is enough. But for them, the men especially, they would eat eight tortillas and *el conque* [what's with it]. That's how they call it up there. *El conque* might be beans, cheese, an egg, or some soup. It isn't that the tortillas accompany the meal, but the other way around. The tortillas *are* the meal and the other things are what go with it, *el conque*. Anyway, I'd go eat with them and then I'd go home—sometimes in the pitch-dark alone, or sometimes the family would send someone to walk me back. No, I was never scared. I felt safe up there with those people. I came to trust them completely. And they trusted me too. By the time I'd been there a few months, I felt very comfortable with them. And I got to know them really well.

It was this process of getting to know these people that affected me deeply. Up until then I'd never known *campesinos*. And up until then the war had been something—how can I put it?—something less personal. Up in San José las Flores, all that I'd been thinking about the so-called national reality took on a personal reality for me.

Back in San Salvador I knew only a few people who'd lost family members in the war. Very few of my friends, and nobody in my family, had suffered directly. But in San José las Flores, it was different. Every family up there—I mean *everyone*—had lost someone from their family. Some people talked openly about what they had gone through and others preferred not to talk about anything. I suppose it was too painful to recall these things. In San José las Flores, everyone had supported the FMLN during the war—many as guerrillas, and the rest as collaborators. Look, in my classes I had a number of girls who had been with the guerrillas. One of them, a seventeen-year-old, had joined when she was twelve, and she'd spent a couple of years fighting alongside the men. She told me that at times she and other women had to carry wounded men on their backs, walking long distances to bring these men for medical help. This particular girl had used a machine gun, she had fought. And when I asked why she had joined, she said, "I couldn't stay on the sidelines and accept our situation. I had to see what I could do."

It was by getting to know people like her, talking to them about the war and their lives, that I came to have a greater understanding. I feel I learned from them. What exactly? *Bueno*, let me put it this way. I saw how much they had suffered during the war, how hard their lives had always been, and yet they somehow never lost their hope for a better way of life. These people never let themselves cave in, and they went on struggling, not letting anything get them too far down. For them, the war was worth it. That's how they see it. Before that, they had reached a point where they felt they had to fight. They couldn't stand how they were living, the exploitation, and so they were willing to fight for change.

And look, let's face it, here in El Salvador there has been so much exploitation and inequality. Like all over Latin America, no? If you know the history of our country, then you know that it's been this way from the beginning here. Ever since the Spanish conquest in the sixteenth century. When the Spaniards came here they regarded themselves as superior to the indigenous people, the Indians, and they exploited them. That's how it started and that's how it has continued. I mean, El Salvador isn't the only place in the world where this goes on. All over, you have people who put themselves above others, take advantage of them. Here, we've had the "fourteen families," right? And there's a number of other families, rich people, who've joined them, and together they have all this power and control. So naturally, there comes a point when those who have been subjugated finally say, "Enough! We won't put up with it anymore!" And if they can't change things through dialogue, then there's a war.

That's how I see it. I know there are other points of view, but to me this is the heart of what went on here. And if you ask me, I think the war might have ended differently—better for the people in Chalatenango and the other poor people in El Salvador—if certain things hadn't happened during the war. What things? Look, I'm not sure I ought to go into all this. Maybe it's foolish to talk so much [*Sara pauses and reflects for a moment*]. Alright, I'll tell you the way I see it. My view is that if the United States hadn't got into the war and thrown its weight to the side of the Fuerza Armada, then the FMLN probably would have won. That's what I've read, and that's what I understood in talking to people up in Chalatenango.

But that's the way the United States acts, no? I mean, speaking frankly, the U.S. advocates democracy, but more than anything else what they want is to be the ones calling the shots, the ones in control throughout this region. Look at what they did in Panama, Nicaragua. And look at what they did here. They don't want a situation to happen like in Cuba, so they intervene and try to control things, make sure it goes their way.

Without the U.S. having got involved here, the FMLN could have won the war outright. Sure, I would have preferred it that way. I know it would be utopian to imagine that the FMLN would have solved everything here. The FMLN has plenty of division within itself, and you can't know for sure how they would have managed things. But yes, I'd prefer it if they were in control. There would have been more sweeping reforms, more benefits for the poor. The land reform that took place after the war would have been more sweeping, better for the *campesinos*. Yes, I know a good deal of land was given over to *campesinos*, but it was done in such a way as to not challenge the real power structure of the country. The rich here still have their land and money—or most of it. And they still have lots of control. Less than before, I think, but still an awful lot.

For the people of San José las Flores, though, and also in many other communities, they *did* get something. They have their *milpas* now, they can make a living. To them, the war brought definite gains. Many of them are disappointed that things didn't work out even better. Yet they did get something, no doubt about it. And if you ask them—which I did—whether they expect another war, they say, "No, we've had enough fighting. We don't want any more war." So from what I've seen, I think the war is over here. At least for now it is.

And from what I could see, there have been important changes, improvements because of the war. Not just economic improvements. Social improvements, too. Take what's happened for the women in these places. All these communities have women's directorates now, and they've become aware of their rights as women. All this is because of the war, I think. The women up there said, "We're not going to stay in the house taking care of the kids, we're going to fight too." From that moment on, when they grabbed rifles and went to fight, things shifted. You know who the majority of the *radistas* were in the war, right? Women! Lots of women fought with the FMLN and contributed to the struggle. That's led to a change in their lives, a change in how they are regarded in their families. I've seen it in Chalatenango, and I'm sure it's happened elsewhere too. To me, this is an undeniable benefit from the war. Not one that was planned, maybe, but one that happened.

Do *I* think I would have joined the women in the guerrillas if I'd been living up there at the time? Well, you know, that's a question I've asked myself several times. Putting myself in their shoes—that is, if I'd been living up there and of the right age—then yes, I think I would have fought. I'm not sure I could have borne the hardship of it, yet I think I would have tried. And I think, even living in San Salvador, if I knew then what I know now, and if I'd been old enough, I would have collaborated with the FMLN. I'd have helped in one way or another. Going off to the *monte* and fighting, I'm not sure. But participate in some way, I'm sure I would have.

To me, the experience of being up in Chalatenango was the most powerful experience in my life so far. I came away from it knowing that I wanted to find a way to contribute more, to go on with that kind of work somehow. I still go up there and visit—maybe three times a year. I spend a week or so, and sometimes my sister joins me now. I don't do much work there. It's more a way of keeping up my connection with the people.

I suppose if I were free to decide, I'd have spent more time there. I might even go back tomorrow—really! But no, I can't do that. I promised my parents I'd finish my university studies before doing anything else, and I owe it to them to do this. They've sacrificed a great deal. It's been a big hardship for them to send all three of us to university, so I feel I must continue. And besides, I can see now that if I have more education behind me, I'll be more effective in whatever I do in the future.

When I came back from Chalatenango and started university, I wasn't exactly sure what I wanted to study at first. I decided to choose communications, and I'm happy with it. It's a five-year program and I'm in my third year now. You have a lot of leeway in this field—there're many directions I can take. By now I've ruled out journalism. You have to be able to write quickly, with pressure on you. I'm no good at that. What interests me more is photography and television. I don't mean being a TV commentator, appearing in front of the cameras. No, that's not for me. But the production side, documenting what goes on here—that's what I think I want to do. Here in El Salvador we're not very developed in this area, in communications. We need much more objectivity and open discussion of what is happening. That's where I want to make a contribution, but exactly how I haven't figured out yet.

I'm lucky, I think, to be having this kind of opportunity—to study, to do something with my life. I mean, my mama has done a lot with her life too. I respect what she's accomplished. But look what happened to the women in my grandmother's generation. Both my grandmas are intelligent women, yet neither had the chance to get educated. Third grade is as far as they went. Or maybe it was only second grade. That's how it was then. Only if you came from the upper class did you have a chance to study more. And even for those women it wasn't a question of studying so you would have a career. It was just so you could read and write. A woman's job then was to be a housewife. And if she was wealthy her job was to supervise the servants in the house, to see to it that her husband was taken care of.

Now all that's changed. Since my mother's generation, I'd say. Women are able to have careers outside the house. More and more, there's been an opening up in this way. This is still a *machista* place, that's sure. Yet if you look around now you see women in almost every area. I think these days we have ten or fifteen women in the Asamblea Legislativa. About seven or eight women *diputadas* are from the FMLN alone. This is a big change here. And in time, there'll be even more improvements in this way. The role of women as just housewives is a thing that's changing. Thank goodness!

In our house—I'm not saying we're typical, but there's more and more families like us—the housework is done by everyone. We used to have a maid when my brother and sister and I were small. No more. We all pitch in now. The sweeping up, the laundry, the cooking—all of us do it. Yes, my father too. He's no *machista*, he pitches in along with everyone else. Actually, it's sort of amusing to see my grandmother when she visits us. My father's mother, I'm talking about. When she comes for a visit and sees my father ironing his own shirt or washing the dishes, well, she winces. She doesn't go along with this way. My father, though, has a deep sense of egalitarianism, and he insists on doing his part. I don't think he enjoys it. He just feels it's his duty to do these things, and he does.

Now, my brother—he actually *likes* doing some of this work around the house. Ironing clothes is something he likes. And cooking too. Especially cooking. He's very good at it. For awhile, a couple years back, he was the one who did most of the cooking in the house. He was home in the mornings and didn't go to university until the afternoon. So he cooked our big meal, our lunch, each day. He's an inventor in the kitchen. He just opens the refrigerator and whatever is there he turns into something. Soups, vegetable dishes, *chile con carne*—you name it, and he can figure out how to make it. He's got a real talent for it. I used to like it when he cooked. It tasted good, and you could see he really enjoyed cooking for all of us.

But my brother is gone from home these days. He left last year for Guatemala. Why? Oh, he's studying there to be a missionary with the Evangelicals. He was studying engineering here, but now he's shifted direction. He wants to work with people, bringing the word of God. It's a good thing to do—even though it means he's not here cooking anymore, right?

No, seriously, I think he's taken a good direction for himself. To bring the word of God to people is a good thing. I'm not part of the Evangelicals myself. I'm more with the Catholic Church, that's been my education. Still, I support what he's doing.

And you know, in a way the Evangelicals have sort of taken their cue from some of what the Catholic Church did here. What I mean is this. During the war the Catholic Church was split, right? Part supported the oligarchy here, and part moved closer to the poor. Those *comunidades eclesiales de base* [Christian-base communities], the ones supported by Monseñor Romero, were formed by the Catholic Church. The nuns and priests in these communities helped the people organize themselves, to work together to better their lives. The *hermanas* I worked with in San José las Flores were all linked with that part of the Church. When I was up there, besides teaching I used to go with the *hermanas* and we'd read the Bible together with people in the community. This brought the Church closer to the people, and I think it strengthened the people's faith in the Church. Many people who fought with the FMLN, they are believers—they're not atheists, not at all.

Anyway, the Evangelicals also gained strength during the war. They saw what the Catholic Church was doing with their *comunidades eclesiales de base,* and they too began to organize more on the community level. They reached out and brought the word of God to people. The Evangelicals have small, unpretentious churches. And their religious service is full of music and song that is really lively, that reaches the people. Unlike the Catholic Church they preach more of a one-to-one relation-ship with God. No saints, no going to confession—just one-to-one with God. And they've been very successful. They're booming here in El Sal-vador. Since the war people have been looking for something to believe in, have faith in. Something besides political parties. And when they ask themselves what they can believe in, it is God they turn to. *Primero Dios* [God first; it's up to God]. And the Evangelicals are benefiting from this trend. They're helping to serve the people in the communities they're in. I think it's a good thing. I'm all for the kind of work they're doing.

❧

What do I do for fun? A good question. I guess I've made it sound like my life is all work and no fun, haven't I? Sometimes I feel that way myself these days. My studies take a lot out of me. Sometimes I only get a couple of hours of sleep at night. In the armchair in the salon. I don't even have the strength to go upstairs and climb into the upper bunk where I sleep. My parents have started to get on my back about this. They think I'm developing bad habits, something like that.

But really, I *do* manage to have fun. Quite a bit. I've got many girl-friends and we do things together—go to the movies, parties. You know, the usual. My sister, Yolanda, she's the one who stays at home more. She's more reserved than I am, less social. My mother tells me I should take her along with me, the way she used to do with my aunt, Doris, who was also more reserved. My mama is always encouraging me, "Look, why not invite Yolanda to go along with you and the others? Be considerate." And I do, really I do. My sister and I are closer these days than ever. I wear her clothes, she wears mine. We *are* close. I guess my mama wants me to do exactly like she did with Doris, and I keep saying, "Look, I'm *me* and you are *you*." I can't do things just like she did. She had her ways, which were a little more conservative than mine. Me, my generation, is a little different in certain ways.

About boys, yes. My generation is a little different from my parents' generation. It's hard for them to accept, but that's how it is. Yes, yes, I have a *novio*. For two years I've been with Enrique. It was hard for them to accept this, at first especially. Now things have calmed down, normal. Though they have their ideas about how one should act, and I have mine.

Before Enrique—Quique, I call him—there were a couple of guys I liked, but it wasn't anything serious. Even back then when things were not serious, I had my parents watching over my shoulder. When I was in high school my father told me, "Male friends, alright. But *novios*, not until you're older—not until you've finished with high school." Then when I finished high school my father was like, "Listen, Sara, it's best for you to finish your university studies before you start with boyfriends. Wait until then!" [*Sara laughs*]. With my father you could see there'd be no end to it. My mother, she felt the same maybe, but the way she went about it was to warn me, "Be careful now, Sara. Don't do anything foolish." And the worst—though the most amusing, I have to say—was my brother. When my brother was here, if Quique or any other guy came around the house, he would snarl at them. Really! He took it on himself to be my protector, and he was nasty to any guy who showed up here.

At this point things are calmer now. My snarling brother is out of the house, right? No, seriously, my parents seem to have accepted the idea that Quique is my *novio*. You see this amethyst? Quique gave it to me when we started going together. I had to hide it at first. But eventually my mother saw it, and we had a conversation, and now all is fine. My parents know I'm involved with him. More than that, I don't really go into with them.

I know that if I went to my mama she'd listen carefully to whatever I told her. She would like me to talk openly with her about Quique and everything else. But a mother is a mother, and she is always going to be offering advice to her daughter. And at times that's exactly what I do *not* want. I only want to be heard, listened to—without being told what to do. I want to figure things out for myself. If I need to have somebody be tough on me, judge me, *I* want to be the one who does it.

So these days the people I talk to are my friends. Some of them have *novios*, and we talk about our experiences. Sometimes very openly. We ask each other, "What do you think about having sexual relations with your boyfriend? Have you done this or that? What would your parents say?" Frankly, I'm a little more closed than some of my friends when it comes to talking about intimate things. Certain intimate things, certain caresses, say, I don't discuss with anyone. Only with Quique. And if I'm having some problems with him, I usually try to figure it out myself. Sometimes I'll sit down and write what I'm feeling, vent things that way. Then I tear up what I've written—it's not poetry or anything like that. I tear it up and burn it.

With my friends, though, I do feel I can talk about important things. Not details so much, but in general. We don't all agree about everything. Some of my friends have this view that they want to stay virgins until they get married. I respect their views, I do. My own thinking is different on that. I know my parents think girls—and boys too, by the way—should stay virgins until they marry. My mama has not really come out and stated this, but she'll say things like, "Remember, it's not all rose-colored or easy. If one gets pregnant it's not so easy, and often it's the parents who get burdened with the situation." And so on, like that. Even my Mama Ia has this view, I think. But if anything happened to me, she wouldn't be so judgmental like my parents, I'm sure of that.

You see, my view—I'll tell you frankly—my thinking is that if a girl is in love with someone, and she has sexual relations because she wants to share this intimacy with him, well, there's nothing wrong with that. I have several friends who think as I do, and some have already had sexual relations. To me, that's fine and I could see that happening to me too. Yes, I could. And if the man I eventually marry couldn't accept me because I wasn't a virgin, I'd feel bad—bad not because I wasn't a virgin, but bad because I'd have chosen the wrong man. What I want to say is that a woman has her value because of who she is, not because she has her hymen intact on her wedding night, right? And, I tell you, from what I can see among my friends, there's a change in thinking along these lines. I'm not talking about jumping into bed with a guy you just meet and feel attracted to, and fummmm!, having sex with him. But with one's *novio*, with someone you love—yes, why not? There's more acceptance of this now, I think, than there was in my mama's time.

❧

To me, all this business about virginity or nonvirginity is not the big issue. To me, a more important question is who you marry and when. And the truth is, I know I'm not ready to get married now. Not next year or the year after that either. My thought is that the earliest I'll get married is when I'm twenty-eight or twenty-nine.

Yes, I've discussed this with Quique. He knows how I feel. I mean, sometimes when we're talking we'll say, "When we get married, then this and that and so on." But it's more a way of talking. And sometimes when I pass a beautiful little church I've thought, "Here's a place I'd like to get married in." And yes, I've thought about how it might be—even what kind of dress and all. Not something white exactly, more cream or pearl colored. Yes, I admit, I think about this now and then. But really, not so much these days.

My view is—I've told this to Quique—we are together now and we are sharing so many experiences together and if someday this leads to marriage, good, great. If not, then at least we've lived our time together well. I don't mean to be negative and fatalistic—just realistic. I don't want to make up fairy tales about my prince. God alone knows who I'll marry. I don't know, and I don't want to know. I've been open with him about this, and he accepts what I'm saying. He's studying psychology, so he's got to be pretty sensitive, no? But really, his way of looking at things is a little more planned out than mine, and he's thinking about marrying me. I don't think it's because he loves me more than I love him. It's just that we have somewhat different ways of looking at things, at our future.

I know lots of girls—not so much my friends, but other girls—who have the idea of getting married quickly. Get married, go to work, have kids, and so on. The *novio* they're with now is the one they're going to marry and spend their lives with. Their whole lives!

Me, I have another way of looking at things. My vision is that—how can I say this exactly?—*bueno*, it's the idea that there is so much to do in life. There're so many things I want to experience *before* settling down into family life. I want to finish my studies, find work, get stabilized economically a little. Yet even before that, I want the chance to have a little freedom. The freedom, I mean, to develop myself more as a person, which is another step in feeling more complete as a woman. For example,

I'd like to travel some. I've never been out of Central America. I'd like to see other places. No, not the United States so much. *Bueno*, if you know anyone who's going to offer me a free airplane ticket to go there, I'll accept! But seriously, more than the U.S., I'd like to go to Europe and South America. I have friends in some of these places, and I'd like to visit. And after that, I'd like to put in another year in Chalatenango. Or if not there, someplace else where I can make a contribution.

Anyway, that's my idea. A real agenda, no? I mean, yes, I want to get married and have children. But not now. I feel I've got so much more to see and learn, and I want to do it. I think I'll manage it. I've been fortunate so far this way. My parents, when all is said and done, they've always gone along with me. I can count on them, and I can count on myself. And I think I know what I want. Yes, I do. *Sí, sí.*

Some Afterwords

This book was originally intended to end on the optimistic note from Sara, her *sí, sí* to life: an incomplete ending perhaps, but one with a certain emotional appeal. However, some of our early readers felt there needed to be more analysis, so in January 1999 the three of us met again to come up with a new ending. We decided to do it in dialogue form. But where, we wondered, should we start?

GLORIA: The main point, it seems to me, is one that rings out loud and clear in all the stories of the women in this book—the *machismo* in our society. And how the women in their various ways have sought to deal with it, and more and more are attempting to fight it.

MARTA: When you came to us that first time, Mike—remember, Gloria and I invited you out to that café where women like to go have tea [*laughs*]—and you suggested doing a book on

Salvadoran women. *Bueno*, I felt, this is a fine idea. Because I'm not aware of any book on Salvadoran women's lives.

GLORIA: There are some books on this aspect or that aspect of women, but no life histories such as we've done.

MARTA: And you know why? It's because nobody has taken women here seriously. Nobody has wanted to read about the lives of women. Not men, for sure. And up until recently, not women either!

GLORIA: Though it's changing now, maybe since the war. It's one of the only good things that came out of our awful civil war here. Women's involvement in the war as combatants seemed to change some views about women, especially among the lower class who fought in the war. And while I'm no leftist, as you know, I do believe there's been a strengthening, an improvement, in the image of women in the last decade or so.

MARTA: Actually, to this day the word "feminist" still has a pejorative meaning even among women themselves, as if it meant they hate men. Many women here strive for social and personal equality with men, but not many would label themselves "feminists."

MIKE: Among the women in our book, not one defines herself as a "feminist." Not even Sara and Dulce, who to me seemed quite obviously to be feminists. Not Lupe either, though that was probably more a question of her not being fully aware of the meaning of the term.

GLORIA: But to me, the main point is that whether women are calling themselves feminists or not, there *is* greater support now for the idea of women having equality with men. Look at the way María and Lupe have managed this in their own households. Compare that with the humiliations and abuses of Lupe's mother, Niña Dolores. She felt she had to put up with those abuses, that there was no other way. I tell you, it was painful listening to her. To her, and to Niña Julia, too. Imagine, she was raped twice and she felt she had to keep her mouth shut, not complain, because *she* would have been the one who got the bad name. And I think it would have gone that way too—she's not exaggerating.

MARTA: Not at all. But you can see how things have changed by looking at how her daughter, Dulce, and her granddaughter, Sara, assume an equality with men.

MIKE: Interestingly, in the upper class, Monica does not assume this equality. Do you think her point of view is unusual for her class?

GLORIA: It depends. In many upper-class families there is a sense of equality, especially when the woman is educated. There is definitely less abuse and humiliation than in the lower class. And if you look at Monica's educated daughter, she doesn't accept her mother's ideas.

MARTA: I feel the main thing to emphasize is a trend that's beginning to support equality between the sexes. I wouldn't want to go so far as to say that *machismo* is about to disappear. It's still a very potent force here, and often women themselves support it. Most especially in the very class where the abuse is worst—the lower class.

GLORIA: Yes, that's true. The lower-class family in our book, because they fought in the war and were exposed to those talks on equality—remember, Lupe is giving talks on this herself—well, they are different from the majority of lower-class women, who have yet to be exposed to this new thinking. These other lower-class women inculcate *machista* values in their children, boys and girls alike.

MIKE: I recall how the midwife, according to Niña Dolores, was getting paid more if she delivered a boy, no?

MARTA: Right. Boys are valued more, especially in the *campo*. They're a social security system for the parents when they get older. The way the *campesinos* look at it, boys will work in the fields, or somewhere else, and hopefully they'll take care of you when you're old. They figure girls can cause problems. They'll come back with their children and need to be taken care of.

MIKE: And yet we can see from the *campesina* women in the book that changes are going on there, even in the *campo*.

MARTA: To my mind, the real issue is one of education. That and exposure to the idea of equal opportunities and social rights for both sexes. And in a way, all classes are now being exposed to these ideas. On TV, for example, programs that come from Europe and the United States. Also, with so many Salvadorans from all classes going to the United States to study or work, well, they come back with these ideas of equality for women, and this is pushing things in a good direction—toward greater fairness and justice for women. But I believe it's among the upper and middle class that the impact is greater. It's women from these classes who are leaders in the various feminist groups and women's organizations, and they're going out to the *campo* and educating the *campesinos*—as in Henríquez. You see how it is with Lupe, right? She gets instruction from women from the capital and she, in turn, is passing on the word to others. Or like Sara, what she is doing out in that community in Chalatenango that she visits. Directly or indirectly, she's getting across the message to women that they have more possibilities, more rights.

MIKE: To me—to an outsider—it seems that since the war there's been a good deal of social legislation supporting women's rights.

MARTA: Yes, the *Codigo de Familia* [family code] came out four or five years ago and is now part of the legal system here. It covers a number of issues, including personal relations within the family, and in essence, it provides more protection for women.

GLORIA: Yes. There's a section in the code stating that nobody—meaning the husband, of course—can limit the right of his partner from working or studying outside the house. And even a phrase stating that the care of the children is the responsibility of *both* parents. I don't suppose it's going to be possible to enforce a lot of this if the husband stands in the way. But the mere existence of this code *is* important, a good step for us.

MARTA: More to the point, maybe, is the fact that women are beginning to realize that they don't have to tolerate physical abuse anymore. We now have hot lines here that women can use to call various agencies if they are being abused. And women can, and sometimes *do*, take their husbands to court. We all know about this from the newspapers. Even women who can't read, they hear this is happening. It's no longer as in Niña Dolores's time, when there was no recourse. She was beaten all the time and there was nothing she felt she could do about it. It was just the way of the world, her world at the time. Today, her daughter Lupe would never stand for that from her husband.

GLORIA: And he knows it. So he wouldn't touch her, I think.

MIKE: Nor María either, she wouldn't put up with it.

MARTA: Absolutely not! She wouldn't bother taking him to court though. She'd beat *him* up!

GLORIA: And he knows that too! Really, *en serio*, there has been a change. More legal protection and more awareness. That's the real point. Women are more aware these days.

MIKE: My impression is that education has been the major influence here. Apart from specific education about how to deal with abuse, there's the vast improvement in educational possibilities for women generally, and this has enabled women to struggle against *machismo* in all its forms. I pointed to this in the introduction, and I think the women's stories, in all three families, indicate how there is growing support for women's education.

MARTA: That's true, no doubt about it. I also look at my family and I can see how true this is, how the trend is going.

GLORIA: Yes, weren't you saying, Marta, how your mother had wanted to study in the university and her father told her, "No way!"

MARTA: That's right. She had wanted to be a physician and she wound up working in my grandfather's bookstore, reading medical books on the side—to this day she still reads anything she sees about medical treatments—but she never got to go to university.

GLORIA: And my mother had wanted to study biology and psychology in the university—which wasn't common for women to do at that time. My grandfather preferred that she study art and music, which were more the usual thing that women studied. So she wound up doing what he wanted.

MARTA: But both our mothers encouraged us to get an education, the kind of training that seemed best to *us*. And I've encouraged my daughters to do likewise. My older daughter is studying economics and my younger one looks as if she's going to take up special education and be a physiotherapist for children.

GLORIA: And me, I have no daughter. My son is only eleven. He's a good student. The only place I'm pushing him these days is to learn how to cook, how to make his own bed—not to expect women to do this for him all the time.

MIKE: And does he complain?

GLORIA: Sometimes, but he does it. And look, it's not so uncommon these days for women to take this approach to their sons. Dulce did it with her son. Lupe is doing it with hers. Maybe Monica wouldn't do it, but I wouldn't be surprised if Paulina does when she becomes a mother. And if you ask me, this represents an enormous shift here. I've known it's going on, but to hear these women talk about it in detail was for me very encouraging.

MARTA: Definitely. And I want to add something we haven't pointed out. Mike, you were asking me before whether I felt there is now a solidarity among Salvadoran women. And I've thought about it, and sad to say, I think there is not. Or put it this way, it exists among *some* of us—Gloria and I have such a feeling, say. And among women like Lupe and María who were exposed to this kind of thinking, through lectures and talks among themselves, yes, there is a sense of solidarity. But not among all women, for sure.

GLORIA: Yes, take Monica, or Niña Cecilia, or Paulina. They're not feeling a solidarity with women of the lower class, say, with the *muchachas* who work for them. Their attitude is not like Dulce's attitude, which, by the way, was unusual for a middle-class woman—I mean, her attitude toward the women who worked for her. She was influenced, I imagine, by the humiliations she experienced when her own mother was working as a *muchacha*.

MIKE: But speaking in general, what you're saying is that the class structure in El Salvador interferes with women's sense of solidarity.

MARTA: You know I'm not so fond of some of your socialist ideas and ideology, Mike. But specifically, in this instance, yes, women from different classes often don't feel on a par with each other and they don't have a sense of solidarity.

MIKE: Within a given social class, do you think there is a sense of solidarity among the women?

GLORIA: Yes, there's a feeling of solidarity with other women who are living the same kind of lifestyle, facing the same kind of daily problems with their lives. Wouldn't you say so, Marta?

MARTA: Yes. And sometimes across classes. Occasionally. Look, in my house I do what Dulce did. The young woman who works for us is pretty much part of our family, a friend to my daughters. She's one of us. Part of our household of women, so to speak. There are no men around to instruct us that this is no way to run things. So we do it our way. Nice, no?

GLORIA: Nice, yes. And by the way, Mike, how should I put this? *Bueno*, don't be insulted, alright? But since we're here in your place, and there's no *muchacha* around for you to call, I'm thirsty, so maybe you'll go get us some water, no?

MARTA: Make it coffee, as long as you're at it, alright?

❧

MIKE: Marta, you were making a point about your "household of women." It's an important point, I think—this whole matter of matriarchies here in El Salvador. The statistics I received indicate about 30 percent of Salvadoran families are headed by women.

GLORIA: I wouldn't be surprised if that's an underestimate. In the city, for sure, the percentage is greater. And among the lower class it's higher than in the middle and upper class.

MARTA: The war pushed this percentage higher. Lots of men were killed. And then too, you've got so many men—like Niña Dolores's sons—who are up in the U.S. trying to make some dollars. So yes, more than ever you have women who are raising families by themselves.

MIKE: And has the shift affected the image women—and for that matter, men—have of women, of their strengths and valor?

GLORIA: One would like to imagine that it has provided a sense of women's strength, yet realistically I'm not sure it has. People, men and women alike, seem to take it for granted that women do this. Maybe up to a point, among women, there is a certain admiration for women like Niña Julia, who managed to raise her daughters with hardly any help from men. But there is also a stigma, a sense that these women are in some way loose women. A woman living alone is very likely to get a bad reputation. So what happens is that many women left alone will look for a man to be together with, to get *ajuntada*. They'll take a bum sometimes, just to have the help, and hope that he'll protect her. And also, that way she can avoid, maybe, getting a reputation as a loose woman. You remember, that's what Niña Dolores did. In the middle and upper class, there's a stigma too, but the women in these classes know better how to take care of themselves. If they don't have their own means of support, then they know better how to protect themselves legally.

MARTA: What Gloria is saying is true, but I would put a somewhat more positive emphasis on the whole matter of matriarchies. It's one of the ironies in our patriarchal culture that women actually are responsible for raising so many families on their own. And the way I see it is that the fact we have succeeded in doing this *does* give us a sense of our own possibilities, our own strength. Look, Gloria and I are both divorced, and we've both had to raise our children by ourselves with the help of our mothers, who are also alone. Gloria has her sister and brother-in-law there. But in my case, there are no men in the house. And I'll tell you honestly, when any one of us does bring a man to the house, a boyfriend, say, we are very hesitant to give him any sway over us. He's got to watch his step. Sure, there's some suspicion there. Not hatred, not even dislike. Just a kind of solidarity between us and a determination that we conduct the household as we see fit. Maybe I'm speaking from my experience alone, but I'm sure the experience gives us a sense of our own capabilities as women. But look, we're not alone in this. Take Niña Julia. Look at her feisty determination to do things her way. She even goes so far as to say that she didn't want to live together with a man—the father of Dulce—because she wasn't about to let him control or abuse her. And she did do it her way. I admire her, really I do.

MIKE: I noticed you hit it off really well with her, you were the one she seemed to confide in the most, Marta. Did you sense there was a comradeship there?

MARTA: I hadn't thought of it in those terms, but now that you mention it—maybe so. I know this, though I haven't talked about it with you, Mike. If there's one part in the book that troubles me, it's the various revelations she made to me regarding her experiences with men, the two times she was raped, which I have misgivings about seeing in print.

GLORIA: It makes me uncomfortable too, but after all, she did give us permission to print it, didn't she?

MARTA: Yes, but her daughters and granddaughters aren't aware of these things, and it troubles me what they will feel on reading it. I mean, I'm aware that the material gives a true sense of her life—truer than if we deleted it.

MIKE: And we do have a certain obligation to the readers, no? To not hide material that renders the lives of the women more revealing and compelling. I understand your dilemma, our dilemma, here. But up to a point I feel these ethical qualms are unavoidable. I know you feel this tie to Niña Julia, but what should we do—delete the material?

MARTA: No. I'm just saying it leaves me uneasy.

MIKE: I tell you, I've got a similar problem. With Monica. Not for
          the same reason as you do, Marta. Actually, for the opposite
          reason. *She* assumed a kind of identity with me, I think, based
          on the fact that I'm from the United States and therefore
          maybe shared her political outlook. And as you know, I
          don't. My views are more leftist than I think she imagined.
          What I tell myself, probably trying to feel less guilty, is that
          I edited her story fairly. Indeed, she read it herself and felt
          so. But my uneasiness, my guilt really, has to do with my
          sense that if she had known my political orientation at the
          start, she wouldn't have consented to the interviews.

GLORIA: Probably not. Or at least she would have been more inhib-
          ited, I think. But I know she liked you, so I think she'll forgive
          you. I think you can rest easy on that one. You, after all, are
          only an intellectual. You didn't go shoot anybody because of
          your beliefs.

MARTA: Now that I know you better, Mike, and I see that you are fair
          despite your socialist ideas, and that the book came out fair,
          well, I can live with your views. In the beginning, though, I
          was pretty worried. I was asking myself, "Who am I getting
          involved with here?"

MIKE: You too, Gloria, you had trouble with my leftist political
          leanings, no?

GLORIA: At first, yes, I was sort of shocked. You weren't here during
          the war, Mike, so frankly it's hard for you to understand
          what we went through. The stories in the book give you some
          idea of how it was for all of us. I don't want to go into my
          family's problems so much. Enough to say, maybe, that the
          guerrillas almost killed my father. They robbed him at gun-
          point as he was driving out to pay the workers on his farm.
          "For the cause," they said. And this is just one incident. So
          it leaves you with a feeling about the guerrillas. To me, the

guerrillas' view that they had to use violence to achieve their political ends is something I can't accept.

MARTA: Yes, it was hard to talk to those who actually had been fighting with the guerrillas. Remember how hard it was for me, and Gloria too, if I'm not wrong, to go out there and speak with the *campesinas* who'd fought with the FMLN? This was the first time I'd ever spoken directly to people who had fought with the guerrillas.

GLORIA: For me too.

MIKE: Yes, I remember how it was. Every time one of them mentioned anything about the war, you tried to change the subject.

GLORIA: It was hard to hear. I didn't want to get into that with them.

MARTA: The same for me. Though by the time we had interviewed them each a few times, I began to see how the political situation looked from their point of view. I think it helped that none of them had gone into the war as a committed ideologue. They drifted into the guerrillas or were drafted—as with Niña Dolores—and for them there was maybe no other way. That's the tragedy of the thing. You see, for them the civil war did make sense, it was their way of being heard. The interviews with them made me see this. Until then I had no sympathy with those people at all. I mean, I'm no leftist. But I do see why *they* took the path they did.

GLORIA: But you know something, Marta? Before doing this book, knowing you as a psychologist at the Student Counseling Services, I'd had the impression you were more sympathetic to the left than you evidently were.

MARTA: What, *me*? Not at all. Actually, I had you figured as more pro-ARENA than you seem to be.

MIKE: You two didn't know each other's political sympathies very much, did you? To me, that's a little hard to imagine.

GLORIA: Look, until recently here in El Salvador, hardly anyone talked openly about politics. If we had tried to interview the middle- and upper-class families only a couple of years back, say, in 1995, they would have dodged all political questions. Only the *campesina* family would have talked, and that's because they were active in fighting for the FMLN. There's still a huge legacy of fear there. And you saw how careful Dulce and Monica were when we brought up the subject. Sara, too, though eventually she felt comfortable enough to reveal her thinking. Maybe because she sensed you were sympathetic, Mike.

MIKE: Yes, I think with Sara I tipped my hand, and it may have helped. Even if it made the two of you somewhat uncomfortable!

GLORIA: By then, no. I'd got used to you—at least regarding your politics. Regarding other things, who could get used to *that*?

MIKE: You're referring to my pushing you hard to meet deadlines, that stuff?

GLORIA: With you—I can speak frankly, can't I?—it's more than just a gringo versus a Latin mentality. Really you're just too perfectionist, too impatient. You refused to accept that sometimes the electricity isn't working in the city, sometimes computers break down. You were too inflexible.

MIKE: My Palestinian woman colleague said the same. I think I was inflexible at times. But to me it seems more a question of a different cultural approach to these things. Was my being a man also a problem? I know it was when I was working with my Palestinian colleague. I felt some deep-seated male chauvinistic attitudes got in the way. I'd like to think I've overcome this, though. Did sexual politics disrupt our working together, do you think?

GLORIA: No, I'll give you credit for that. I feel you were sensitive on those issues. What do you think, Marta?

MARTA: I agree. Except for one thing. I've never gone into this with you, though perhaps I should have. When you first told us you thought we would have to ask our subjects questions about sex—honeymoon experiences, virginity, and all that. Well, I gulped when I heard that. I couldn't imagine myself asking Salvadoran women, particularly older women, that type of question. It's one thing to do this as a psychologist with a patient who comes for counseling, but it's quite another matter to ask such questions to women who are simply talking about their lives. I felt very, very reluctant to do it.

MIKE: Did you sense—let me put it in the most blunt way—did you feel in a way that I was forcing my views, myself, on the two of you?

MARTA: The truth? Yes. I didn't see how I could ask.

GLORIA: Me neither. I also felt you were, as you put it, "forcing" yourself on us. And you notice, I never did go through with it. I couldn't get the questions out, even though I understood the material would be important. To ask the grandmothers was impossible for me. Not for you, Marta, you somehow managed it.

MARTA: Yes, somehow. I wouldn't say the women went into great detail. They were rather reserved, don't you think?

MIKE: The details were not so important—and actually I would have edited them out. What seemed important to me was to get some idea about their sentiments and feelings about some of their sexual experiences. How they approached the whole matter of sex, their thinking about virginity. And I feel we did get that material. That *you* did, Marta. And to me what they said rang true.

MARTA: Oh, I think what they said was accurate. It took time before they, and I, really could talk about it. But, in retrospect, I think the sexual material was worth asking, and I've long ago forgiven you for pushing us to do it.

MIKE: I appreciate that. Actually, I don't know how readers will react to the dialogue we've been having—our disagreements and all that. Personally, I feel a lot of this kind of thing is unavoidable, no matter how you try to avoid it. The gringo in me, perhaps, does want to think that it has ended well between us. And I do feel it has.

MARTA: I agree.

GLORIA: Same here. But let me ask you this, Mike. How do you feel about closing the book with this dialogue? You seemed to have your hesitations at first, no?

MIKE: I did, yes. But I think it adds something, some further analysis of various points in the book. It's just that I might have preferred to end with one of our subjects speaking. And I especially liked Sara's final words, her optimistic note about her life. But closing with this dialogue might work too. What do you think?

GLORIA: *Sí.*

MARTA: *Sí, sí.*

Chronology

1524   As part of Spain's conquests in the New World (starting in 1492), the Spanish commander Pedro de Alvarado and his troops entered the territory of what today is El Salvador. At the time its two major indigenous peoples were the Pipil tribe in western and central El Salvador and the Lenca tribe in the east. The Indians quickly fell victim to the superior weaponry of the Spanish and to the various diseases that the conquerors happened to be carrying.

1821   In the wave of independence movements that swept through the Spanish-controlled territories of the entire region, the territory of Guatemala—which included El Salvador—declared independence from Spain in 1821 and within two years formed the Federal Republic of Central America. In 1840 El Salvador began its existence as a separate independent political entity.

1876–85 Coffee became El Salvador's principal export, and an elite of coffee growers, producers, and exporters—sometimes called the "fourteen

251

families"—effectively consolidated its control and rule in the country. Over the next half-century, this elite expanded its economic power into additional areas, including banking, industry, and other agricultural production (e.g., sugar, cotton).

1929–31   The Great Depression created an economic crisis in El Salvador that threatened the coffee elite's rule. A coup in 1931 overthrew the elected government, and General Maximiliano Hernández Martínez assumed the presidency (military-led governments ruled El Salvador, with the support of the economic elite, until the 1980s).

1932   A planned peasant uprising led by the founder of the Communist party in El Salvador, Farabundo Martí, was discovered and crushed. General Martínez carried out the killing of some 30,000 people, primarily *campesinos* (peasants), who were suspected of being sympathetic to the uprising.

1950   The constitution granted women the right to vote.

1968   In the wake of the Second Vatican Council (1962–65) and the 1968 conference of Latin American bishops in Medellín, Colombia, a growing number of Catholic nuns and priests in El Salvador became involved in forming "Christian-base communities" in poor rural areas. These clergy members interpreted the Bible in a manner such as to encourage *campesinos* to join in a struggle against their poverty. The political right in El Salvador deplored this new ecclesiastical approach, and many priests and nuns involved in these communities were attacked and murdered.

1973   During this year's "stolen election"—as it is sometimes called—in which the politically moderate engineer José Napoleón Duarte appeared to be leading in the vote count for the presidency, a military-led government halted the vote count, declared its candidate the winner, and forced Duarte into exile (he reemerged in 1980 as part of a civilian-military government, and in 1984 as the country's president). Many observers cite this "stolen election" as a watershed that made a revolution in El Salvador likely, if not inevitable.

1979   The leftist Sandinistas assumed power in neighboring Nicaragua after the fall of Anastasio Somoza, giving a potent impetus to the Salvadoran leftist forces.

1980   In an attempt to head off revolution, the government instituted a land reform program. Also in this year five revolutionary political-military organizations joined to form the Frente Farabundo Martí para la Liberación Nacional (FMLN). And on March 24, 1980, assassins murdered the archbishop of San Salvador, Monseñor Romero, who in his sermons had supported the Christian-base communities and spoken out against human rights abuses by the government. Clashes between the FMLN and government army, the Fuerza Armada, became frequent and brought the country to civil war.

1989   "The final offensive" of the FMLN occurred and—despite its forces' capture of some of the capital's suburbs—ended in a military stalemate. The rightist political party, Alianza Republicana Nacionalista (ARENA, formed in 1981), won a victory in the parliamentary election this year, and its candidate, Alfredo Cristiani, a wealthy businessman, won the presidency.

1992   Under the auspices of the United Nations, on January 16, 1992, the Cristiani-led government and the FMLN signed a peace agreement in Chapultepec, Mexico, thus ending twelve years of civil war in El Salvador. As part of the settlement, the FMLN was recognized as a legal political party.

1997   In this year's parliamentary elections the FMLN won 27 of the 84 seats in the Asamblea Legislativa, its greatest political success to date and just one seat fewer than the leading political party, ARENA (whose leader, Armando Calderón Sol, had won the presidency of El Salvador in 1995). In the 1997 elections, the FMLN also succeeded in having its candidates elected as mayors of several Salvadoran cities, including the capital, San Salvador.

Glossary

ajuntada/o	to be tied, joined; this term is used to describe a common-law marriage
atole	drink prepared of cornmeal gruel
bolo	a drunk
brujería	witchcraft, sorcery
bueno	good, well
campesina/o	peasant woman/man
campo	countryside, field
colón	Salvadoran currency; as of 1998, 8.75 colones = $1.00, and 100 centavos = 1 colón
comal	clay dish on which tortillas are made
comedor	dining room or hall
curandera/o	faith healer
chicha	alcoholic beverage made of corn and sugar
dulce	sweet; (pl.) candies
empleada doméstica	domestic employee
finca	farm, piece of property

frijol	dried bean; (pl.) *frijoles*; in El Salvador, peasants often refer to beans in the singular
Fuerza Armada	Armed Force
gringo	North American (slightly pejorative)
Guardia	National Guard; rural police force (disbanded in 1992)
hermana	sister; nun
maíz	corn
mandador	work boss
manzana	1.7 acres
marquesote	cake made of corn or rice flour, sugar, and eggs
masa	lump of dough
militar	military man
milpa	small plot of land, usually for growing corn and beans
molendera	grinder; that is, a person who grinds corn to make tortillas
monte	mountain, woods
muchacha	girl, maid
mujerero	womanizer, skirt-chaser
niña	young girl; in El Salvador the term is used as one of respect for a woman but is less formal than Doña and Señora
novia/o	girlfriend/boyfriend; fiancée/fiancé
partera	midwife
petate	straw or reed sleeping mat
quesadilla	cornmeal pound cake made with cheese
radista	radio operator
tamal	cornmeal delicacy, usually made with chicken or meat and wrapped in a banana leaf or corn husk

Text: 10/14 Palatino
Display: Bauer Bodoni
Composition: Binghamton Valley Composition
Printing and binding: Haddon Craftsmen